VITAL
PROPHETIC
ISSUES

Examining Promises and
Problems in Eschatology

THE VITAL ISSUES SERIES

VITAL ISSUES SERIES

VITAL

PROPHETIC

ISSUES

*Examining Promises and
Problems in Eschatology*

ROY B. ZUCK
GENERAL EDITOR

kregel
RESOURCES

Grand Rapids, MI 49501

Vital Prophetic Issues: Examining Promises and Problems in Eschatology by Roy B. Zuck, general editor

Copyright © 1995 by Dallas Theological Seminary

Published by Kregel Resources, an imprint of Kregel Publications, P.O. Box 2607, Grand Rapids, MI 49501. Kregel Resources provides timely and relevant resources for Christian life and service. Your comments and suggestions are valued.

Cover Design: Sarah Slattery
Book Design: Alan G. Hartman

Library of Congress Cataloging-in-Publication Data
  Roy B. Zuck.
  Vital prophetic issues: examining promises and problems in eschatology / Roy B. Zuck, gen. ed.
     p.   cm. (Vital Issues Series–vol. 5)
  1. Millennialism. 2. Dispensationalism. 3. Prophecy—Christianity. 4. Prophets. I. Zuck, Roy B. II. Series: Zuck, Roy B., Vital Issues Series.
BT891.V58   1995   236'.9—dc20   95-35768
                                              CIP

ISBN 0-8254-4067-x (paperback)

1 2 3 4 5 Printing / Year 99 98 97 96 95

This volume is affectionately dedicated to

Dr. John F. Walvoord

Distinguished Theologian
Leading Authority on Premillennial Eschatology
Outstanding Seminary President
Exemplary Christian Leader

Contents

Part 1: Millennialism

Part 2: Dispensationalism and the Tribulation

Contributors

Roy L. Aldrich
  President Emeritus, William Tyndale College,
  Farmington, Michigan

Craig A. Blaising
  Professor of Theology,
  Southern Baptist Theological Seminary,
  Louisville, Kentucky

Larry V. Crutchfield
  Mentor, Faraston Theological Seminary,
  Colorado Springs, Colorado

Michael A. Harbin
  Visiting Professor of Biblical Studies,
  Taylor University, Upland, Indiana

Thomas D. Ice
  Executive Director, Pre-Trib Research Center,
  Washington, D.C.

Ramesh P. Richard
  Professor of Pastoral Ministries and World Missions,
  Dallas Theological Seminary, Dallas, Texas

Charles C. Ryrie
  Professor of Systematic Theology, Emeritus,
  Dallas Theological Seminary, Dallas, Texas

Jeffrey L. Townsend
    Senior Pastor, Woodland Park Community Church,
    Woodland Park, Colorado

John F. Walvoord
    Chancellor, Minister-at-Large, and Professor of Systematic
    Theology, Emeritus, Dallas Theological Seminary,
    Dallas, Texas

Bruce A. Ware
    Professor of Biblical and Systematic Theology,
    Trinity Evangelical Divinity School, Deerfield, Illinois

Preface

Everyone seems to be interested in the future. In their search to know what lies ahead, many people consult astrology charts and scan the daily horoscope columns in the newspapers. Others read tarot cards or go to palm readers. Well-known psychics find an eager audience for their annual New Year's predictions in the supermarket tabloids. Investors and speculators analyze trends and try to make a profit on "futures" contracts.

With the rapid pace of technological change, not knowing what may happen next week, next month, or next year creates feelings of uncertainty and insecurity—a situation one modern author has labeled "future shock."

God, however, knows all things—past, present, and future. He has given us glimpses of what is to come in the Scriptures. In fact, one-fourth of the Bible deals with prophetic issues. What lies ahead in God's program for the world includes the rapture of the church, the terrible seven-year tribulation, the return of Christ to the earth followed by His one-thousand-year reign, and then the eternal state.

Eschatology, the study of what the Bible predicts for the days ahead, entails numerous issues. How does the Abrahamic Covenant relate to God's program for the future of Israel? Is the millennium a future era, or does it exist now? What differences are there between premillennialism and amillennialism? How does dispensationalism relate to this issue? Will the church go through the tribulation?

These and many other intriguing questions addressed in this volume call for concerned study and diligent watchfulness for that day when the trumpet will sound and death will be swallowed up in victory.

"Amen. Come, Lord Jesus."

ROY B. ZUCK

About *Bibliotheca Sacra*

Aflood is rampant—an engulfing deluge of literature far beyond any one person's ability to read it all. Presses continue to churn out thousands of journals and magazines like a roiling, raging river.

Among these numberless publications, one stands tall and singular—*Bibliotheca Sacra*—a strange name (meaning "Sacred Library") but a journal familiar to many pastors, teachers, and Bible students.

How is *Bibliotheca Sacra* unique in the world of publishing? By being the oldest continuously published journal in the Western Hemisphere—1993 marked its 150th anniversary—and by being published by one school for sixty years—1994 marks its diamond anniversary of being released by Dallas Seminary.

Bib Sac, to use its shortened sobriquet, was founded in New York City in 1843 and was purchased by Dallas Theological Seminary in 1934, ten years after the school's founding. The quarterly's one-hundred-and-fifty-year history boasts only nine editors. Through those years it has maintained a vibrant stance of biblical conservatism and a strong commitment to the Scriptures as God's infallible Word.

I am grateful to Kregel Publications for producing a series of volumes commemorating both the journal's sesquicentennial (1843–1993) and its diamond anniversary (1934–1994). Each volume in the Kregel *Vital Issues Series* includes carefully selected articles from the thirties to the present—articles of enduring quality, articles by leading evangelicals whose topics are as relevant today as when they were first produced. The chapters have been edited slightly to provide conformity of style. As Dallas Seminary and Kregel Publications jointly commemorate these anniversaries of *Bibliotheca Sacra*, we trust these anthologies will enrich the spiritual lives and Christian ministries of many more readers.

ROY B. ZUCK, EDITOR
Bibliotheca Sacra

For *Bibliotheca Sacra* subscription information, call Dallas Seminary, 1-800-992-0998.

PART 1

Millennialism

CHAPTER 1

Basic Considerations
in Interpreting Prophecy

John F. Walvoord

The wide diversity in the interpretation of prophecy alerts anyone who approaches this field of biblical exegesis that there are also widely differing principles of interpretation. How can it be that reputable scholars who agree on many basic Christian doctrines interpret the prophetic portions of Scripture with such differing results? How can this be explained?

Differing Views of the Bible

One of the most obvious reasons for difference in interpretation in prophecy is that scholars do not all regard the Bible as having the same authority and accuracy. Liberal theologians tend to regard the Bible as a human instrument written by fallible men, and therefore conclude that the Scriptures are not infallible. It is understandable that liberals have no clear conclusions about the future. Some question the validity of prediction itself on the grounds that no one knows the future. Others accept the premise that prophecy is in some cases true and in other cases not true. This leaves the interpreter with the difficult question of sorting out the true from the false. Generally, there is little scholarly discussion of prophecy among those who are clearly liberal in their approach to the Bible.

Among conservatives who regard the Bible as authoritative in prophecy as in history, a more serious attempt is made to try to determine what the Bible actually reveals. Here the diversity is not based on the premise that the Bible in some respects is untrue; instead, the difficulty arises in various schools of interpretation.

Major Schools of Interpretation

Most Bible scholars recognize at least three major approaches to prophecy, all dealing primarily with the doctrine of the millennium. The most ancient view, that of the church of the first few centuries, was what is known today as premillennialism or chiliasm. Premillenarians assert that the second coming of Christ will precede a millennium or a thousand-year reign of Christ on earth. Chiliasm is another word (derived from the Greek χιλιός, "one thousand") that affirms the same doctrine. Most impartial interpreters of the history of doctrine agree that premillennialism was the doctrine of the early church. Adherents of this view hold that Christ taught that His second coming would be followed by His kingdom on earth, as indicated in such passages as Matthew 20:20–23; Luke 1:32–33, 22:29–30; Acts 1:6–7. In the first two centuries of the church there seems to have been an absence of any controversy on this point.

Premillenarians cite many early adherents of their interpretation, such as Papias, who was acquainted with the apostle John and many others such as Aristio, John the Presbyter, and a number of the twelve apostles including Andrew, Peter, Philip, Thomas, James, John, and Matthew. Peters also lists in the first two centuries premillenarians such as Clement of Rome, Barnabas, Hermas, Ignatius, and Polycarp.[1] It was not until the close of the 2d century and the beginning of the 3d century that specific opposition to this view seems to have arisen. In the 2d and 3d centuries, however, many other premillenarians surfaced in their writings, including Cyprian (200–258), Commodian (200–270), Nepos (230–280), Coracion (230–280), Victorinus (240–303), Methodius (250–311), and Lactantius (240–330). While the premillennial views of some of these have been challenged, it is unquestionably true that Nepos was an ardent defender of premillennialism in North Africa and he was joined by Commodian. Even opponents of premillennialism concede that there was a broad premillennial teaching in the first three centuries.

A second prominent approach to prophecy is the view that has been called amillennialism since the 19th century. It is basically a nonmillennial view, which teaches that there will be no literal millennium after the second advent of Christ. While amillenarians tend to avoid identification of any adherents of their view, they usually find the first strong advocacy of amillennialism in the school of theology at Alexandria, Egypt, with the first adherents appearing about A.D. 190. A few writers claim that amillennialism existed earlier. Landis, for example, tries to trace amillennialism back to Christ and the apostles.[2] Most amillenarians, however, claim that it had its beginning in the second and third centuries.

And yet even careful scholars like Berkhof[3] tend to slur over the facts by claiming that amillennialism was prominent in both the 2d and the 3d centuries, when actually it was practically all in the 3d century except for the last 10 years of the 2d century.

Early amillenarians include Gaius, whose writings come from the 3d century, and Clement of Alexandria, a teacher in the school at Alexandria, from 193 to 220. Clement's disciple Origen (185–254) and Dionysius (190–265) led the opposition to premillennialism in the 3d century.

Amillenarians usually concede that the basic approach of the Alexandrian school was to take Scripture, especially prophecy, in a nonliteral sense. They regarded the entire Bible as one great allegory in which the real meaning is hidden behind the actual statements of Scripture. They attempted to combine the idealism of Plato with Scripture which was only possible if Scripture were interpreted in a nonliteral sense.

Amillenarians admit that the school at Alexandria was heretical inasmuch as they challenged almost all the principal doctrines of the Christian faith. For instance, W. H. Rutgers, an amillenarian, wrote the following concerning Clement of Alexandria:

> Clement, engrossed and charmed by Greek philosophy, applied this erroneous, allegorical method to Holy Writ. It was a one-sided emphasis: opposed to the real, the visible, phenomenal, spatial and temporal. A platonic idealistic philosophy could not countenance carnalistic, sensualistic conceptions of the future as that advanced by Chiliasm. It shook the very foundation on which Chiliasm rested. Robertson observed that "it loosed its [Chiliasm's] sheet-anchor — naive literalism in the interpretation of Scripture."[4]

In spite of the fact that the major thrust of amillennialism in the 2d and 3d centuries was provided by those who were heretics, Rutgers offers the questionable proof that amillennialism was the prevailing view in the 2d century simply because many of the church fathers never discussed the issue at all. On the basis of this, and without citing those definitely committed to amillennialism, Rutgers states, "Chiliasm found no favor with the best of the Apostolic Fathers, nor does it find support in the unknown writer of the Epistle to Diognetus."[5]

While it is true that many early church fathers simply do not discuss the millennial question, the fact that specific adherents to premillennialism can be cited makes the almost complete silence of any advocates of amillennialism until A.D. 190 most significant.

While there is dispute as to whether Barnabas, an early church father, is amillennial or premillennial, even those in the amillennial camp usually do not claim Barnabas. Up until A.D. 190, no clear adherent to amillennialism can be found. This fact is in stark contrast to the fact that many held to the premillennial point of view.

For this reason, most amillenarians trace their view to Augustine (354–430), the famous bishop of Hippo in North Africa. Augustine was the father of amillennialism because he discarded the allegorical system of interpretation of the Bible as a whole as advanced by the school at Alexandria in favor of limiting allegorical interpretation to prophetic Scriptures only. He held that other Scriptures should be interpreted in their natural, grammatical, historical sense. With Augustine began general acceptance of the modern approach of recognizing the basic and normal interpretation of Scripture as literal and grammatical (as held by the Protestant Reformers such as Calvin and Luther) but at the same time holding that prophecy is a special case requiring nonliteral interpretation. This difference with premillennialism is the basic problem in the continued discussion between premillenarians and amillenarians.

The third broad view of prophetic interpretation is postmillennialism. It holds that Christ will return at the end of the millennium. Postmillenarians hold that the "millennium," such as it is, must be fulfilled before the second coming of Christ, and in this, amillennialism and postmillennialism agree. The difference between the two schools is the more optimistic approach of postmillennialism, which regards the gospel as being increasingly triumphant until the world is at least Christianized, and this victory is climaxed by the second coming of Christ and the immediate introduction to the eternal state. While some leaders throughout the history of the church, such as Joachim of Floris, a 12th-century Roman Catholic, held views close to postmillennialism, most postmillenarians trace their view to Daniel Whitby (1638–1725). While some amillenarians tend to emphasize the earlier postmillennialism, Strong, a postmillenarian, states clearly, "Our own interpretation of Revelation 20:1–10, was first given, for substance, by Whitby."[6]

Postmillennialism related to the optimism of the 18th and 19th centuries, which coincided with the general hope of a better world. While largely discarded now, it was a prevailing view among many conservative theologians in the 19th and 20th centuries, of which Charles Hodge is an example.

The Needed Return to Basic Hermeneutics

For students of prophecy seeking to weigh the relative cogency of premillennialism, amillennialism, and postmillennialism, the first requirement is a clear view of ordinary rules of interpretation as normally advanced in hermeneutics. Adherents of all views of prophecy tend at times to forget that basic rules for exegesis have been established in the history of the church at least by conservative scholars, and one is not free to disregard them in favor of establishing his own particular interpretation. Conservative scholars tend for the most part to agree on these basic principles, which include the following:

1. Words are to be understood in their normal, natural sense unless there is firm evidence in the context that the words are used in some other sense.

2. Each statement of Scripture should be interpreted in its context. This usually means that a word should be interpreted in its immediate context, although sometimes usage in other passages is also relevant. A common fallacy, however, is to read into a passage something that is found elsewhere in the Bible instead of allowing the immediate context to have primary weight.

3. A text of Scripture must always be seen in its historical and cultural contexts, and the intended meaning of the author is important. Conservative scholars, however, recognize that the Bible is not only a work by human authors, but is also inspired by the Holy Spirit, and in some cases even the human author did not understand entirely what he was writing.

4. Scripture should be interpreted in the light of grammatical considerations including such important matters as tense and emphasis.

5. If the language of Scripture is figurative as is sometimes the case, this should be clearly established by the context itself and not by prior considerations.

The science of hermeneutics, the interpretation of Scripture, is by no means simplistic, but in general the consensus has been that the normal interpretation of Scripture should be according to its literal, grammatical, and historical sense. For the purpose of this discussion the general rules commonly accepted in hermeneutics are considered a basis for judging prophetic portions of Scripture.

Interpreting Prophecy Is a Special Case

Though the nonliteral interpretation of the Bible as a whole arose in the heretical school of theology at Alexandria, Egypt, in the late 2d and 3d centuries, most conservative interpreters agree that the Bible is not an extensive allegory in which the normal sense is not the real sense. The point of departure is the view of Augustine that while Scripture normally should be interpreted in the literal sense, prophecy is a special case. To some extent adherents of all views of prophecy concede that special problems exist in the interpretation of prophecy.

In unfulfilled prophecy questions about the exact meaning of the text are often left unanswered. In the history of prophetic interpretation there have been so many erroneous views which were later exposed by actual fulfillment that any student of prophecy must necessarily be cautious. Occasionally some people have carelessly made wild and unrealistic claims regarding the meaning of certain prophetic passages. Accordingly careful expositors generally are conservative in their interpretation of prophecy regardless of which school of thought they follow. However, several major considerations tend to focus on the real problem as it exists today in correct interpretation of prophecy.

One-fourth of the Bible was prophetic when it was written, and interestingly about one-half of these prophecies have been fulfilled, often with amazing accuracy. The Old Testament is full of predictions concerning future events and especially concerning the coming of Christ. The fulfillment of many of these in His first coming illustrates that prophecy is intended to be interpreted in its normal and literal sense.

For instance the birth of Christ was to be supernatural. His mother was to be a virgin (Isa. 7:14). His place of birth was Bethlehem, pinpointed in Micah 5:2 about seven hundred years before He was born. He was to be the seed of the woman (Gen. 3:15) who would have victory over Satan. His lineage is described in the Old Testament as extending through Seth, Noah, Abraham, Isaac, Jacob, Judah, and then through Boaz, Obed, Jesse, and David. All this is pointed out in the genealogies of the New Testament (Matt. 1:1–16; Luke 3:23–38). The Old Testament abounds with prophetic details about Jesus as prophet, priest, and king (Deut. 18:15–18; 1 Sam. 2:35: Ps. 110:4; cf. Gen. 49:10; 2 Sam. 7:12–16; Zech. 6:13; Heb. 5:6). Isaiah 9:6–7 summarizes His birth, Person, and deity. All these prophecies have been literally fulfilled. Even His death on the cross is anticipated in Psalm 22 and Isaiah 53, and His resurrection is predicted in Psalm 16:10. In all these cases the prophetic Scriptures have been fulfilled historically in a literal way.

In view of these fulfilled prophecies it seems reasonable to conclude that yet unfulfilled prophecies will have the same literal fulfillment, especially when they are couched in terms that make sense literally.

In general, conservative expositors have agreed on the literal interpretation of Scripture when it comes to broad doctrines such as the deity of Christ, the humanity of Christ, His life on earth, His death, His resurrection, and His second coming. They agree that there is a literal heaven and a literal hell. In discussion of prophetic interpretation, it soon becomes evident that the crux of the matter is whether there is a future, literal millennial reign of Christ on earth. It is here where conservative scholars differ, going in general in three directions: premillennialism, amillennialism, or postmillennialism.

Further Definition of the Interpretive Problem

Although it is generally agreed that amillennialism sprang from the theology of Augustine and that postmillennialism derived from it, it is quite clear in current discussion that the problem is more than a general rule that prophecy should be interpreted in an allegorical or nonliteral sense. As has been pointed out, as a matter of fact, both amillenarians and postmillenarians often interpret prophecy in a literal way. What, then, is the real point of distinction?

The abundant literature in the field supports the concept that the major problem is the doctrine of the millennium or a thousand-year reign of Christ. If the millennium precedes the second coming of Christ as amillenarians and postmillenarians contend, it is also clear that many of the precise predictions related to the millennium cannot be clearly fulfilled. The present world is not under the political direction of Jesus Christ, and evil as such is not being immediately judged by God as it will be in the millennial kingdom.

By contrast the premillennial view anticipates a second coming of Christ followed by His thousand-year reign on earth. This is the historic interpretation held by the early church fathers and which has continued in contemporary premillennialism.

Current discussion on the subject, however, has tended to blur some of these time-honored distinctions. For instance, Arthur H. Lewis denies that he is amillennial but at the same time he prefers not to be known as premillennial or postmillennial.[7] Lewis holds that the millennium must be before the second coming because there is sin in the millennium and for him there can be no sin on earth after the second coming of Christ. His problem is in his premise that the millennial kingdom is perfect. This, of course, is contradicted by many Old Testament passages which he ignores.

Others have followed the lead of Lewis by claiming to be historic premillennialists and then proceeding to view the millennium as preceding the second coming of Christ. Often the problem arises because they are forced in their denominations or schools to agree to a premillennial statement.

Bilezikian is typical of those who blur the distinctions on the doctrine of the millennium. He writes, "Peter, reading about God's oath to David to set one of his descendants upon his throne (Ps. 132:11), interpreted the promised messianic rule as having been fulfilled in the resurrection of Christ and his exaltation in heaven (Acts 2:30–31)."[8] This view is obviously not historical premillennialism, for it allows for no literal thousand-year reign of Christ after His second coming. This he makes clear later in the same article, when he states that "the essential features accompanying the second coming of Christ" are "the general resurrection, the universal judgment, and the inauguration of the reunion of the redeemed in eternity."[9] He further adds insult to injury by accusing those who differ with him as being guilty of "shoddy exegesis consisting of facile scissors-and-paste patchworks of fragments of biblical texts," which he claims is motivated by their desire to reap monetary gain.[10] He discards the testimony of a millennial reign in Revelation 20 because it is found in one of "relatively unclear passages where figurative and symbolic motifs are present (such as the thousand years' rule of Revelation 20)."[11] What can be said of this type of "premillennial" interpretation? Actually this approach brings confusion rather than clarity to the subject. Any system that says the millennium is fulfilled before the second advent and also teaches that the eternal state begins at the second advent cannot accurately be labeled premillennialism. It would be far better for a scholarly discussion of the problem to accept the time-honored terms rather than attempt to redefine prophetic interpretation in a way that does not correspond to the historic handling of the problem.

It is clear that the major problem in the interpretation of prophecy is the doctrine of the millennium. Along with this is the corresponding difficulty of whether many Old Testament prophecies relating to Israel will be fulfilled before or after the second coming of Christ. The doctrine of a future millennium following Christ's second advent is inevitably related to the question as to whether promises given to Israel will have a literal fulfillment.

CHAPTER 2

The Premillennial Interpretation of History

Ramesh P. Richard

The requirements for any philosophy of history[1] are comprehensiveness, coherence, and complementariness. Nonbiblical philosophies are inadequate because none of them is comprehensive.[2] But even among biblical ones some are more comprehensive and more consistent than others.

It is the contention of this writer that premillennialism, especially dispensational premillennialism, provides the best substantive philosophy of history. Roberts, however, disagrees. He writes, "The tendency toward over-assurance has frequently been found among Christian historians within the evangelical tradition. Its most blatant and popular form is that interpretation of history called 'dispensationalism.'"[3] In a footnote he continues:

> It is the opinion of the editors that, despite the popularity of dispensationalism, it is not really successful as an effort to relate Christianity and history in a scholarly way. It is probably fair to suggest that dispensationalism largely ignores the accepted canons of historical scholarship in its rather facile attempts to relate the Bible to current and future events.[4]

Roberts is right when he says that dispensationalism is an interpretation of history. If ever there was need for a biblical one, dispensational premillennialism does provide for it. But a word such as "over-assurance" is highly relative. And pejorative words such as "blatant" or "facile attempts" are unnecessary. It is easier to be analytical than to be substantive. And that is exactly what Roberts is doing. He thinks that dispensationalism is too simple to be right (as though simplicity is wrong in itself), but he does not articulate his own position except in a loose, indefinite way. He asserts that this "tendency towards over-assurance" may also be found in such Christian historians as Latourette and Dooyeweerd, but he suggests that they are more modest and academically respectable. But modesty and over-assurance are a strange couple in any case. Further, Roberts implies that Dooyeweerd's "academically respectable" over-assurance should be more acceptable than untrained "over-assurance." Is Roberts faulting the tendency to over-assurance or the training of the philosophers? To say that dispensationalism "ignores the accepted canons of historical scholarship" is to imply that there are such canons. But the present state of philosophizing about history is as skeptical as it has ever been. Historians and historical canons have to limit themselves wholly to the past, which has accompanying problems of selectivity, objectivity, and others. Therefore the battle between Christians over a comprehensive historical scheme cannot wholly be on the level of historiography, but must also be on the level of the authority and interpretation of the Scriptures — which gives the only objective, beyond-history, propositional perspective on all of time.

The Interpretation of the "Future"

History is past and future. The whole of history is more than the past. "It covers, as well, the whole future or, if it is important to make this qualification, the whole *historical* future."[5] Historical future means "in-time" future, just as historical past means "in-time" past. The beyond-time future is as crucial to a philosophy of history as a beyond-time past, that is, it is not crucial at all. History is concerned with time and the temporal process. To appeal to "beyond-time" history (a contradiction in terms) as the basis for writing a philosophy of history is to undermine totally the continuing apologetic significance of Christianity. Hinduism can compete with Christianity on this "metachronological, metatemporal" level. Also Islam could conceivably compete with Christianity on the level of the past only. It is the "in-time" fulfillment of prophecy (past or future) that enabled the covenanted people of Israel to believe their God and that tempted outsiders to "look in."

The crucial debate between premillennialism and amillennialism is whether the prophecies concerning the future (especially, the kingdom) are to be interpreted literally. On the basis of literal interpretation, the premillennialist sees an actual first coming of Christ to Bethlehem and an actual earthly kingdom established at His second coming. As Walvoord states, the premillennial prophecies are "to be taken literally, the exact interpretation following the pattern of the law of fulfillment established by prophecies already fulfilled and in keeping with the entire doctrine."[6] Walvoord continues, "Prophecies fulfilled in the past are found to sustain the principle of literal fulfillment."[7] Now if all prophecies are interconnected by virtue of the omniscience of God and are a homogeneous whole, there is no reason to expect some to be fulfilled literally and others nonliterally.

> Biblical prophecy is not made up from scattered and unrelated predictions, but forms a grand design, in which each individual unit finds a place. It is not necessary however, that we should formally systematize the material before we are convinced of its homogeneity. . . . The coherence and interconnection [*sic*] of prophecy in all its parts is implied in its origin, and casts us back upon the foreknowledge of God.[8]

Thus if prophecy makes sense and finds fulfillment mainly in the context of history and is a homogeneous whole, to see past history as literal fulfillment and future history as not necessarily literal is to introduce a disjunction which ultimately reflects on the knowledge and simplicity of God.

Thus premillennialism does not contradict itself (as amillennialism does) in reference to time (i.e., in speaking of past-time history) nor in reference to prophesied history (i.e., in taking some events to be literal and others to be nonliteral). The premillennialist on this account has a more adequate philosophy of *history*; he sees a literal fulfillment of a millennium in time.[9]

The Unifying Principle of History

Amillennial and premillennial philosophies of history have unifying principles in their interpretation of universal history. For the amillennialist and the covenant theologian, the unifying principle is the soteriological covenant of grace, the essence of which is never changed throughout history.[10] The dispensationalist on the other hand emphasizes the doxological method of God in all His dealings under different dispensations. Ryrie notes, "In dispensationalism the principle is theological or perhaps better, eschatological, for the differing dispensations reveal the glory of God as He manifests His character in the differing stewardships culminating in history with the millennial glory."[11]

Therefore both systems have a unitary emphasis. But the problem with the covenant theologian is that he does not adequately deal with the "fragmentary" aspects of history. The overriding principle is imposed on all God's creatures and history. It does not give due recognition to aspects outside *Heilsgeschichte*. The process of history and the progress of revelation are virtually ignored, with only formal acknowledgment given to them. The problem is that the principle is not as comprehensive as it should be in order to qualify as a requirement for an adequate philosophy of history.

By contrast dispensationalism gives proper recognition to the unitariness and fragmentariness of history. The "doxological" principle states that God is manifesting His glory through His multidimensional relationships with man and creation. God was dealing with man even before man fell, and before Abraham, and before the Law. God has plans for other creatures of His, though they are nonsoteriological plans, for example, fallen angels and Satan. He providentially directs history and brings glory to Himself. Certainly soteriology is an important part of the doxological principle, but the manifestation of His glory is not limited to the provision of salvation for man.

Is this true unity? The dispensationalist answers yes. He claims that only the doxological principle is comprehensive enough to include all facets of history and creation. For instance, in the realm of soteriology, salvation is the constant factor, faith is the constant method, and obedience is the constant test in all the dispensations. "These are so framed together that they constitute one harmonious whole, each part contributing to the other and dependent on it. The successive ages grow out of the previous age . . . as God has purposed from the beginning, and Christ has appointed."[12] Unity is also found in the continuity between the ages. It must be noted here that nondispensationalists have to agree with at least three dispensations—"before the Law," "Law," and "church." The principles used in determining these three are similar to the ones used in determining the five or the seven which others hold. Thus it is illegitimate to charge the dispensationalist with disunity when he gives adequate recognition to the diversity within unity.

While pursuing this theme of the unitariness and fragmentariness of history in the dispensationalist system, mention should be made of the cross-sectional and longitudinal views of history in dispensationalism. It is possible to see extreme antitheses between the ages and to enunciate the differences. This is the cross-sectional view. But "from another viewpoint, the dispensational system can be regarded from a longitudinal perspective. Seen from this angle are certain long-range principles continuing from one dispensation to the next and giving coherency to the whole course of history."[13] This longitudinal perspective provides the unitary aspect of history.

In questioning the dispensationalist's unifying principle, one may ask how glory is so vital to the millennium, and how God will be glorified in the millennium in a way in which He is not now glorified. First, all notions as to adding glory to the perfections of God must be rejected. What He possesses, He possesses perfectly and fully. The best that man could do is to reflect His glory in a better way, and appreciate His name among *men* while ascribing praise to Him. Second, all that is being argued from this unifying principle is that the greatest *display* of God's glory on earth will be during the millennium. God's glory is not fully visible now. It will be, beginning with the Parousia. Third, the comprehensiveness of the doxological principle as especially evident in the millennial kingdom is seen in its relation to all aspects of creation. In relation to the earth, there will be a removal of the curse before it is thoroughly renovated in the formation of the new earth (cf. Rom. 8:18–25). The zoological world will live in harmony (Isa. 11:6–9). Man will live in subjection to the King of glory. The church will share in the glory of Christ's redemption (Rev. 19:7–9) as the bride of Christ. Satan will be absent during this time (Rev. 20:1–3), and Christ's glory will not be hidden. Sin will be judged immediately and man will be under the last and greatest test in God's program for history.

In conclusion this doxological principle leaves no aspect of reality untouched, and includes them coherently. On the other hand the soteriological principle is not all-inclusive and does not include all aspects of creation or history.

The Goal of History

History is directional and goal-oriented. Dispensational premillennialists contend that it is moving toward the messianic kingdom as the final phase of time.

A VIEW OF TIME

The linear concept is upheld by premillennialists. But it is divided into successive ages, not repetitive cycles. These divisions may be called ages, dispensations, or eras. They all show that history is graded, "The Holy Scripture is plainly not a spiritual-divine-uniform block, but a wonderfully articulated historic-prophetic-spiritual organism. It must be read organically, age-wise, according to the Divine ages."[14] Each age is given its due emphasis. There are two emphases here. The first is that each age has its own self-justification. It has been specially placed there and planned by God. In its particular context it reflects the purposes of God. However, the second emphasis is that the final stage justifies each of the other stages, because the long-range purposes finally find culmination.

Occasionally these stages are charged with being cyclical. But this accusation is not correct for there is genuine progress and novelty. The dispensations should be seen as stages in a symphonic movement, or steps on a staircase, or rungs on a ladder. There is a new beginning each time, there is progress within each age, and each age is an advance over the previous one.

TIME: THE ARENA OF GOD'S VICTORY

Dispensational premillennialists maintain that the goal of history should be within history. And historical ends are within time. The first temporal focus was at the Incarnation—it divided time. The second temporal focus will be at the millennium—the final phase of time. This final phase must not be confused with eternity when time and delay as known now shall be no more.

While the eternal state has its own glory, there are reasons why historical ends should be within history even where glory is concerned. First, the purpose of creation and history is the glory of God. The millennium allows for this purpose to be consummated within history itself. Second, time is the arena of God's conflict with Satan. "To place the ultimate triumph in eternity would mean a defeat for God in time. God has chosen the earth to fight the battle with Satan."[15] The earth will be the venue of God's victory. Third, historical ends beyond history are an unaffirmable contradiction. Ends beyond time and history are not historical. History must have fulfillment within time.[16] And only the premillennial scheme brings ultimate glory to God within the realm of time.

Theodicy and a Philosophy of History

"The free existence of evil in a world originally created good is the great contradiction within history."[17] This is absolutely true. And the theologian who does not posit a millennium will have to say that this world is the best of all possible worlds. He cannot appeal to eternity for his answer, for an eternal "world" is not historical. And despite the great achievements of man, one has great doubts that this is the best *possible* world. But a premillennial framework allows one to posit "the best possible way to the best possible world" theodicy.[18] Even though the world is evil, God is bringing about His glory and man's good, and this will be displayed on the earth—a historical salvation and a historical theodicy.

Also each dispensation proves that humanity failed under all possible situations, freely bringing evil on itself. Thus both the immediate and ultimate divine reconstruction do justify God. Sauer remarks that "the history of salvation will thus be an historical self-justification of God, an 'historical Theodicy,' and the course of revelation will constitute the proof of its own necessity."[19] As McClain asks, if some evils have been conquered now, then why should there not be an age when *all* evil will be rooted out?[20] And he concludes, "If there be a God in heaven, if the life which he created on the earth is worthwhile, and not something evil per se, then there ought to be in history some worthy consummation of its long and arduous course."[21] Thus a theodicy, as an aspect of an adequate philosophy of history, renders premillennialism viable.

Heilsgeschichte (Salvation History) and Premillennialism

While it is true that dispensational premillennialism holds to salvation as a *means* to God's glory, salvation does occupy an *integral* part of God's strategy in history. It is possible to prove that the history of salvation corroborates and supports dispensationalism as a system. Sin is the reason for salvation. Man has morally departed from God. The dispensations prove that he failed God's tests in every situation. If man were ever to protest that had he not known sin he would not have sinned, God can direct him to examine the pre-Fall period. Perhaps man needed conscience or human government to check him, but man failed under those systems also. Or man could argue that if he were given a divine prescription, he would know how to please God. But the Law was given and man failed. Or he may argue that if the Law were only taken away he would not sin. But the church age was effected and man still failed. Mankind cries for one more chance. "The devil made me do it," he complains. "If the devil were locked away, I would not be tempted to sin." So God will lock the devil away for a thousand years and give man the ideal environment. And yet the evil heart of man will still rebel against

God. The answer to sin then is God's provision, not human ingenuity or effort. Man cannot excuse himself and God is vindicated, for man has failed under every conceivable circumstance. So the dispensational premillennial position adequately explains man's sin and God's way of dealing with it in history, focusing on the cross of Christ.

Utopian Consciousness and Premillennialism

Man has always dreamed of a Utopia. He longs for a time when the earth will be all that he conceives of as the ideal state, which he is not able to bring about now. According to the Scriptures the millennial kingdom, which includes material features, will be ushered into this earth. After man has marred the earth, bringing it to a humanly irretrievable state (contra postmillennialism), God will step in and bring in the millennium. Material Utopian aspects of the kingdom still await the future.[22] This is the future kingdom promised to Israel, into which individuals who are rightly related to God can find privileged acceptance and blessing.

Conclusion

A dispensational premillennial philosophy of history is comprehensive, coherent, and complementary. The establishment of a kingdom on earth as the last phase in time and the climactic self-revelation of the glory of God is the purpose of history. The premillennial system has a comprehensive unifying principle and a goal within time. It also meets the demands of a theodicy, a *Heilsgeschichte*, and a Utopia, all resulting in God's glory. Only dispensational premillennialism has "an *eschaton* that delimits, a *telos* that affords meaning, and a finish that marks finality."[23] It covers all of history, from the beginning of time (creation) to the end, when the kingdoms of the world will become the kingdom of the Lord (Rev. 11:15).

CHAPTER 3

The Hermeneutics of Covenant Theology

Michael A. Harbin

The question of authority is probably the key question of this generation. Conservative Christianity has struggled to resist numerous attempts to erode the base of authority rediscovered during the Reformation, when the Reformers proclaimed *sola Scriptura*, rather than the pope, as the base of authority.

Following this standard, the Reformers built on the principle of a literal interpretation of Scripture.[1] This hermeneutical principle is more than just a guideline for Bible study. It is also a powerful control on what Scripture may or may not be construed to say. In other words the principle of literal interpretation is what makes Scripture, and not some interpreter, the authority.

However, the issue is more complex than this. Obviously the Scriptures contain many kinds of figurative speech. In addition several books of the Bible are devoted almost exclusively to prophecy. Properly interpreting this mass of material has challenged conservative Christianity since the Reformation. Two schools of interpretation have arisen in an attempt to maintain this authority.

These two schools, popularly known as covenant theology and dispensationalism, are often set at odds with one another. Unfortunately they are also often misunderstood. At times members of both camps have gone to extremes in their zeal to uphold their systems.

What Is Covenant Theology?

Confusion abounds in the minds of many people about several terms. Apparently many people use the terms "Reformed tradition," "Calvinism," "covenant theology," and "amillennialism" interchangeably. For this reason it is necessary to define these terms.[2]

REFORMED TRADITION

"Reformed tradition" is a term often used by Presbyterians and people in related groups to reflect their theological system. This is a catchall term that reflects all the various facets of theology that arose as part of the Reformation. The "Reformed tradition" seems to include Calvinism, covenant theology, and amillennialism, as well as the Presbyterian form of church government. Arriving at a more technical definition is difficult. As de Witt observes, "There is no single source to which we can turn for an authoritative expression of Reformed faith."[3] He cites several sources of the Reformed faith, including John Calvin, Martin Luther, the Canons of Dort, and even pre-Reformation men such as Augustine and Anselm.

It would appear then that the Reformed tradition is not an explicit system of doctrine but a history or development of doctrine. That is, the Reformed tradition is the *historical process of the church clarifying views on specific points of theology by dealing with issues as they arose.* As issues came to the fore, the church, through debate and consultation with the standards of Scripture clarified what was truth and what was heresy.[4] This may lead one to suspect that there may yet be areas where the church has not delineated the limits of orthodoxy.[5] This is addressed in the *Westminster Confession of Faith*, which states that "it belongeth to synods and councils, ministerially to determine controversies of faith" (chap. 31). Furthermore the same chapter warns that "all synods or councils, since the apostles' times, whether general or particular, may err; and many have erred. Therefore they are not to be made the rule of faith, or practice; but to be used as a help in both."

De Witt lists seven themes that he argues could be construed as delineating the Reformed faith or tradition: (1) its doctrine of Scripture, (2) its high view of the sovereignty of God, (3) its view of the invincibility of the grace of God, (4) a doctrine of the Christian life that places a high view on holy living, (5) a distinction between law and grace, (6) a positive view of the relationship between the kingdom of God and the world (a view of a cultural mandate), and (7) a distinctive view of preaching.[6]

One cannot help but wonder how these characteristics are peculiarly "Reformed" in the traditional sense of the word. De Witt notes this himself on the last point: "There is much that all evangelicals, from whatever period of history, have in common here. That, of course, is true with respect to the other areas I have mentioned as well."[7]

In evangelicalism today the distinctions that set the Reformed tradition apart are questions more of degree or emphasis rather than absolute differences. So caution must be exercised in the use of the term as a distinguishing label.

CALVINISM

Calvinism is the system of theology developed from the writings of John Calvin. As usually delineated, it is set forth in five points which were the points of remonstrance postulated by the followers of Jacob Arminius. The argument primarily focused on the question of predestination, especially in relationship to salvation. Properly speaking, then, Calvinism follows up the question facing the first Reformers (viz., the issue of salvation by faith) and is an attempt to reconcile the sovereignty of God with salvation.[8]

COVENANT THEOLOGY

Covenant theology is a system developed by two men, Johannes Cocceius (1603–1669) and Hermann Witsius (1636–1708). It was an attempt to tie the Old and New Testaments together by two covenants. The first was called the covenant of works, defined as the covenant instituted by God with Adam after creation. This was abrogated by the Fall and was replaced by the covenant of grace. The covenant of grace is the covenant of salvation, a single covenant for all men after the Fall.[9] Thus the unifying feature of the Bible in this system is God's grace. An evaluation of the hermeneutical base for this system will be given later.

AMILLENNIALISM

Amillennialism is a system of interpretation of prophetic Scripture. Basically it holds that the Bible does not predict a literal thousand-year period of universal peace and righteousness before the end of the world.[10] For example Berkhof states:

> The Amillennial view is, as the name indicates, purely negative. It holds that there is no sufficient Scriptural ground for the expectation of a millennium, and is firmly convinced that the Bible favors the idea that the present dispensation of the Kingdom of God will be followed immediately by the Kingdom of God in its consummate and eternal form.[11]

Others, while agreeing with Berkhof regarding the characteristics of that system of interpretation, dislike the negative implications of the title. For example Adams renames the "unhappy term" with a title he feels is more accurate and positive—"realized millennialism."[12]

What Is Dispensationalism?

Dispensationalism is an effort to interpret Scripture on the basis of the distinctives of God's demands for and relationships with mankind. This pertains to man's stewardship toward God. A basic corollary of this is the assumption of the same literal, historical-grammatical method of interpretation followed by many other schools of thought in evangelical Christianity.[13] Like other sections of evangelicalism, it recognizes the use of figures of speech and symbols as an important aspect of the literal method.[14]

Dispensationalism, then, is not per se a method of interpreting only prophecy. Premillennialism seems to flow naturally from the hermeneutical assumptions of dispensationalism, but it is not a direct or necessary corollary.

Also, as delineated, dispensationalism is not necessarily incompatible with covenant theology, if one wishes to view the various dispensations as being aspects of the covenant of grace, which encompasses all time after the Fall. In fact this has been true of covenant theology from its inception. For example Witsius notes that it was "dispensed 'at sundry times and in divers manners,' under various economies for the manifestation of the manifold wisdom of God."[15] He suggests that the Old Testament includes four distinct periods between the Fall and Christ: Adam to Noah, Noah to Abraham, Abraham to Moses, Moses to Christ.[16] Berkhof states that the covenant of grace "is essentially the same in all Dispensations, though its form changes."[17]

The distinctions between the various periods noted by Witsius cannot be denied. The real question lies in their significance and the amount of emphasis one wishes to accord them. Dispensationalism suggests that the distinctions are significant, whereas covenant theology suggests that they are in reality minimal.

"Reformed tradition" is a broad term. "Calvinism" reflects a perspective on soteriology. "Amillennialism" and "premillennialism" reflect one's eschatological perspective. "Dispensationalism" and "covenant theology" reflect one's perspective on the unity and purpose of Scripture. Therefore it is possible, theoretically at least, to be an amillennial dispensationalist or a premillennial covenant theologian.

Dispensationalism, however, because of its focus on a consistent hermeneutic, is difficult to harmonize with an amillennial view of prophecy, and covenant theology is traditionally associated with the amillennial view and more naturally fits with it. So in this article covenant theology is considered as including amillennialism as an adjunct, and dispensationalism is viewed as including premillennialism as an adjunct.

The Beginning of Covenant Theology

As already noted covenant theology was first developed in the 17th century by Johannes Cocceius (1603–1669). His work, viewed with suspicion, was not accepted until it was republished much later in a somewhat different form.[18] Apparently he built on Beza's work (1519–1605) on the eternal decrees. Rogers states that "Beza was the first supralapsarian among the Reformers who rooted all theological affirmations in God's eternal decrees."[19]

MacKay has suggested that Cocceius's work was not initially accepted because of his opposition to some of the more extreme teachings on predestination. Cocceius wrote during the period after the Synod of Dort (1618–1619), which delineated but did not settle the issue. Van der Waal suggests that a factor was Cocceius's premillennial views, which Van der Waal placed in the same category as those of Hal Lindsey.[20]

Cocceius's hypothesis was revised by Hermann Witsius (1636–1708), and in this form it gradually gained acceptance. Even before this, however, statements on the decrees of God were included in the *Westminster Confession of Faith* (1647, a year before Cocceius published his major work).[21]

This was not the only attempt to explain how the Scriptures together. For example the Englishman William Cave (1637–1713) wrote from a dispensational perspective. The Frenchman Pierre Poiret (1646–1719) published a six-volume set in 1687 in which he presented a "fully systematized teaching on premillennial dispensationalism with six distinct economies."[22]

The doctrine of the covenants then became a part of the Reformed tradition. This perspective of theology was essentially completed with the "Formula Consensus Helvetica," adopted in 1625. It is significant that Seeburg sees this as the completion of the doctrines of the Reformed church,[23] which would suggest that Reformed theology has been essentially fixed for more than three hundred years.

The Hermeneutical Base of Covenant Theology

HISTORICAL-GRAMMATICAL METHOD
OF INTERPRETATION

Covenant theologians generally begin with a literal or historical-grammatical method of interpretation. This came in conjunction with rejecting the Roman Catholic viewpoint that the church is to interpret Scripture and that church tradition is on a par with Scripture.[24] The Roman Catholic Church views this rejection as effectively removing all controls on interpretation. For example O'Brien states that Luther's Ninety-five Theses "set loose in the religious world a principle which was destined to produce consequences far beyond the ken of himself or his fellow reformers. It was the principle of the supremacy of private judgment in the interpretation of the Scriptures and as a guide in the religious life."[25]

Protestantism has three controls, however. The first is the testimony of the Holy Spirit in the believer (John 14:26; 1 John 2:27). Even the most mature Christian, however, does not consistently follow the leading of the Holy Spirit, even in the area of interpretation. Reasons for this are the depravity of man, presuppositions one may hold from before regeneration, and cultural values which are often difficult to sort out. A second control is the combined testimony of the body of believers. By comparing interpretations, honest students of the Word have a clearer understanding of the truth. This builds on the first control and assumes that all in the body of Christ indeed have the testimony of the Holy Spirit within them. Even here, however, a group or an individual may go astray in some interpretation. A third control is the literal method of interpretation. This is the most reliable of the three, since it is the least dependent on frail human instruments. This is the method adopted by the church in the Reformation. This is not to say that it was not an accepted method before that time. In actuality it dates back to the early church (cf. Acts 17:11). The loss of this control at the time of Augustine led to the institutional church considering itself the final control.

The *Westminster Confession* states the following in its first chapter:

> ix. The infallible rule of interpretation of Scripture is the Scripture itself, and therefore, when there is a question about the true and full sense of any Scripture (which is not manifold, but one) it must be searched and known by other places that speak more clearly.

x. The supreme judge by which all controversies of religion are to be determined, and all decrees of councils, opinions of ancient writers, doctrines of men, and private spirits, are to be examined, and in whose sentence we are to rest, can be no other but the Holy Spirit speaking in the Scripture.

This historical-grammatical method is the basic hermeneutical method of covenant theology. However, many writers on hermeneutics would suggest that there are areas that require "special literary methods." These include similes, metaphors, proverbs, parables, allegories, types, prophecy, and apocalyptic literature (though not everyone would necessarily include all these categories).[26]

The point these writers make is that the interpretation of figurative speech requires something other than an explicit, straightforward, dictionary meaning of each word. A figure, in whatever sense, requires recognition of the fact that it is a figure, and that its interpretation transcends the explicit word value. This would seem to imply that the interpretation of figurative language is beyond the scope of the literal method of interpretation.

Historically, however, scholars have allowed figures of speech as an integral part of the historical-grammatical, or literal, method. This is true, no matter which view one takes of the interpretation of prophecy, which will be discussed later.

A thorough knowledge of the varieties of figures of speech employed in the Scriptures is necessary for accurate interpretation. The literal method calls for an understanding of the word or phrase in the figure of speech which corresponds to the passage's intended meaning. This problem relates to the purpose of the passage.

PURPOSE OF SCRIPTURE

In addition to the sheer mass of material in the Scriptures is their depth. One of the aids to understanding Scripture is the delineation of its purpose. The statement of purpose of any piece of literature must be broad enough to encompass all the data, yet narrow enough to reflect its distinctive characteristics.[27] This purpose becomes a key for interpretation in that it provides a foundation for understanding overall themes, which then provides clarification of obscure passages. This is especially relevant for figures of speech and for extended figurative passages.

A variety of purposes have been proposed for the Bible.

Augustine apparently suggested "purity of life." "Whatever there is in the Word of God that cannot, when taken literally, be referred either to purity of life or soundness of doctrine, you may set down as figurative."[28]

Calvin said the revelation of Christ for man's salvation is the purpose of Scripture. "Calvin cautioned that we must not interpret Scripture as having any other purpose than of revealing Christ for our Salvation."[29]

Voetius suggested that the Synod of Dort was the key for figurative interpretation.[30] Cocceius saw the key as Christ.[31] Milton saw charity as "the end of all Scripture." On this basis, he built "an extraordinarily flexible hermeneutical principle."[32]

Luther said that Christ as Judge and Savior was his criterion for interpretation.[33] Berkhof suggested that a possible foundation for interpretation is Matthew 21:43,[34] in which Jesus stated that the kingdom of God would be given to a "nation producing the fruit of it." This is the principle, he said, that the church has replaced the nation of Israel in God's program.

Van der Waal cites both the covenants and the confessions of the Reformation. To him these two seem to be synonymous or at least closely related.[35] MacKay suggested that dispensationalism "proposes the glory of God as the all-inclusive principle for the divine activities."[36]

This is a broad spectrum of suggestions. Two major purposes of Scripture held today are "salvation by Christ" and "the glory of God." The former is held predominantly by covenant theologians, and the latter predominantly in dispensational circles. Which of these two is appropriate?

Salvation is certainly a major theme throughout the Bible, appearing first after the Fall in the protevangelium (Gen. 3:15), and continuing up to the removal of the curse (Rev. 22:3). However, the glory of God is also emphasized throughout Scripture.

The salvation or redemption of the world by Christ could be subsumed under the subject of the glory of God. For an overriding purpose of the Scriptures, salvation is too narrow a theme, for several reasons.

First, some passages of Scripture (e.g., some of the psalms) do not fit into the theme of salvation. Calvin observed this and rejected Luther's contention that Christ could be found everywhere in Scripture.[37]

Second, because of this difficulty, certain portions of Scripture have been interpreted nonliterally to seek to relate them to the salvation theme. One such portion is the Song of Solomon, which has often been construed as an extended allegory representing the relationship of Christ and His church. The problem is that this approach is not presented in the book itself. Instead the book is written as a straightforward love relationship between a man and a woman. Any allegorical interpretation of the Song of Solomon has no controls. Who decides which details do or do not represent "spiritual" values? When two commentators disagree on a given allegorical interpretation, how does a person decide which one to follow?

Third, this view does not take into account God's role as Judge (Matt. 7:23; 25:41; 2 Cor. 5:10; Rev. 20:11; etc.).

Therefore a more appropriate theme is the glory of God, which is suggested by Hebrews 1:1–3. Interestingly this theme fits well with Westminster standards. It is seen in the *Westminster Confession* in 1.6; 4.1; 6.1; and 18.1. It is also seen in the Westminster catechisms. The first answer in the *Larger Catechism* is "Man's chief and highest end is to glorify God and fully to enjoy Him forever." The first answer of the *Shorter Catechism* says essentially the same thing.

THE QUESTION OF A SPECIAL INTERPRETIVE METHOD FOR PROPHECY

As already noted, many writers suggest that prophecy calls for a special method of interpretation. This is the foundation for the distinction between amillennialism and premillennialism. For example Terry states:

> A thorough interpretation of the prophetic portions of the holy Scripture is largely dependent upon a mastery of the principles and laws of figurative language and of types and symbols. . . . It is principally those portions of the prophetic Scriptures which forecast the future that call for special hermeneutics."[38]

While it is acknowledged that many prophetic passages do contain figurative language and that they are often written in poetic style, one must question whether the method for interpreting prophecy should be distinct from the method for interpreting other kinds of biblical literature.

As Virkler has observed,

> The question is not between a strictly literal versus a strictly symbolic approach: even the strictest literalist takes some things symbolically . . . conversely, even the most thoroughgoing symbolist interprets some things

literally. Thus the differences between literalists and symbolists are
relative, rather than absolute, involving questions of "how much" and
"which parts" of prophecy should be interpreted symbolically rather than
literally.[39]

Therefore instead of a "special hermeneutics" of symbolism
for prophecy, as is suggested by covenant theologians, the question
is, How much and which parts are to be understood symbolically?

Several factors are involved in determining where a given
Bible passage may lie in the spectrum between the "absolutely
allegorical" and the "absolutely literal."

Virkler notes that context and historic word usage are two such
factors. Another key factor is that of presuppositions. An additional
factor is the question of past or future fulfillment. Some writers
will accept a literal fulfillment of prophecy in history, and yet will
deny a literal future (from a present perspective) fulfillment of
prophecies that may be found in the same passage. By what
criteria can one determine that yet unfulfilled prophetic sections
are symbolic or allegorical while asserting that already fulfilled
prophetic sections are literal?

Crucial to this question is the issue of authority. Regardless of
one's position on the allegorical-literal spectrum, one must have a
standard by which to determine whether an interpretation of a
given passage is valid. This standard in effect becomes one's
ultimate authority. This is why the *Westminster Confession* deferred
councils and synods (including those that developed the
Westminster Confession and the Synod of Dort) to Scripture.

If one accepts an "absolutely literal" perspective, the text itself
becomes the clear-cut authority without question. Unfortunately
this absolute view is impossible to maintain, not only because of
the nature of language (and even more so the language of Scripture),
but also because of the size and complexity of Scripture. As one
moves away from this end of the spectrum, a greater degree of
subjectivity of interpretation enters the picture until one reaches
the opposite extreme of absolute subjectivity with each individual
and his interpretations being his own authority.

Here is where Calvin's dictum that Scripture interprets Scripture
is helpful. For example Ryken notes that in interpreting the Book
of Revelation, one must be aware that the symbols in it were
addressed to an audience that knew the Old Testament and that
the book contains approximately three hundred fifty allusions to
the Old Testament.[40] So it is crucial that a reader studying

Revelation be aware of the Old Testament Scriptures and symbols for a valid control on interpretation.

Some Old Testament prophecies, regardless of how symbolical, have been interpreted in the New Testament. These, of course, are ones that were fulfilled in the first coming of Christ. A prime example is Isaiah 61:1–2a. Jesus read this passage in the synagogue in Nazareth and proclaimed that this Scripture had been "fulfilled" in the hearing of His listeners (Luke 4:17–21).

The Old Testament was often used by New Testament writers to demonstrate God's dealings or to prove a point. In the case of the fulfillment of prophecy, the Old Testament predictions provide a foundation for understanding further prophecy. The understanding and hope of New Testament prophecy is built on the foundation and fulfillment of Old Testament prophecy. As Hoekema has stated, "Christian eschatology, therefore, involves an expectation for the future which is rooted in what has already happened in the past."[41]

Also the New Testament often explains aspects of Old Testament prophecy. For example no interpreter of Isaiah should bypass the explanation of Isaiah 61:1–2a given by Jesus. This interpretation in Luke 4:17–21 has put a control on the possible ways of understanding the Isaiah passage. This does not necessarily say that Isaiah himself understood all the implications of what he wrote.

As one moves toward figurative and symbolic language, the built-in controls decrease and the need for an external control heightens. According to Roman Catholicism this external control is church tradition and authority, focused ultimately in the pope.

The Reformers broke with this, in their acceptance of the historical-grammatical method. This returned Scripture to its role as one's ultimate authority. However, this break was not complete. Amillennialism was the prophetic understanding of medieval Catholicism. It was also the prophetic understanding of Calvin and Luther, who were educated in the medieval Catholic Church. Eschatology was not an issue of the Reformation; soteriology and ecclesiology were.

Consequently it is not surprising that scholars who followed Calvin sought a new control as they studied Scripture. Two controls were suggested—one typified by Cocceius, and the other typified by Poiret. The former became the one accepted by most of Protestant Christianity for the next two and one-half centuries.

The other, though accepted in some circles, was not revived on a large scale until the 19th century. One cannot help but wonder how much of that revival was also a result of the awareness of the inadequate controls exhibited by an emerging liberal theology.

The control accepted in the circles of the Reformed tradition was that of the covenants. This was an attempt to demonstrate the unity of Scripture. However, it is suggested that this control served more as a stopgap measure to clarify a prophetic understanding already present, and thus was not a clear Reformed reevaluation of the issue. This is not to say that the concept of the covenants is invalid. The covenants are an attempt to understand the thinking of God and the relationship of the Persons of the Trinity to each other and to man in the manifestation of God's grace in the redemption process. As such, there is value in their consideration.

However, to base the interpretation of all Scripture on the covenants is inadequate. Van der Waal appears to exhibit such a view when he states, "Our understanding of the covenant must come to fruition in our understanding of Scripture,"[42] or when he writes, "Dispensationalism must stand or fall with its view of the covenants."[43] He views the covenants as the ultimate truth and authority, and suggests that even Scripture must be interpreted in consonance with this theological construct.

Interestingly he senses a certain degree of frustration in the amillennial interpretation of the Book of Revelation. He calls it being "trapped in a blind alley."[44] This admits a sense of inadequacy in the entire system.[45]

Dispensational theology is more objectively based. As such, it has the necessary external control while at the same time recognizing the place of figures of speech. On the other hand the control of the covenants is insufficient to prevent a person from slipping further away from a literal understanding of the text.

Conclusion

Covenant theology is built on a weak hermeneutical base which consists of theological constructs. These constructs were established during the 17th century by serious scholars who no doubt genuinely sought to understand God's Word and how it fits together. But it was done without sufficient evaluation of the basic issue of authority and hermeneutical foundations. Conversely dispensationalism is built on the strong hermeneutical base of literal interpretation. As such it has a strong external authority and a consistent method. Since Scripture is the believer's authority, dispensationalism is concluded to be a more effective hermeneutical system.

CHAPTER 4

Ages and Dispensations in the Ante-Nicene Fathers

Larry V. Crutchfield

It is possible to find in the writings of the Fathers divisions of human history based on God's dealings with mankind. These are systems based not on an arbitrary division of human existence into predetermined chronological ages, as Kraus charges,[1] but on God's program for humanity within the context of salvation. The early church fathers recognized that at various times the method of God's dealings with men and the content of the divine revelation to them had undergone change to counteract the creature's failure and to facilitate his approach in obedience to God. Yet these Fathers saw but one basis throughout human history for man's justification before God: faith in Jesus' sacrificial death on the cross.

Among those whose doctrine of ages and dispensations has survived from the ante-Nicene period are Justin Martyr, Irenaeus, Tertullian, Methodius, and to a minor degree Victorinus of Petau. This study focuses on Justin and Irenaeus, with occasional references to Tertullian and Methodius as appropriate. The dispensational outline found in Victorinus of Petau is similar to the others (see Appendix A), but the absence of detail in his scheme makes meaningful evaluation of it virtually impossible.

The Early Concept of Ages and Dispensations

Barnabas' year-day tradition is the earliest budding of the dispensational understanding of God's dealings with man. Barnabas indicated that boundaries have been set for the times of man, the kingdom rest, and the beginning of eternity.[2] Furthermore within the time of man's allotted six thousand years, God has had His special people Israel, who failed. Therefore He established a new people with whom He deals on the basis of newly revealed principles. While sacrifices, burnt offerings, and oblations were the acceptable means of approach to God in the old era, according to Barnabas, Christ Himself is the "human oblation" in the present age.[3] This latter age, suggested Ignatius, is "a dispensation founded on faith in [Jesus Christ] and love for Him, on His Passion and Resurrection."[4] It is distinct from what Clement terms "every age that has passed,"[5] and as Hermas implies, from "the age that is to come, in which the elect of God will dwell."[6]

JUSTIN MARTYR (ca. A.D. 100–165)

The data by which to reconstruct Justin Martyr's doctrine of dispensations is abundant though it is not presented systematically. The stage for a dispensational system was set with his reply to a question on whether God always taught the same righteousness. Justin remarked,

> For if one should wish to ask you why, since Enoch, Noah with his sons, and all others in similar circumstances, who neither were circumcised nor kept the Sabbath, pleased God, God demanded by other leaders, and by the giving of the law after the lapse of so many generations, that those who lived between the times of Abraham and of Moses be justified by circumcision, and that those who lived after Moses be justified by circumcision and the other ordinances—to wit, the Sabbath, and sacrifices, and libations, and offerings.[7]

Elsewhere Justin made three things clear in this regard: (1) God is always the same; (2) the righteous actions (righteousness) that He expects are always the same;[8] but that (3) the manner in which they are expressed or that man is to respond to God changes from dispensation to dispensation, and that change is precipitated by man's sin and failure. Justin warned of

> fall[ing] into foolish opinions, as if it were not the same God who existed in the times of Enoch and all the rest, who neither were circumcised after the flesh, nor observed Sabbaths, nor any other rites, seeing that Moses enjoined such observances; or that God has not wished each race of mankind continually to perform the same righteous actions [obedience to the will of God]: to admit which, seems to be ridiculous and absurd. Therefore we must confess that He, who is ever the same, has commanded these and such like institutions on account of sinful men.[9]

Justin set forth four distinct phases[10] through which the human race passes in God's progressive, revelatory program of salvation: the first, from Adam to Abraham; the second, from Abraham to Moses; the third, from Moses to Christ; and the fourth, from Christ presumably to the eternal state. Each phase has one or more chief representatives, distinct characteristics marking it off from all others, a specific reason for which change is instituted, and a clear basis on which salvation rests (see Appendix B).

Justin identified Enoch and Noah as the chief representatives of the first dispensation extending from Adam to Abraham. He wrote of "Enoch, Noah with his sons, and all others in similar circumstances"[11] and of "Enoch and those like him."[12] Elsewhere Justin named Adam, Abel, Lot, and Melchizedek as also belonging to this dispensation,[13] which included all those "righteous and pleasing to Him, who lived before Moses and Abraham." He distinctly marked the next dispensation when he wrote, "After them Abraham with all his descendants until Moses"[14] and spoke of "those who lived between the times of Abraham and of Moses."[15]

Justin identified the chief dispensational characteristic during this first period as the nonobservance of rites. He said, "All these righteous men already mentioned,"[16] "neither were circumcised, nor kept the Sabbath,"[17] "nor any other rites."[18] Yet the means of their salvation, as is the case in all dispensations, by Justin's reckoning, is the individual righteousness that comes through faith in God, as evidenced by the keeping of His commands. Those from Adam to Noah, though observing no rites, were declared righteous and pleasing to God[19] because of their possession of true circumcision—the circumcision of the heart. "Though a man be a Scythian or a Persian, if he has the knowledge of God and of his Christ, and keeps the everlasting righteous decrees, he is circumcised with the good and useful circumcision, and is a friend of God, and God rejoices in his gifts and offerings."[20] And again, "We, who have approached God through Him [Christ], have received not carnal, but spiritual circumcision, which Enoch and those like him observed. . . . and all men may equally obtain it."[21]

This dispensation of nonobservance of rites, however, came to an end. But since Justin's focus was on Israel as the people of God, he said nothing directly here about the personal failure of those between Adam and Abraham. He wrote only in general terms of the need for new "institutions on account of sinful men"[22] and "the hardness of your people's heart."[23] This he said with reference to the two dispensations to follow. Failure in each of these periods was presented by Justin primarily in terms of God's chosen people, the Jews, while the Gentiles and those who preceded Abraham were mainly ignored. As was the custom of these early Fathers, the canvas of theological debate is covered only by the broad strokes of apologetic or polemic necessity with little attention given to nonexpedient detail.

In the second dispensation, from Abraham to Moses, Abraham was the chief representative. Since "circumcision began with Abraham,"[24] Abraham was representative of those who followed him, until the time of Moses.[25]

The primary identifying mark of this dispensation is the rite of circumcision. Justin explained to Trypho that this rite was unnecessary before Abraham's time, but because of the foreseen sin of Israel it became a necessary sign.[26] It would seem that, according to Justin, as a type of the true circumcision to come, circumcision of the flesh also served as the means of approach to God and as a symbol of Abraham's obedience in faith.[27]

Justin explained the reason for the change in dispensational arrangement in the following way. On the basis of God's foreknowledge of Israel's sin, the rite of circumcision ("of the flesh") was given as a sign.[28] This sign was given so that Israel might be distinguished from all other nations "and that you alone may suffer that which you now justly suffer."[29] He maintained further that "these things [various sufferings of the Jews] have happened to you in fairness and justice, for you have slain the Just One, and His prophets before Him; and now you reject those who hope in Him, and in Him who sent Him . . . cursing in your synagogues those that believe on Christ."[30] But in another place Justin suggested that this circumcision of the flesh "was a type of the true circumcision by which we are circumcised from deceit and iniquity through Him who rose from the dead on the first day after the Sabbath [namely, through] our Lord Jesus Christ."[31]

As in all dispensations justification in this period between Abraham and Moses was by faith. And faith results in individual righteousness which is manifested by obedience to the revealed will of God. "For when Abraham himself was in uncircumcision," wrote Justin, "he was justified and blessed by reason of the faith which he reposed in God, as the Scripture tells."[32] And again he said, "For Abraham was declared by God to be righteous, not on account of circumcision, but on account of faith [Gen. 15:6]."[33]

The chief representative of the third dispensation, that from Moses to Christ, was Moses himself. This is the "legal dispensation,"[34] the dispensation of Law. Again, as Justin explained, certain rites "were enjoined on account of the hardness of [the] people's heart."[35] The rites that characterized this dispensation included the continuation of circumcision, with the addition of Sabbaths, sacrifices, offerings, libations (or ashes), and feasts.[36]

As was true with circumcision, Justin maintained that these new rites were given as signs and not for a work of righteousness. At the same time, however, he viewed the rites as a means of approach to God, as a prod toward piety and away from idolatry. On the significance of the rites as signs, Justin wrote, "Moreover, that God enjoined you to keep the Sabbath, and impose on you other precepts for a sign, as I have already said, on account of your unrighteousness, and that of your fathers—as He declares that for the sake of the nations, lest His name be profaned among them, therefore He permitted some of you to remain alive."[37]

But while Justin claimed that these rites were given as signs because of Israel's hardness of heart, he also insisted that they were given to lead the Jews into obedience to God and away from idolatry. With regard to sacrifices, for example, he said that "it was for the sins of your own nation, for their idolatries, and not because there was any necessity for such sacrifices, that they were likewise enjoined."[38] He quoted Amos 5:18–6:7; Jeremiah 7:21–22; and Psalm 1 in support. Then he added, "For indeed the temple . . . in Jerusalem, He admitted to be His house or court, not as though He needed it, but in order that you, in this view of it, giving yourselves to Him, might not worship idols."[39] Commenting on the same theme elsewhere, Justin wrote, "You were commanded to observe the Sabbath, and to present offerings, and that the Lord submitted to have a place called by the name of God, in order that, as has been said, you might not become impious and godless by worshiping idols and forgetting God, as indeed you do always appear to have been."[40] The Sabbath itself was to serve as "a memorial of God."[41]

Justin also stated that the Jews had indeed forgotten God and once again demonstrated their disobedience, despite God's efforts to encourage them in righteous conduct. Justin maintained that under Moses, all those descended from Abraham "appeared unrighteous and ungrateful to God, making a calf in the wilderness: wherefore God, accommodating Himself to that nation, enjoined them also to offer sacrifices, as if to His name, in order that you might not serve idols. Which precept, however, you have not observed."[42] Justin indicted Israel further: "You were commanded to abstain from certain kinds of food, in order that you might keep

God before your eyes while you ate and drank, seeing that you were prone and very ready to depart from His knowledge."[43]

Those who lived under the Mosaic dispensation were saved as others are: by individual righteousness through faith in God on the basis of Christ's atoning work. Trypho had asked Justin, "Tell me, then, shall those who lived according to the law given by Moses, live in the same manner with Jacob, Enoch, and Noah, in the resurrection of the dead, or not?" Justin replied,

> each one . . . shall be saved by his own righteousness. . . . those who regulated their lives by the law of Moses would in like manner be saved. For what in the law of Moses is naturally good, and pious, and righteous, and has been prescribed to be done by those who obey it; and what was appointed to be performed by reason of the hardness of the people's hearts; was similarly recorded, and done also by those who were under the law. Since those who did that which is universally, naturally, and eternally good are pleasing to God, they shall be saved through this Christ in the resurrection equally with those righteous men who were before them, namely Noah, and Enoch, and Jacob, and who ever else there be, along with those who have known this Christ, Son of God.[44]

The fourth dispensation in Justin's outline of human history is the period from Christ to presumably the eternal state. While it is certain that Justin looked for a distinct one-thousand-year millennial reign of Christ on earth, he did not discuss it in dispensational terms. He seemed rather to include it under the dispensation of Christ.[45]

However, Justin did speak pointedly about the end of the dispensation under Moses and the beginning of that under Christ. Because of Israel's sin, "it was necessary, in accordance with the Father's will, that they [all rites] should have an end in Him who was born of a virgin, of the family of Abraham and tribe of Judah, and of David; in Christ the Son of God."[46] In response to Trypho's questioning, Justin admitted that Christ "was both circumcised, and observed the other legal ceremonies ordained by Moses," but he hastened to add that "He endured all these not as if He were justified by them, but completing the dispensation which His Father . . . wished Him [to complete]."[47] Obviously Christ is the chief Representative of the present dispensation.

Justin characterized this dispensation under Christ as one in which the rite of circumcision instituted with Abraham, and the rites of Sabbath-keeping, sacrifices, offerings, and feasts, which came in under Moses, have ceased.[48] Now God provides spiritual circumcision of heart[49] and gifts of the Holy Spirit.[50] The prophets

of old received "some one or two powers from God," by which
they were enabled to speak what has been set down in Scripture.
After citing several instances of this as evidence, he said,

> Accordingly [the Holy Spirit] rested, i.e., ceased, when *He* [Christ] came,
> after whom, in the times of this dispensation wrought out by Him amongst
> men, it was requisite that such gifts should cease from you; and having
> received their rest in Him, should again, as had been predicted, become
> gifts which, from the grace of His Spirit's power, He imparts to those
> who believe in Him, according as He deems each man worthy thereof.[51]

The reason given by Justin for the change in God's governmental
arrangement of things with men is that with the advent of the
sinless Christ there is no longer any need for the former rites.[52]
The blood of that former circumcision, asserted Justin, is obsolete.
For now "we trust in the blood of salvation; there is now another
covenant, and another law has gone forth from Zion. Jesus Christ
circumcises all who will . . . with knives of stone; that they may be
a righteous nation, a people keeping faith, holding to the truth, and
maintaining peace."[53] In Christ believers have "the everlasting
law and the everlasting covenant."[54]

Concerning the promised New Covenant and its relation to the
old, Justin made a significant statement about God's methods of
dealing with mankind. To Trypho, Justin said,

> did not the Scriptures predict that God promised to dispense a new
> covenant besides that which [was dispensed] in the mountain Horeb? . . .
> Was not the old covenant laid on your fathers with fear and trembling, so
> that they could not give ear to God? . . . God promised that there would
> be another covenant, not like that old one, and said that it would be laid
> on them without fear, and trembling, and lightnings, and that it would be
> such as to show what kind of commands and deeds God knows to be
> eternal and suited to every nation, and what commandments He has
> given, suiting them to the hardness of your people's hearts, as He exclaims
> also by the prophets.[55]

The means of salvation in this dispensation, as in the previous
ones, according to Justin, is individual righteousness. In every
instance obedience to the decrees of God results in salvation
through Christ.[56] Those who have approached God in this
dispensation, Justin maintained, have received the same spiritual
circumcision received by Enoch and others like him. "And we
have received it through baptism," said Justin, "since we were
sinners, by God's mercy; and all men may equally obtain it."[57]
While his terminology is not always consistent and his presentation
of the subject is not systematic, it is nevertheless clear that Justin

is in essential agreement with Ryrie's statement that "the basis of salvation is always the death of Christ; the means is always faith; the object is always God . . . but the content of faith depends on the particular revelation God was pleased to give at a certain time."[58]

IRENAEUS (ca. A.D. 120–202)

Like Justin Martyr, Irenaeus saw human history not merely as parcels of time patterned after the six plus one days of creation, but in terms of the dispensational arrangements of God. Even though Irenaeus's presentation of the dispensations is not as full as Justin's, he did make some interesting statements about and arguments for God's ordered program for man's salvation. Irenaeus's four dispensations are (1) Creation to the Deluge (or Adam to Noah), (2) Deluge to the Law (or Noah to Moses), (3) the Law to the Gospel (or Moses to Christ), (4) the Gospel to presumably the Eternal State (or Christ to the Eternal State).

The method by which Irenaeus arrived at the number of dispensations is interesting as it is based on quadriplex prototypes, both in nature and in Scripture.[59] He reasoned that the Gospels can be neither greater nor fewer than four in number because of the analogy of the quadriform structure of creation. Irenaeus maintained that there are four zones of the world inhabited by mankind and four principal winds. He concluded, therefore, that

> while the Church is scattered throughout all the world, and the "pillar and ground" [1 Tim. 3:15] of the Church is the Gospel and the spirit of life; it is fitting that she should have four pillars [1 Tim. 3:15], breathing out immortality on every side, and vivifying men afresh. From which fact, it is evident that the Word, the Artificer of all, He that sitteth upon the cherubim, and contains all things, He who was manifested to men, has given us the Gospel under four aspects, but bound together by one Spirit.[60]

Irenaeus developed this reference to Christ sitting on the cherubim (Ps. 80:1) in conjunction with the "four living creatures" of Revelation 4:7. Observing that the cherubim were four-faced, Irenaeus contended that "their faces were images of the dispensation of the Son of God." As seen in the following summary of Irenaeus's position,[61] he saw the dispensational arrangements of God culminating in the final dispensation brought in by Christ.[62]

1. *First living creature: like a lion* = "His effectual working, His leadership, and royal power" (characterized by the Gospel of

John). "And the Word of God Himself used to converse with the ante-Mosaic patriarchs, in accordance with His divinity and glory" (reference to the first and second dispensations).

2. *Second living creature: like a calf* = "[His] sacrificial and sacerdotal order" (characterized by the Gospel of Luke). "But for those under the Law he instituted a sacerdotal and liturgical service" (reference to the third dispensation).

3. *Third living creature: like a man* = "His advent as a human being" (characterized by the Gospel of Matthew). "Afterwards, being made man for us" (reference to the fourth dispensation).

4. *Fourth living creature: like a flying eagle* = "Pointing out the gift of the Spirit hovering with His wings over the church" (characterized by the Gospel of Mark). "He sent the gift of the celestial Spirit over all the earth, protecting us with His wings" (reference again to the fourth dispensation).

Irenaeus advanced his thesis by saying that just as the living creatures and the Gospel are quadriform so also is "the course followed by the Lord." He contended that this is the reason God gave four principal covenants to mankind. It should be kept in mind that Irenaeus often employed the term "covenant" in a broad sense to refer to some specific economy in God's program of salvation. Thus in some contexts the terms "covenant" and "dispensation" signify essentially the same thing. Since there is some variation in the dispensational system of Irenaeus in the Latin and Greek versions of the text under consideration, both are presented below in parallel and summary fashion.[63]

1. *First*, "prior to the deluge, under Adam."
   Greek version: "first covenant as having been given to Noah, at the deluge, under the sign of the rainbow."
2. *Second*, "that after the deluge, under Noah."
   Greek version: "the second as that given to Abraham, under the sign of circumcision."
3. *Third*, "the giving of the Law, under Moses."
   Greek version: "the third, as being the giving of the Law, under Moses."
4. *Fourth*, "that which renovates man [under Christ], and sums up all things in itself by means of the Gospel, raising and bearing men upon its wings into the heavenly kingdom."
   Greek version: "the fourth, as that of the Gospel, through our Lord Jesus Christ."

In the Greek version, the less authoritative of the two,[64] the outline is exactly the same as that found in Justin Martyr.

Irenaeus held firmly to the belief that the divine program of salvation for mankind is worked out in an orderly fashion by the Triune God. And this orderly system he cast in dispensational terms. Irenaeus spoke of the various gifts, "adapted to the times," which have been bestowed on the human race by the "prophetic Spirit." "Thus, therefore," he concluded, "was God revealed; for God the Father is shown forth through all these [operations], the Spirit indeed working, and the Son ministering, while the Father was approving, and man's salvation being accomplished."[65] For Irenaeus, Christ is especially prominent in this dispensational drama. It is the eternal Son, he said,

> who did also show to the human race prophetic visions, and diversities of gifts, and His own ministrations, and the glory of the Father, in regular order and connection, at the fitting time for the benefit [of mankind]. For where there is a regular succession, there is also fixedness; and where fixedness, there suitability to the period; and where suitability, there also utility. And for this reason did the Word become the dispenser of the paternal grace for the benefit of men, . . . revealing God to men through many dispensations, lest man, falling away from God altogether, should cease to exist.[66]

Irenaeus gave relatively little information on the first two dispensations, Creation to the Deluge, and the Deluge to the Law. But the information he did include is redolent of Justin's teaching on the subject. Irenaeus explained that circumcision (Gen. 17:9–11) and Sabbath observance (Ex. 31:13; Ezek. 20:12) were both given as signs. The former was given so that the "race of Abraham might continue recognizable." But he explained further that these signs had symbolic meaning and real purpose beyond the sign. Physical circumcision, for example, was a type of the circumcision of the heart performed by the Holy Spirit (Col. 2:11; Deut. 10:16, LXX). Sabbath observance, on the other hand, taught continual service to God. It spoke too of the millennial rest to come, after the type of the seventh day of rest following the creation.[67]

Like Justin, Irenaeus insisted that no man was justified by these rites. For proof of this he mentioned Abraham, Lot, Noah, and Enoch, all of whom were uncircumcised yet pleased God. Also "all the rest of the multitude of those righteous men who lived *before Abraham*, and of those patriarchs who *preceded Moses*, were justified independently of the things above mentioned, and without the law of Moses." Here Irenaeus obviously followed the

Greek version of the dispensational system outlined earlier, and was in agreement with Justin's dispensational arrangement.[68]

Irenaeus asked, "Why, then, did the Lord not form the covenant [Law given to Moses] for the fathers?" His answer was to the effect that the fathers prior to Moses had the Law (meaning here primarily the Decalogue) written in their hearts and the righteousness of the Law in their souls, and they lived by it.[69] Therefore there was no need for an external Law written on stone. However, said Irenaeus,

> when this righteousness and love to God had passed into oblivion, and became extinct in Egypt, God did necessarily, because of His great goodwill to men, reveal Himself by a voice, and led the people with power out of Egypt, in order that man might again become the disciple and follower of God. . . . And it [the Decalogue] enjoined love to God, and taught just dealing towards our neighbor, that we should neither be unjust nor unworthy of God.[70]

This passage suggests the principle of a new dispensation precipitated by failure. The principle is also set down that with the new dispensation is an attendant new revelation, the purpose of which is to assist man in gaining justification before God.

In another place, on the theme of failure and differing covenants, Irenaeus pointed out that one person may, more accurately than another, be able to explain

> the operation and dispensation of God connected with human salvation; and show that God manifested longsuffering in regard to the apostasy of the angels who transgressed, as also with respect to the disobedience of men; and set forth why it is that [by] one and the same God . . . more covenants than one were given to mankind; and teach what was the special character of each of these covenants.[71]

Irenaeus blamed the error of Simon Magus, Marcion, Valentinus, and others on their "ignorance of the Scriptures and of the dispensation of God." He, on the other hand, promised in the progress of his treatise to address the cause of the differences between covenants and to touch on their unity and harmony. For those were perfected, he maintained, "who knew one and the same God, who from beginning to end was present with mankind in the various dispensations."[72]

In speaking of the various covenants, especially that under Moses (the legal dispensation) and that under Christ (the gospel dispensation), Irenaeus emphasized the fact that throughout history there is but one God and one means of salvation. But at the same time he believed in the progressive nature of both revelation and the precepts by which salvation is understood and God approached. "The Lord is the good man of the house, who rules the entire house of His Father."[73] It is He, according to Irenaeus, who delivers what is suited to man in each dispensation. For example the old covenant was suited to those who were slaves and undisciplined. But the same householder brought forth a New Covenant, the Gospel, as fitting for free men, justified by faith. This, he said, is "the new dispensation of liberty, the covenant, through the advent of His Son."[74]

The former covenant, the legal dispensation,[75] resulted in bondage, whereas the latter, the greater of the two dispensations, brought forth liberty and multiplied grace.[76] This New Covenant and He who was to carry it out, Irenaeus continued, were both preached by the prophets and revealed to men as it pleased God. This was done in order that "they might always make progress through believing in Him, and by means of the [successive] covenants, should gradually attain to perfect salvation. For there is one salvation and one God; but the precepts which form the man are numerous, and the steps which lead man to God are not a few."[77]

As failure was the reason the Mosaic or legal dispensation was substituted for that under Abraham, Irenaeus believed that here too failure resulted in mankind

> enter[ing] upon a new phase, the Word arranging after a new manner the advent in the flesh, that He might win back to God that human nature (*hominem*) which had departed from God; and therefore men were taught to worship God after a new fashion, but not another god [contra Gnostic teaching], because in truth there is but "one God, who justifieth the circumcision by faith, and the uncircumcision through faith" [Rom. 3:30].[78]

Irenaeus employed the imagery of a vineyard to explain the reason for the transfer from the former dispensation to the present. After explaining that the God who called those of the former dispensation of Law (which involves bondage) also called those of the latter dispensation (by means of adoption), he added, "For God planted the vineyard of the human race when at the first He formed Adam and chose the fathers; then He let it out to husbandmen when He established the Mosaic dispensation." Irenaeus observed that God then "hedged it round about" (i.e., gave special instructions for worship), "built a tower" (i.e., chose Jerusalem), and "digged a winepress" (i.e., prepared a medium for the prophetic Spirit). God sent the prophets to seek the fruits of righteousness and then He sent His own Son. But the wicked husbandmen killed His Son and cast Him out of the vineyard. Thus God, having justly rejected these evil men, has unhedged the vineyard, throwing it open to husbandmen (i.e., Gentiles) throughout the world. Now the beautiful "elect tower," the church, is being raised everywhere and the winepress is being digged everywhere, for everywhere there are those who are receiving the Spirit.[79]

This last dispensation, the "dispensation of His coming," was clearly announced by Moses (Num. 24:17) as being from Jacob and from among the Jews.[80] There are some, he pointed out elsewhere, who "despise the coming of the Son of God and the dispensation of His incarnation, which the apostles have transmitted to us."[81] And further, "certain persons, because of the disobedient and ruined Israelites, do assert that the giver . . . of the law was limited in power, they will find in our dispensation that 'many are called, but few chosen'" (Matt. 22:14). Nevertheless "those who have believed on Him should be honored with immortality."[82]

A Word about the Number of Dispensations

While it is true that the number of dispensations to which one holds is not a decisive issue, it is nevertheless an important one. The claim made by Kraus, that for the Fathers "there is only one basic dispensational division,"[83] is inaccurate. It was of course true then as now that the basic division between the Old and New Testaments—God's programs before and after Christ—was recognized. But it is also true, as has been demonstrated, that several of the Fathers held to a multi-staged (or dispensational) dealing of God with man based generally on a cycle of failure and the consequent need for new revelation to aid mankind in his endeavor to please God in obedient faith. Though some Fathers set forth only four such dispensations, others came very close to making nearly the same divisions modern dispensationalists do. In Irenaeus, Victorinus of Petau, and Methodius the number of dispensations is artificially restricted to four because of the quadriplex types adduced from both nature and Scripture which seemed to require it. Without such an artificially self-imposed constraint, the result is more like that found in Tertullian.[84]

While it makes little essential difference whether the Fathers held to four or more dispensations, it is nevertheless instructive to determine how they arrived at the number of dispensations to which they held. It is also of interest to observe how their dispensations relate to those held by contemporary dispensationalists. The dispensations are most often spoken of in the early Fathers in terms of the prominent persons—Adam, Noah, Abraham, Moses, and Christ—with whom God dealt individually, and to whom He imparted new revelation for the collective good of His people. Often the name of Abel is associated with that of Adam, while Enoch is often connected with Noah. Dispensational divisions were customarily made along the boundaries of these five men's lives and times.

If a church father held to only four dispensations, there is frequently confusion as to where to draw the boundaries for the first two dispensations. The Fathers recognized the distinctive part that Adam, Noah, and Abraham played in God's dispensational arrangements. But if there can be only four dispensations and the Law under Moses and the Gospel under Christ are assumed,[85] the first two economies must be manipulated to fit the predetermined number. The result is that, depending on which fourfold system one examines, one patriarch (usually Adam or Abraham) was absorbed into one of the others when the actual divisions were set forth. In general discussions of God's economies, however, the fivefold division continued to be observed. And these five are roughly equivalent to Scofield's dispensations of Innocence (Adam), Government (Noah), Promise (Abraham), Law (Moses), and Grace (Christ).[86]

But how did the Fathers deal with what modern dispensationalists call the dispensation of conscience (from the Fall to the Flood) and the millennial dispensation (the second coming of Christ to the eternal state)? Since the Fathers tended to think of the dispensations in terms of prominent men, it is easy to see how Abel and Enoch (two of the prominent men of the dispensation of conscience)[87] could be absorbed into the economies under their more illustrious contemporaries (Abel under Adam and Enoch under Noah), men to whom greater portions of the biblical narrative are devoted. In the case of the millennium the Fathers alternated between calling it a "new" dispensation and the "future" dispensation,[88] and simply regarding the whole period from the Incarnation to the eternal state under Christ, the prominent figure throughout. Regardless of the number of economies to which the Fathers held, the fact remains that they set forth what can only be considered a doctrine of ages and dispensations which foreshadows dispensationalism as it is held today. Their views were certainly less well defined and less sophisticated. But it is evident that the early Fathers viewed God's dealings with His people in dispensational terms.

Conclusion

John Nelson Darby (1800–1882) was the first to give systematic form to the doctrine of ages and dispensations. But he was by no means the first to recognize and employ the basic principles on which this doctrine stands. Ehlert's valuable work, *A Bibliographic History of Dispensationalism*,[89] shows that this doctrine has a history almost as old as the church itself. In every major area of importance in the early church one finds rudimentary features of dispensationalism that bear a striking resemblance to their contemporary offspring. But this doctrine does not depend on the historical consensus of human opinion—devout or otherwise—for its existence. Believers have one authority, and one authority only. As Charles L. Feinberg aptly puts it, "The final issue is, 'What saith the Scripture?'"[90]

Appendix A

Comparison of Dispensational Systems of Fathers in the Ante-Nicene Age

Justin Martyr (ca. 100-165)	Enoch/Noah	Abraham	Moses	Christ	Millennium
	(Adam to Abraham)	(Abraham to Moses)	(Moses to Christ)	(Christ to Eternal State?)	(Seventh millenary of years)
(Dialogue with Trypho)	(Chap. 92; cf. chap. 27)	(Chap. 92; cf. chap. 19)	(Chap. 92; cf. chap. 43)	(Chap. 23, 43, 45)	(Chap. 81; Frag. 15)

Irenaeus* (ca. 120-202)	(3. 11. 8) Four Covenants (4. 9. 3)				Millennium
	Adam to Noah	Noah to Moses	Moses to Christ	Christ to Eternal State	(Seventh millenary of years)
(Against Heresies)	(3. 11. 8; 4. 16. 2)	(3. 11. 8; 4. 16. 2)	(3. 11. 8; 4. 16. 2-3)	(3. 11. 8-9; 4. 9. 1-3)	(4. 16. 1; 5. 30. 4; 5. 33. 2)

Tertullian (ca. 150-225)	Adam (Adam and Eve; Paradise; Abel)	Noah (Noah and Enoch; Patriarchs)	Abraham (Lot; Jews; Melchizedek; Patriarchs)	Moses (Jews; the Prophets)	Christ ("more faithful worshipers)	"millennial interspace" prior to "eternal economy"
(An Answer to the Jews)	(Chaps. 2, 4, 5)	(Chaps. 2, 4)	(Chaps. 2-6)	(Chaps. 2-6)	(*Apology* chap. 21)	(*Apology* chap. 49)
(Against Praxeas)	(Chap. 16)	(Chaps. 16)	(Chaps. 16)	(Chaps. 16)	(*Ag. Marc.* 3-4, 20)	(*On the Res.* 59, 61)

Victorinus of Petau (d. ca. 304)	Four Generations of People				Millennium
	Adam to Noah	Noah to Abraham	Abraham to Moses	Moses to Christ	(Seventh millenary of years)
(On the Creation of the World)					

Methodius (died 311)	(Judg. 9:8-15) Four Trees / Laws (Disc. 10, chap. 2)				Millennium
	Adam to Noah (Fig tree)	Noah to Moses (Vine)	Moses to Christ (Olive Tree)	Apostles to Millennium (Bramble)	(Seventh millenary of years)="new dispensation"
(Banquet of the Ten Virgins)	(Disc. 10, chaps. 2-4; disc. 7, chaps. 4-5, 7)	(Disc. 10, chaps. 2-4; disc. 7, chaps. 4-7)	(Disc. 10, chaps. 2-4; disc. 7, chaps. 4-5, 7)	(Disc. 10, chaps. 2-3; disc. 7, chaps. 4-5, 7)	(Disc. 4, chap. 5; disc. 7, chap. 3; disc. 8, chap. 11; disc. 9, chap. 2)

* Alternate system for Irenaeus (based on Greek text) = first covenant under Noah; second covenant under Abraham; third covenant (Law) under Moses; and fourth covenant (Gospel) under Christ (Roberts and Donaldson, eds., *Ante-Nicene Fathers*, 1:429, n. 3).

Appendix B *The Dispensations of Justin Martyr (ca. 100-165)*

	I (Dial. Chaps. 27, 92) **Adam to Abraham**	II (Dial. Chaps. 19, 92) **Abraham to Moses**	Old Covenant: Law (Dial. Chaps. 67) III (Dial. Chaps. 43, 92) **Moses to Christ**	New Covenant: Gospel (Dial. Chaps. 67) IV (Dial. Chaps. 222, 42, 45) **Christ to Eternal State?**
Representative(s) of Dispensation	1. **Chief representatives:** Enoch and Noah (*Dial.* chaps. 43, 92).	1. **Chief representative:** Abraham (*Dial.* chaps. 23, 43, 92).	1. **Chief representative:** Moses (*Dial.* chaps. 23, 67, 92).	1. **Chief representative:** Christ (*Dial.* chaps. 23, 43).
Characteristic(s) of Dispensation	2. **Chief Dispensational characteristic:** non-observance of rites, i.e., no circumcision, sabbaths, sacrifices, offerings, or feasts (*Dial.* chaps. 19, 23, 27, 46, 92).	2. **Chief Dispensational characteristic:** circumcision (*Dial.* chaps. 23, 43, 46, 92).	2. **Chief Dispensational characteristic:** circumcision plus sacrifices, feasts, sabbaths, and offerings (or oblations) (*Dial.* chaps. 23, 43, 92).	2. **Chief Dispensational characteristic:** all former rites, i.e., circumcision, sacrifices, etc., ended; there is now no circumcision of heart and gifts of the Holy Spirit (*Dial.* chaps. 43, 87).
Reason for Change in Dispensation	3. **Reason for change in dispensation:** new institutions were commanded because of sin / hardness of heart / failure (*Dial.* chaps. 16, 23, 43, 67, 92).	3. **Reason for change in dispensation:** circumcision given as sign for evil done to Christ, prophets, Christians; type of true circumcision (*Dial.* chaps. 16, 41).	3. **Reason for change in dispensation:** sacrifices /oblations instituted to combat idolatry; sabbaths to be memorial to God (*Dial.* chaps. 19, 21-22, 92).	3. **Reason for change in dispensation:** with advent of Christ, no further need for circumcision, sabbaths, etc.; new covenant promised (*Dial.* chaps. 23, 43).
Means of Salvation in Dispensation	4. **Means of salvation:** individual righteousness, i.e., they were circumcised of heart (*Dial.* chaps. 27-28, 43).	4. **Means of salvation:** individual righteousness, i.e., Abraham declared righteous / justified by faith, not circumcision (*Dial.* chaps. 23, 92).	4. **Means of salvation:** individual righteousness, i.e., those who lived by the Law shall be saved through Christ (*Dial.* chaps. 27-28, 43).	4. **Means of salvation:** individual righteousness, i.e., spiritual circumcision of heart like Enoch, et. al.; all may obtain it (*Dial.* chaps. 43, 45).

The means of salvation in every age is individual righteousness, resulting from faith in God and through the death of Christ (Dial. chap. 45).

———— 7,000 Years ————

(*Dialogue* chap. 81; Frag. 15; *Voice of the Church*, p. 59)

CHAPTER 5

The Abrahamic Covenant and Premillennialism

John F. Walvoord

A ll serious students of the Bible recognize that the covenant of God with Abraham is one of the important and determinative revelations of Scripture. It furnishes the key to the entire Old Testament and reaches for its fulfillment into the New. In the controversy between premillenarians and amillenarians, the interpretation of this covenant more or less settles the entire argument. The analysis of its provisions and the character of their fulfillment[1] set the mold for the entire body of scriptural truth.

Most of the discussions on the issue are distinguished for their disregard of the specific provisions of the covenant. Pieters in his closely reasoned book on this subject[2] is no exception. Like Berkhof,[3] Allis,[4] and other amillenarians, he finds it convenient and suited to his purpose to overlook the details of the promise and seize on its general promises of blessings. This is of course necessary for the amillennial interpretation which does not provide any fulfillment of the details. The premillennial interpretation on the other hand is able to account for the entire prophecy and its ultimate complete fulfillment.

The issue, in a word, is the question of whether Israel as a nation and as a race has a prophesied future. A literal interpretation of the Abrahamic Covenant involves the permanent existence of Israel as a nation and the fulfillment of the promise that the land should be their everlasting possession. Amillenarians generally deny this, remillenarians affirm it. What, then, are the provisions of the covenant with Abraham and do they promise what premillenarians affirm?

The Provisions of the Covenant

The language of the Abrahamic Covenant is plain and to the

point. The original covenant is given in Genesis 12:1–3, and there are three confirmations and amplifications as recorded in Genesis 13:14–17; 15:1–7; and 17:1–18. Some of the promises are given to Abraham personally, some to Abraham's seed, and some to Gentiles, or "all families of the earth" (Gen. 12:3).

THE PROMISE TO ABRAHAM

Abraham himself is promised that he would be the father of a great nation (Gen. 12:2), compared to the dust of the earth and the stars of the heaven in number (13:16; 15:5), and including kings and nations other than the "seed" itself (17:6). God promises His personal blessing on Abraham. His name shall be great and he himself shall be a blessing. All of this has had already the most literal fulfillment and continues to be fulfilled.

THE PROMISE TO ABRAHAM'S SEED

In addition to the promises to Abraham, the covenant includes blessings for Abraham's seed. The nation itself would be great (12:2) and innumerable (13:16; 15:5). The nation is promised possession of the land with its extensive boundaries described in detail (15:18–21). In connection with the promise of the land, the Abrahamic Covenant itself is expressly called "everlasting" (17:7) and the possession of the land is defined as "an everlasting possession" (17:8). It should be immediately clear that this promise guarantees both the everlasting continuance of the seed as a nation and its everlasting possession of the land.

Miscellaneous promises are included in the covenant. God is to be the God of Abraham's seed. It is prophesied that they would be afflicted, as fulfilled in the years in Egypt, and that afterward they would "come out with great substance" (15:14). In the promise to Abraham, "In thee shall all families of the earth be blessed," it is anticipated that the seed should be a channel of this blessing. In particular this is fulfilled in and through the Lord Jesus Christ.

All the promises to the "seed" in Genesis are references to the physical descendants of Abraham. General promises of blessing to Abraham's seed seem to include all his physical lineage, but it is clear that the term is used in a narrower sense in some instances. Eliezer of Damascus, while according to the customs of the day regarded as a child of Abraham because he was born in his house, was nevertheless disqualified because he was not the physical seed of Abraham (15:2). Further, not all the physical descendants of Abraham qualify for the promises to the seed. Ishmael was put aside. When Abraham pleaded with God, "O that Ishmael might live before you!" God replied, "Sarah thy wife shall bear thee a son indeed; and thou shalt call his name Isaac: and I will establish my covenant with him for an everlasting covenant, and with his seed after him" (17:18–19). The line of the seed and its promises is narrowed to the one son of Abraham. Later when Jacob and Esau are born, God in sovereign choice chose the younger as the father of the twelve patriarchs and confirmed the covenant to Jacob. The particular Abrahamic promises and blessings are thereafter channeled through the twelve tribes.

While the promises to the "seed" must be limited in their application according to the context, it is clear that much of the general blessings attending the Abrahamic Covenant such as the general blessing of God on men is larger in its application. Thus the sign of circumcision (17:10–14, 23–27) was administered not only to Isaac later, but also to Ishmael and the men in Abraham's house either born in the house or bought with money. Circumcision is wider in its application than the term "seed," as far as the use in Genesis is concerned.

THE PROMISE TO GENTILES

As a part of the Abrahamic Covenant, "all families of the earth" are promised blessing (12:3). It is not specified what this blessing shall be. As a general promise it is probably intended to have a general fulfillment. Abraham himself has certainly been a blessing to all nations and has the distinction of being honored alike by Jew, Mohammedan, and Christian. The seed of Abraham or the nation of Israel itself has been a great blessing as the channel of divine revelation and the historic illustration of God's dealings with men. *The* seed of Abraham, the Lord Jesus Christ Himself, has also been a blessing to all nations. The blessing bestowed includes not only the salvation of many but also the revelation of God, the revelation of moral law, and the many byproducts of biblical Judaism and Christianity. The promise has already been abundantly fulfilled.

A solemn part of the covenant as it deals with the Gentiles is the provision, "I will bless them that bless thee, and curse him that curseth thee" (12:3). This of course would be true even of an Israelite, but the primary application is to Gentiles. Long sections of the Old Testament pronouncing judgment on the Gentiles for their ill-treatment of Israel enlarge on this provision. History has recorded graphic fulfillment in the downfall of Nineveh, Babylon, and Rome, to say nothing of smaller groups and peoples. Down to modern times, the nation that has persecuted the Jew has paid dearly for it.

FURTHER DISTINCTIONS

The promises to Abraham, to Abraham's seed, and to "all families of the earth" are to be distinguished clearly. It breeds utter confusion to ignore these scriptural divisions and to muddle the whole by reducing it to a general promise. Not only should these distinctions be observed, but also what is omitted from the covenant should be carefully noted. While Abraham was personally justified by faith because of his trust in God's promise concerning his seed, it is obvious that the Abrahamic Covenant itself is not the Gospel of salvation even though the promised blessing anticipated the Gospel (Gal. 3:8). Those in the covenant are promised that God will be their God in the general and providential sense. It is true that Christ is the fulfillment of the promise of blessing to all nations. But the covenant does not contain the covenant of redemption, a revelation of the sacrifice of Christ, a promise of forgiveness of sin, a promise of eternal life, or any of the elements of salvation. The promise to Adam and Eve in Genesis 3:15 is, by way of example, a far clearer picture of the promise of redemption than any of the long passages dealing with the Abrahamic Covenant. While the Abrahamic Covenant is essentially gracious and promises blessings, it deals for the most part with physical blessings and with a physical seed. To make the covenant a phase or a statement of the covenant of redemption is hardly justified by the study of its precise provisions.

Literal Versus Spiritual Interpretation

While the premillennial interpretation of the Abrahamic Covenant distinguishes the promises to Abraham, to Abraham's seed, and to "all families of the earth," the amillennial view largely blurs this distinction. To understand the amillennial view, it is necessary to summarize its main arguments.

THE AMILLENNIAL POSITION

Pieters summarized the amillennial position as follows: "The expression 'Seed of Abraham,' in biblical usage, denotes that visible community, the members of which stand in relation to God through the Abrahamic Covenant, and thus are heirs to the Abrahamic promise."[5] In other words, all who are heirs of the covenant in any sense are the seed of Abraham. In discussing the circumcision of Abraham's entire house including the servants, Pieters concludes, "Yet they were all accounted, for covenant purposes, to be 'The Seed of Abraham.'"[6] He states the following in regard to the question of whether promises were made to Abraham's physical seed:

> Whenever we meet with the argument that "God made certain promises to the Jewish race, the above facts are pertinent. God never made any promises to any race at all, as a race. All His promises were to the continuing covenanted community, without regard to its racial constituents or to the personal ancestry of the individuals in it.[7]

The expression "seed of Abraham" under this interpretation loses its literal meaning and is considered only in a spiritual sense. Coupled with this spiritualizing of the terms is the general assumption that the covenant as a whole is entirely conditioned upon the faith of the individual. Hence the promise of everlasting possession of the land by the seed of Abraham is thrown out as having been forfeited by Israel's failure in the Old and New Testaments. According to amillennialism the Abrahamic Covenant has its fulfillment in the church.

THE PREMILLENNIAL VIEW OF THE COVENANT

As distinguished from the amillennial position, the premillennial interpretation of the Abrahamic Covenant takes its provisions literally. In other words, the promises given to Abraham will be fulfilled by Abraham; the promises to Abraham's seed will be fulfilled by his physical seed; the promises to "all families of the earth" will be fulfilled by Gentiles, those who are not the physical seed. While possession of the land forever is promised to the physical seed, the promise of blessing is to "all the families of the earth." Both are to be fulfilled exactly as promised.

While the premillennial position insists on fulfillment of promises to Israel as the physical seed, and thereby its national preservation and future hope of possession of the land, the premillenarian recognizes that there is a spiritual as well as a natural seed of Abraham. The New Testament in numerous passages refers to the spiritual seed of Abraham. Abraham is called "the father of all them that believe" (Rom. 4:11). In Galatians 3:7, it is noted, "Know ye therefore that they which are of faith, the same are the children of Abraham." Again in Galatians 3:29 it is revealed, "And if ye be Christ's, then are ye Abraham's seed, and heirs according to the promise." These passages teach beyond doubt that there is a spiritual seed of Abraham, those who like Abraham of old believe in God, and are children of faith.

Premillenarians also recognize the distinction between the natural and the spiritual seed within Israel itself. In Romans 9:6, this is stated in a few words, "For they are not all Israel, which are of Israel." This is defined later, "That is, They which are children of the flesh, these are not the children of God: but the children of the promise are counted for the seed" (9:8). Within Israel, then, there is a believing remnant who are both natural and spiritual children of Abraham. These inherit the promises.

There are, then, three different senses in which one may be a child of Abraham. First, there is the natural lineage, or natural seed. This is limited largely to the descendants of Jacob in the 12 tribes. To them God promises to be their God. To them was given the Law. To them was given the land of Israel in the Old Testament. With them God dealt in a special way. Second, there is the spiritual lineage within the natural. These are the Israelites who believed in God, who kept the Law, and who met the conditions for present enjoyment of the blessings of the covenant. Those who ultimately possess the land in the future millennium will also be of spiritual Israel. Third, there is the spiritual seed of Abraham who are not natural Israelites. Here is where the promise to "all the families of the earth" comes in. This is the express application of this phrase in Galatians 3:6–9, "Even as Abraham believed God, and it was accounted to him for righteousness. Know ye therefore that they which are of faith, the same are the children of Abraham. And the Scripture, foreseeing that God would justify the heathen through faith, preached before the gospel unto Abraham, saying, In thee shall all nations be blessed. So then they which be of faith are blessed with faithful Abraham." In other words spiritual children of Abraham who are Gentiles fulfill that aspect of the Abrahamic Covenant which dealt with Gentiles in the first place, not the promises pertaining to Israel. The only sense in which Gentiles can be Abraham's seed in the Galatians context is to be "in Christ Jesus" (Gal. 3:28). It follows, "And if ye be Christ's, then are ye Abraham's seed, and heirs according to the promise" (Gal. 3:29). They are Abraham's seed in the spiritual sense only and heirs of the promise given "to all the families of the earth."

While premillenarians can agree with amillenarians concerning the fact of a spiritual seed for Abraham which includes Gentiles, they deny that this fulfills the promises given to the natural seed or that the promises to the "seed of Abraham" are fulfilled by Gentile believers. To make the blessings promised to all the nations the same as the blessings promised to the seed of Abraham is an unwarranted conclusion.

The weakness of the amillennial position is shown by examination of their exegesis of such passages as Genesis 15:18–21, where the exact boundaries of the Promised Land are given, and the kindred passage in Genesis 17:7–8 where the covenant is called everlasting and the land is promised as an everlasting possession. Pieters, in his discussion of "The Seed of Abraham in the Patriarchal Period,"[8] finds it convenient to pass over these passages entirely. His argument is that modern Jews have lost their lineage and therefore no one today is qualified to claim the promises given to the Jews anyway—a radical and questionable line of argument to say the least. Most amillenarians as well as premillenarians recognize the modern Jew as having some racial continuity with ancient Israel, however polluted by intermarriage with Gentiles.

Allis,[9] on the other hand, while an ardent amillenarian, faces these promises on an entirely different basis. His argument is that the promises have either been fulfilled literally for Israel or that they were conditional promises and Israel failed to meet the conditions. The contrast between the approach of Allis and that of Pieters illustrates that amillenarians are quite at odds among themselves not only on details of their interpretation but also on the main principles.

The issue that divides premillenarians and amillenarians in the interpretation of the Abrahamic Covenant is the familiar question of literal versus spiritualized interpretation. If taken in its ordinary literal sense, the sense in which Abraham no doubt understood it, the covenant promised Abraham's seed that the land would be a lasting possession and that the nation in a special way would be the object God's care, protection, and blessing. The Scriptures indicate that the Abrahamic Covenant was intended to be interpreted literally as seen in its partial fulfillment and the frequent prophetic revelation of Israel's glorious future and repossession of the land.

CHAPTER 6

Is the Present Age the Millennium?

Jeffrey L. Townsend

The word "millennium" comes from the Greek phrase χίλια ἔτη ("one thousand years"), which is found six times Revelation 20:2–7. Premillennialists generally point to these verses as strong support for their understanding that after the present age Jesus Christ will return to this earth and rule over the world from the throne of David in Jerusalem for one thousand years.

On the other hand amillenarians traditionally have identified the "one thousand years" in Revelation 2:2–7 as the present age between the first and second comings of Christ. This identification of the present age and the millennium has been put forth in a new way in a book that focuses on the implications of the revolt of the nations in Revelation 20:7–10. The book, *The Dark Side of the Millennium: The Problem of Evil in Revelation 20:1–10*, is authored by Arthur H. Lewis, professor of Old Testament at Bethel College in St. Paul, Minnesota.

Lewis claims that in looking to Revelation 20 for proof of the millennium, premillennialists have overlooked its "dark side." In the words of the preface,

> For whatever reasons, premillennial commentaries on Revelation and books about Bible prophecy have paid meager attention to the fact that Revelation 20 presents the millennial society as a mixture of saints and sinners. The Gog and Magog nations revolt against the King at the end of the thousand years, but they exist as groups of wicked people throughout the entire course of the age.[1]

For Lewis the implications of this evil aspect of the millennium are crucial. "This aspect immediately raises a doubt about the correlation of the millennium with the other kingdom passages in the Bible, which invariably speak of its glory and perfection."[2] Lewis's purpose, then, is to show that the allegedly under-emphasized aspect of millennial evil is sufficient reason to deny the identification of the one thousand years of Revelation 20 with the glorious future messianic kingdom of Jesus Christ.[3] Lewis aims to show that the one thousand years should be identified with the present age and that the glorious messianic kingdom refers to the eternal state pictured in Revelation 21–22.[4]

Lewis's argument could be summarized in a syllogism with two corollaries:

Major premise:	The millennium of Revelation 20 is not a perfect state.
Minor premise:	The future messianic kingdom is a perfect state.
Conclusion:	Therefore the millennium of Revelation 20 is not the glorious future messianic kingdom.
Corollary 1:	The millennium is the present age.
Corollary 2:	The kingdom age is to be equated with the eternal state in Revelation 21–22.

The present study will consider the validity of corollary 1, equating the present age with the millennium.

Though this identification is a typical amillennial assertion, Lewis approaches it in a novel way by starting with what he sees as the implications of the Satan-led revolt following the one thousand years.[5] The evaluation of Lewis's reasoning will proceed by asking and answering three questions that correspond to the major points of his logic.

Is the Millennium of Revelation 20:1–10 an Imperfect State?

Though Lewis claims that premillennialists pay "meager attention" to the fact of evil in the millennium, he quotes five prominent premillennialists, all of whom do recognize and seek to explain the presence of evil in the millennium.[6] The explanation given by these premillennialists focuses on unconverted offspring born during the millennium to those in natural bodies. Contrary to Lewis's claims that this premillennial explanation of evil in the millennium is "inferential at best" and amounts to a substitution of logic for exegesis,[7] is the scriptural evidence that those in natural bodies capable of bearing offspring who rebel will populate the millennium (cf. Ezek. 20:33–38; Matt. 25:31–46) and that Satan will deceive many when he is loosed (Rev. 20:7–10). Thus premillennialists agree with Lewis on his first premise. The fact that the millennium is not a perfect state is nothing new to premillennialism. Where premillennialists differ with Lewis is in the implications he draws from this imperfection.

Before considering Lewis's second major premise, a reply should be given to two specific assertions made by Lewis in his discussion of millennial evil.

Lewis states that "it is important . . . to understand what the millennium is, according to the *one passage* in the Bible that defines it."[8] He also says, "Again it is essential that the meaning of millennium be restricted to the language given it in Revelation 20."[9] While it is true that Revelation 20:2–7 is the only passage in the Bible that indicates the exact duration of that age, Lewis patently assumes his conclusion in asserting (wrongly) that Revelation 20 is the only passage in the Bible to describe the millennial age.

A second problem is that Lewis repeatedly leaves the impression that premillennialists hold that wicked people enter the millennial age and therefore have a second chance to be saved. For example in criticizing the pretribulational explanation for evil in the millennium, Lewis writes, "Logic is never a substitute for exegesis, particularly when other passages raise serious doubts concerning the survival of any wicked persons after the Messiah's return for the express purpose of judging 'the quick and the dead' (Acts 10:42, KJV)."[10] But pretribulationists hold that all the wicked survivors of the tribulation are put to death at the beginning of the millennial age so that only saved persons enter the thousand-year period.[11] During the millennium the offspring of these saved entrants will be saved or lost according to their response to Jesus Christ. Such a system in no way vitiates the urgency of the many passages Lewis mentions (e.g., Luke 14:23; John 3:3, 36; Acts 10:42; 2 Peter 3:8–10), which call on sinners in this age to repent in view of the Lord's coming in judgment.

Is the Future Messianic Kingdom a Perfect State?

Lewis devotes 21 pages to the second premise in his argument, namely, that the future kingdom age of Scripture is *always* presented as a perfect state. Granted, says Lewis, "the smiting of the wicked . . . is associated with the kingdom, but it is not typical of the *course* of the kingdom; rather, it has to do with the elimination of all injustice at its *inception*."[12] Consequently Lewis argues that the kingdom age cannot be equated with the millennial age which has evil elements. Rather, the future kingdom of Christ must be fulfilled in the eternal state.

The crux of the issue is clear. Do the Scriptures always present the messianic kingdom as a perfect state? Are there any passages that clearly indicate imperfection, rebellion, or judgment during the course of the kingdom? Lewis deals with some of the passages premillennialists normally cite to demonstrate that imperfection will manifest itself and evil will be judged by Christ during the kingdom age (e.g., Pss. 2; 110; Isa. 11; 65; Zech. 12–14; 1 Cor. 15). Admittedly the Scriptures do extol the glories and perfections of the messianic age. No doubt certain passages do emphasize the judgments at the beginning of the earthly reign of Jesus Christ (though it is very convenient for Lewis to assign any apparent rebellion during the kingdom to its inception).[13] But several passages clearly place rebellion, judgment, and imperfection in the kingdom age.

Isaiah 65:20 presents a problem for Lewis. A literal rendering of the verse clearly places death, the wages of sin (Rom 6:23), in the messianic kingdom. "No longer will there be in it an infant who lives but a few days, or an old man who does not live out his days; for the youth will die at the age of one hundred and the one who does not reach the age of one hundred shall be thought accursed." Isaiah writes that premature death will be unknown in the kingdom age. But death will be experienced, though the one who dies at the age of one hundred, accursed because of sin, will be considered but a youth because of the longevity of those days. As Fausset notes, "This passage proves that the millennial age to come on earth, though much superior to the present, will not be a perfect state. Sin and death shall have place in it (cf. Rev. 20:7–8), but much less frequently than now."[14]

While agreeing that "Isaiah 65:20 is without doubt a passage that concerns the age to come, the messianic kingdom,"[15] Lewis claims that because surrounding verses speak of various blessings (cf. Isa. 65:19, 23, 25), "the literal sense is denied by the total context of the passage."[16] He asks, "How could parents in that day have any joy or hope, knowing that their children will die when they reach the age of one hundred? Such an environment would become a horror instead of a paradise!"[17] But that is not what the passage says. Isaiah 65:20 stresses increased longevity and the *exceptional* nature of death, which is judgment on sin in the person's life. With elimination of those who rebel and fullness of life for those who do not, the environment would not be a horror but a heaven on earth.

Admittedly Isaiah 65:17–25 is problematical for both premillennialists and the amillennialists. The difficulty is that the new heavens and the new earth (v. 17) seem to be described in terms appropriate only for the present order (e.g., labor pains, childbirth, babyhood, death as judgment for sin, things wearing out). Lewis, like the amillennialist Hoekema, solves the problem by taking verse 20 as figurative of life and longevity.[18] But can even a figurative understanding of the terms of verse 20 eliminate the meaning of death from the verse? And what about the references to things that wear out (v. 22) and to childbearing (v. 23)? It seems better to understand Isaiah as including references to the millennial age which is preliminary to the new heavens and the new earth. This allows the terms of the passage to be taken in their literal, normal sense.

Isaiah 65:20 is not an "isolated text" as Lewis claims.[19] Another clear indication of imperfection in the future messianic kingdom is Psalm 110:2, "The LORD will stretch forth Thy strong scepter from Zion, saying, 'Rule in the midst of Thine enemies.'" After mentioning the King's present session in heaven (v. 1), the psalmist wrote of the King's reign on the earth from Zion (v. 2: cf. Ps. 2:6). The King's universal dominion based in Jerusalem will be a rule in the midst of enemies though the converted Jewish remnant will provide willing subjects for His kingdom.

Lewis's explanation is that "both Peter [Acts 2:34–35] and Paul [1 Cor. 15:25] use this psalm [110:1] to describe the Lord's present-day task of shattering his enemies. . . . For both the psalmist and the apostles, the throne is a heavenly one and the battle is a spiritual one, but the age is this present one!"[20] But Lewis does not deal with the transfer of dominion to Zion in Psalm 110:2. In addition, Paul's use of Psalm 110:1 in 1 Corinthians 15:25 is not a quotation but an allusion which the apostle seems to apply to the kingdom age.

Numerous other Old Testament passages could be mentioned which indicate various imperfections in the kingdom age.[21] But since Lewis does not deal with each of these verses, it is appropriate that the discussion move on to 1 Corinthians 15 to which Lewis devotes considerable attention.

Lewis objects to the premillennial understanding of εἶτα ("then") in 1 Corinthians 15:24 as allowing for the millennial age. He claims that "the natural flow of Paul's language" would indicate that εἶτα should be understood transitionally not temporally.[22]

But as Johnson has noted, "Every Pauline use of *eita* involves an interval. Note that the *epeita* of verse 23 has already covered an interval of at least 1,900 years!"[23] Significantly Paul clearly uses εἶτα in the temporal sense in verses 5 and 7 of this same chapter. Ladd adds the thought that "there is a temporal adverb used of concurrent events, *tote*; but this word is not used in this passage."[24] So in discussing the order of the resurrection in 1 Corinthians 15:23–24 Paul sets forth a premillennial chronology: (1) Christ's resurrection; (2) "after that" (ἔπειτα, indicating a period of at least 1,900 years) the resurrection of believers (those that are Christ's) at His coming; (3) "then" (εἶτα, allowing for the millennial age of Rev. 20:4–6) the end of the mediatorial kingdom (cf. 1 Cor. 15:25); and (4) the eternal state.

The implication of this chronology for the issue of imperfection in the kingdom is amplified by a comparison of verses 24 and 25. In verse 24 the two ὅταν clauses describe the end, temporally, as the time when Christ will deliver up the mediatorial kingdom to the Father and at that same time all rule, authority, and power will be finally abolished (cf. Rev. 20:7–10). The reason (δεῖ γάρ) Christ cannot relinquish the kingdom until its appointed end is that all His enemies must be subjugated during the earthly messianic reign. As mentioned earlier, Paul here alludes to Psalm 110:1, but the chronology of the context demands that the apostle was applying Psalm 110:1 to the millennial reign of Christ. As Tenney puts it:

> This passage [1 Cor. 15:23–25] requires a period after Christ's return during which He will reign until He can complete the subjugation of evil and bring his enemies completely under His sovereignty. Such a period coincides quite exactly with the thousand years of Revelation.[25]

Of course this is fatal to Lewis's view that the future earthly kingdom of Christ is always presented as a perfect state. The millennium, though glorious in many ways, will not be perfect, as the Old and New Testament passages indicate.[26]

Lewis's rebuttal to this chronology is that Paul identifies "the day of resurrection as the day when the 'last enemy'—death—is to be destroyed (1 Cor. 15:26, 54–55). This fact by itself is sufficient evidence to deny the millennialists the right to break the sequence of verses 23 and 24."[27] But Lewis is assuming that there is but one resurrection.[28] If 1 Corinthians 15:54–55 is understood as the church's victory over death at the resurrection and rapture of the church (cf. 15:51–52), these verses cannot be identified with the abolishing (καταργέω) of death at the end (1 Cor. 15:24–26; cf. Rev. 20:11–15).

Whereas premillennialists agree with Lewis's first premise that the millennium is not a perfect state, they do not agree with his second premise that the future messianic kingdom is always presented as a perfect state. The distinction Lewis would draw between the thousand years and the kingdom age cannot be sustained.

Does Revelation 20:1–10 Refer to the Present Age?

In the final and longest chapter of his book, Lewis attempts to prove that the millennium of Revelation 20 is the present age. The chapter provides a suitable climax to the book since the meaning of the millennium is the most crucial issue addressed in Lewis's work. This is where he must prove his case. But does he?

Though space does not allow interaction here with every aspect of Lewis's presentation on Revelation 20, five key interpretive issues in Revelation 20: 1–10 will be considered.

THE CHRONOLOGY OF REVELATION 19–20

Lewis admits that Revelation 19–20 appear to be in sequential and chronological order. But he claims that

> . . . a number of features will appear to challenge this order. There is good reason to conclude that at this point [20:1] John broke the sequence to reiterate the great themes of victory for the saints and defeat for the forces of evil. Thus, chapter 20:1–10 maybe taken as a return to the present age leading up to the second advent of Christ.[29]

But the only "features" Lewis presents are his understanding of the details of Revelation 20:1–10. He never deals specifically with the chronology of chapters 19–20. In effect Lewis argues that since the particulars of 20:1–10 fit the present age, verse 1 therefore reverts to the present age.

Such reasoning is inferior to a direct consideration of the chronological details of the passage. But Lewis avoids this because the particulars confirm the opposite. Revelation 19–20 is in chronological order. The reasons are as follows.

First, though it is true that καὶ εἶδον ("and I saw") in 19:11, 17, 19, 20:1, 4, 11 refers to the sequence of visions as John saw them, nonetheless the events described do seem to follow each other. Thus the burden of proof is on those, such as Lewis, who disagree. As noted already, this is a burden Lewis fails to bear.

Second, the details of the passage confirm rather than deny the apparent chronological progression of chapters 19–20. For example, the chronological order of the visions in 19:17–18 and 19:19–21 is apparent from the fact that "in the former the birds are called together for the feast; in the latter they actually eat. If there is progression between these two visions, why not in the others?"[30]

Another indication of chronological progression is the ὅταν clause beginning in 20:7. It could be argued that the temporal clause merely indicates progress within the vision of 20:4–10. But the fact that 20:10 assumes the presence of the beast and the false prophet in the lake of fire (19:20) indicates that the ὅταν of 20:7 marks progression within the overall sequence of chapters 19–20.[31]

Third, Deere has pointed out that the events described in Revelation 19:11–20:6 parallel the events in Daniel 7.[32] Since there is no indication of recapitulation in the sequence of Daniel 7, it is best to understand the same of Revelation 19:11–20:6.

In short, the apparent logical dependence of one event on another in Revelation 19–20 is confirmed by the chronological implications of this passage and other Scripture. Though Revelation as a whole is not in strict chronological order, 19:11–20:15 evidently is. Thus Lewis's appeal to recapitulation is invalid.

THE MEANING OF THE ONE THOUSAND YEARS

Lewis passes over the most impressive feature of Revelation 20 with a question: "Could not even the famous 'thousand years' be a figure of speech for an extended, but indefinite, period of time?"[33] The answer, of course, is yes, John could have employed the term χίλια ἔτη in a figurative way. But did he?

The interpreter must look for clues in the biblical text that indicate whether a term is used literally or figuratively. In this case the interpreter must ask, Are there clues that indicate that χίλια ἔτη stands for an indefinite period of time? In Revelation 20:2–7 χίλια ἔτη is used six times in connection with a number of chronologically interrelated events.[34] John seems to have set up a definite timetable of events relative to the one thousand years. There is no indication in these verses that χίλια ἔτη means anything but a definite span of one thousand years.

The literal meaning of χίλια ἔτη is confirmed by the fact that in verse 3 the duration of Satan's release after the thousand years is described by the indefinite phrase μικρὸν χρόνον ("a short time"). So when John designated indefinite time he used indefinite terms.

It would seem most natural therefore to understand χίλια ἔτη as a definite one-thousand-year period since in the same context the author used an indefinite term for an indefinite period of time. The context indicates a literal not a figurative use of temporal terms in Revelation 20:2–7.

Therefore Lewis's claim that "a 'present-day millennium,' stretching from our Lord's first coming to His second, can be just as literal as a millennium which hasn't started yet"[35] must be denied. Lewis has substituted the concept of reality for literalness and the two are not identical. A present-day millennium of indefinite length may indeed be just as real as a future thousand-year millennium, but it is not an equally literal understanding of χίλια ἔτη in Revelation 20:2–7. Since, as argued, Revelation 20:2–7 requires that a literal meaning be given χίλια ἔτη, the millennium cannot be the present age commencing at the first advent of Christ as Lewis claims.

THE STRUCTURE OF REVELATION 20: 1–10

Lewis's view of the structure of Revelation 20:1–10 is unique: "There are three scenes running concurrently through the thousand years of Revelation 20:1–10."[36] He defines these as the binding of Satan (vv. 2–3, an earthly scene), the reign of the saints in the intermediate state (vv. 4–6, a heavenly scene), and the nations in revolt (vv. 7–10, an earthly scene).[37] The effect of this scheme is to deny the premillennial sequence of the binding of Satan following Armageddon (vv. 1–3), then the thousand years (vv. 4–6), followed by the loosing of Satan, the revolt of the wicked, and the battle of Gog and Magog (vv. 7–10). Can Lewis's structural analysis be sustained by the evidence? It cannot be upheld for the following reasons.

As in Lewis's treatment of the larger context, so also in analyzing the structure of Revelation 20:1–10, he gives no proof for his position other than attempting to show that the binding of Satan, the reign of the saints with Christ, and the revolt of the nations could apply to the present age. Lewis does not deal specifically with the structure of those verses. Again the reason is obvious. A careful analysis of the structure of these 10 verses does not support Lewis's view of three concurrent scenes, one heavenly and two earthly.

For example, though the καὶ εἶδον in verses 1 and 4 introduces two visions which could describe concurrent events, this is not the impression gained from the content of the visions. Rather, the binding of Satan seems to occur before (and as the cause of) the events of verses 4–6. As Walvoord states, "The most obvious fact of Revelation 20 is that the binding of Satan makes the millennium possible, i.e., there is a causal relation—the millennium would be impossible without Satan bound."[38] One wonders how Lewis's view of the binding of Satan with respect to the nations on earth (20:1–3) could have any bearing on a heavenly reign of the saints (Lewis's view of Rev. 20:4–6).

Lewis's view also fails at the opening clause of verse 7, καὶ ὅταν τελεσθῇ τὰ χίλια ἔτη . Verses 7–10 are not another vision (καὶ ὅταν , "and when," not κα εἶδον , "and I saw"). Rather, the verses record what will happen temporally only after the thousand years are completed. The structural evidence weighs heavily in favor of a sequence of events rather than a concurrence of events in Revelation 20:1–10. Lewis's structuring of these verses fails to make sense of the passage.

THE BINDING OF SATAN

Lewis claims that one of the evidences that the millennium is in existence today is the applicability of Revelation 20:1–3 to the present age. He sees two lines of thought in the New Testament. On the one hand "the devil's operations in our world today are too obvious to deny."[39] On the other hand "in some very real sense the devil is 'bound' and no longer free to deceive the nations as he did before Christ."[40] In other words Lewis is saying that there is a sense in which Satan is now bound and that this is consistent with Revelation 20:1–3. What is the premillennial reply?

Walvoord cuts to the heart of the issue.

> The Scriptures present, then, on the one hand the great power of Satan and on the other that this power is limited and under the sovereign control of God. . . . The premillennialist . . . does not for one moment deny that the power of Satan is limited in the present age, in fact, in any age. . . . Whether this *limitation* should be identified with the *binding* of Satan in Revelation 20:1–3 is quite another issue.[41]

The issue then is as follows: Is the binding of Satan (Rev. 20:1–3) the same as what the New Testament refers to elsewhere as limitations on Satan's power? The premillennialist says no for the following reasons.

While Lewis emphasizes the passages that speak of Satan's limitations (e.g., Matt. 12:29; Luke 10:18; John 12:31; 2 Thess. 2:7;

Rev. 9:2–6; 11:7–8; 13:7),[42] he fails to give due consideration to the absolute terms of the binding of Satan in Revelation 20 and the New Testament passages that speak of Satan's present power.

In Revelation 20:1–3, 7 the binding of Satan is described in the following terms: (1) he is bound with a great chain for a thousand years (vv. 1–2); (2) he is thrown (ἔβαλεν) into the abyss (v. 3), the abode of demons (cf. 9:1; 11:7), which acts as a secure prison (φυλακῆς, v. 7); (3) the abyss is shut (ἔκλεισεν), locked (cf. "key" in v. 1), and sealed (ἐσφράγισεν) over him (v. 3); (4) he will be released (λυθῆναι/λυθήσεται) but not until the thousand years are completed (vv. 3, 7). In other words Satan is completely cut off from the earth during the millennium. As Mounce comments, "The elaborate measures taken to insure his custody are most easily understood as implying the complete cessation of his influence on earth (rather than a curbing of his activities)."[43]

But what does the New Testament say about the activity of Satan in the present age? Yes, there are limitations on Satan's activity as there have been in the past (cf. Job 1:12; 2:6). Yes, Satan was judged at the cross (John 16:11). But his confinement awaits the millennial age (Rev. 20:2–7) and his execution will follow the millennium (20:10). The following facts (which Lewis ignores) are evidence of the present power of Satan: Satan filled Ananias's heart to lie to the Holy Spirit (Acts 5:3); Satan tempts (1 Cor. 7:5); he hinders and afflicts believers (2 Cor. 12:7; 1 Thess. 2:18); he is as great and real an adversary as a hungry lion on the loose (1 Peter 5:8). He lies, tempts, hinders, afflicts, and devours—and all in the present age. As Walvoord asks, "Is this a picture of Satan bound?"[44]

During the millennium (Rev. 20) Satan will be completely cut off from the earth but during the present age he is vigorously active on the earth. Therefore the millennium cannot be the present age.

One can anticipate objections that might be raised to the premillennial approach to the binding of Satan. It is often asserted that Jesus' illustration concerning the binding of the strong man (Matt. 12:29; Mark 3:27) indicates that Satan is at least partially bound during this age and that the common use of δέω ("to bind") in the Gospel passages and Revelation 20:2 implies that the bindings are identical.[45]

While most premillennialists would agree that Jesus' ministry did have a limited binding effect on Satan, the fact remains that any so-called binding of Satan during Christ's first-advent ministry was not absolute. For example Hendriksen says that the binding of Satan began with the victory at the temptation.[46] But according to Matthew 4:10–11 Satan left the temptation scene defeated but unbound. This is confirmed by Luke's notation that the devil departed "until an opportune time" (Luke 4:13). When this is compared with the absolute terms used of Satan's imprisonment in the abyss, it becomes apparent that any restriction on Satan in the Gospels is not to be equated with his binding in Revelation. During Jesus' first-advent ministry Satan was not bound. Only during Christ's millennial ministry following His second advent will Satan's binding be absolute.

Another common rejoinder by amillennialists is that the ἵνα clause in Revelation 20:3 limits Satan's binding to the deception of the nations, and that in other respects he is unbound during the millennium.[47] But it does not necessarily follow that if Satan is bound with respect to the nations that he is otherwise unbound. Such a conclusion violates the absolute confinement described in Revelation 20:1–3. Twice the apostle John wrote that Satan will be released only after the thousand years are completed (Rev. 20:3, 7). Regardless of the purpose of the confinement, the passage makes it clear that Satan will be in the prison of the abyss for one thousand years, completely cut off from the earth.

Moreover, in light of 2 Corinthians 4:3–4 and Ephesians 6:12 it is difficult to see how a current binding of Satan with respect to the nations can be allowed. The New Testament clearly indicates that Satan is now very much involved in the deception of the nations, for what is the deception of the nations if it is not the deception of individuals who make up the nations?[48]

Berkouwer, an amillennialist, provides a telling conclusion to the debate on the binding of Satan.

> Those who interpret the millennium as already realized in the history of the church try to locate this binding in history. Naturally, such an effort is forced to relativize the dimensions of this binding, for it is impossible to find evidence for a radical elimination of Satan's power in that "realized millennium." . . . The necessary relativizing of John's description of Satan's bondage (remember that Revelation 20 speaks of a shut and sealed pit) is then explained by the claim that, although Satan is said to deceive the nations no more (v. 3), this does not exclude satanic activity in Christendom or individual persons. I think it is pertinent to ask whether this sort of interpretation really does justice to the radical proportions of the binding of Satan—that he will not be freed from imprisonment for a thousand years.[49]

So it seems clear that Revelation 20:1–3 does not describe the present age as Lewis claims.

THE FIRST RESURRECTION

Another interpretive issue focuses on Revelation 20:4–6 and the events that will take place during the millennium. Here more than anywhere else it becomes apparent that the millennium does not fit the present age.

In attempting to explain how Revelation 20:4–6 could be true of the present age, Lewis makes a number of unproved assumptions: "the apostle John had a message with direct application to the suffering Christians of his own day"; "the throne scene here is linked directly to the other throne scenes in the Book of Revelation"; "the Book of Revelations [*sic*] prophecies the entire age and its end events. . . . John should not be faulted for doing exactly what our Lord did in this regard by moving abruptly from his own time to the final events. . . . Every period of martyrdom should be included [in the great tribulation]"; "Whatever one makes of the phrase 'first resurrection' in Revelation 20:6. it has to be inclusive of all who reign with Christ."[50] In assuming these presuppositions rather than proving them from Revelation, Lewis allows himself a tremendous amount of latitude in the interpretation of the first resurrection. He can very easily assign the meaning of various features as it suits his argument or position.

Lewis states that "the search for the true meaning of the 'first resurrection' in the text is not an easy one"[51] (for the amillennialist!). After noting the wide variety of amillennial views,[52] Lewis casts his lot with Warfield, who held that the first resurrection of Revelation 20:4–6 stands for the glorification and intermediate state of believers following death.[53] Lewis's proof for his position is a dogmatic denial of Alford's classic argument[54] based on the assertions that "the 'aliveness' of the saints is the point of the scene"; that "the new life in Christ is frequently called a 'resurrection' (Rom. 6:11; Eph. 2:4, 5; Col. 3:1)"; and that "Revelation 20 was given to the churches to comfort them in respect to loved ones who had died and gone to be with Christ."[55]

Missing from Lewis's defense is any mention of the details of the text at hand. This is because the textual and contextual evidence does not support the idea that the first resurrection is the glorification of the believer at death in the intermediate state. The evidence is as follows.

"The crux of the entire exegetical problem is the meaning of one word: *ezesan*."[56] At issue is whether the word means a literal, bodily resurrection or, as Lewis would claim, a resurrection of the soul at death. Several arguments strongly support the premillennial view that ἔξησαν (Rev. 20:4–5) refers to physical resurrection. Most interpreters, including Lewis,[57] agree that ἔξησαν in verse 5 refers to bodily resurrection at the great white throne judgment. It would seem natural, then, to take the same bodily meaning for ἔξησαν in verses 4–5.[58] This understanding is fortified in verses 5–6 where the coming to life is plainly referred to as the first resurrection. The word John employed is ἀνάστασις. In over 40 occurrences in the New Testament, with only one clear exception (Luke 2:34), ἀνάστασις always refers to bodily resurrection.[59] Thus the language of Revelation 20:4–6 demands that the first resurrection be understood as a premillennial, bodily resurrection of saints.

Additional arguments in favor of the premillennial understanding of the first resurrection may be stated briefly as follows. Revelation 5:10 indicates that the reign of the resurrected saints in 20:4, 6 is "upon the earth" (not in heaven as Lewis claims). As mentioned previously, unless verses 4–6 speak of an earthly scene, the casting of Satan out of the earth in verses 1–3 hardly seems a necessary preparation for the millennium. One must also question whether the judgmental and priestly functions indicated for the saints in verses 4 and 6 are appropriate to the intermediate state, especially in light of the fact that, according to Lewis's system, the saints are not themselves judged until after the thousand years.

It seems that Lewis's primary reason for rejecting a premillennial first resurrection is John 5:28–29. He writes, "The general resurrection at the end of this world was his [John's] basic view and needs to be kept in mind at all times when reading through his Book of Revelation."[60] But two observations weigh in favor of premillennialism. First, Jesus, as recorded by John, did mention *two* resurrections in John 5:29, "a resurrection of life" and "a resurrection of judgment." These two resurrections are discussed in more detail in Revelation 20 where only blessing is associated with the coming to life in verse 4 and only judgment is associated with the coming to life in verse 5 (which is developed further in vv. 11–15). Second, it must be emphasized that the resurrection at the great white throne is not presented as a general resurrection but as a resurrection of judgment. At best all Lewis can do is assume the presence of the just at the great white throne by implication from the conditional εἰ ("if") in verse 15. That might be acceptable if the resurrection of the just had not been discussed earlier as occurring before the thousand years.

The five lines of evidence presented from Revelation 20 weigh decidedly against the view that the millennium is the present age. On the other hand the premillennial understanding of the thousand years does justice to the terms of Revelation 20 taken in their normal, literal sense.

Conclusion

This study has evaluated a recent formulation of the classic amillennial position that the present age is the millennium of Revelation 20:1–10. Arthur H. Lewis has attempted to show that the millennium is *not* a perfect state but that the future messianic kingdom *is* a perfect state. Therefore he concludes that the two cannot be identified. Lewis then tries to demonstrate that the millennium should be identified with the present age and the messianic kingdom with the eternal state.

The critique of this view that the millennium and the present age are the same focused on three questions that parallel Lewis's logic. (1) Is the millennium of Revelation 20:1–10 an imperfect state? Premillennialists say yes, though they draw different implications from this fact than does Lewis. (2) Is the future messianic kingdom, described in the Old and New Testaments, a perfect state? No, the kingdom age in Scripture is not always presented as a time void of all evil. (3) Does Revelation 20:1–10 describe events in the present age? No, the thousand years simply cannot be made to fit the current period of the earth's history. Rather, the premillennial understanding of the millennium (as a future thousand-year kingdom of Jesus Christ on this earth following His second coming but before and preparatory to the kingdom of the new heavens and the new earth) better accounts for the details of Scripture. Indeed there is a "dark side of the millennium," but this fact is better handled by the premillennial system than by any system that equates the millennium with the present age.

CHAPTER 7

Is Satan Bound?

John F. Walvoord

There are many approaches to the field of eschatology which includes the consideration of all that was prophetic in the Scriptures when they were written. Prophecy can be studied from the viewpoint of the purposes of God, with all history in its detail being a fulfillment. Prophecy can be examined as portraying Christ in His Person and work, a most fruitful field of study because every important aspect of prophecy has some relation to Christ. Prophecy can be viewed as an unfolding picture of human sin and a divine remedy of grace or judgment. Prophecy can be traced as it deals with Israel and the Gentile nations, a most illuminating study of God's program. Prophecy can be viewed, also, from God's program for the angels, as revealed in the Scriptures, including the course and destiny of Satan. Each approach has its own contribution to the total of prophecy. The present subject involves the consideration of the last named, the place of Satan in the prophetic program. While any of the other approaches would be as suitable, the present subject has been selected because it establishes so simply and directly the point in God's program today. If the question in regard to the binding of Satan can be answered, as it can, a forward step of great importance has been taken in establishing the whole point of view.

Most systems of interpretation of prophecy can be classified by their interpretation of the millennial doctrine. The Old Testament has frequent allusions to the glory and righteousness of a future kingdom. The New Testament reveals that this kingdom will continue for one thousand years. The nature of this millennium, or thousand-year period, and its relation to other prophesied events constitute a determining factor in any system of prophetic interpretation.

There have been at least four important millennial views, all involving the relationship of Christ to the millennium. Three of these are mutually exclusive concepts. Postmillennialism had its rise in the aftermath of the Protestant Reformation, during the 16th and 17th centuries. Berkhof lists as its originators, "Coccejus, Alting, the two Vitringas, d'Outrein, Witsius, Hoornbeek, Koelman, and Brakel."[1] In its original form postmillennialism held that Christ would return to the earth after a millennium or period of time of great blessing during which the Gospel triumphed and righteousness and peace characterized the world. Postmillennialism constituted a rejection of premillennialism, admittedly an early doctrine of the church, and a rejection of the amillennialism which characterized the eschatology of many Roman Catholics. Postmillennialism was particularly popular during the 19th century. The hope for a millennium on earth to be ushered in by the progress of the church was rudely shattered, however, by World War I and succeeding events. The prospect of converting the world to an era of righteousness and peace by human effort is no longer a prominent factor in theology or preaching. A modern type of postmillennialism has persisted, however, though it is quite divorced from an attempt to expound the Scriptures. It may be identified with the evolutionary hypothesis that man is gradually evolving to a higher state. Adherents of this modern type of postmillennialism deny that there is much connection with world-betterment and the Gospel of salvation by grace. They advance the theory that it is the duty of mankind to better his condition by a constructive policy of world improvement. Just as human disease is being conquered by improvement in medical methods, so, they say, social problems can be solved by improved sociology and political science.

With the passing of the old type of postmillennialism, those who continued to preach a scriptural message have turned back to the eschatology that characterized the period of stagnation before the Protestant Reformation, giving it the more or less new designation of amillennialism, by which is meant that there will be no millennium on earth. While the term is relatively new, the idea that there would be no earthly millennium was quite suited to the moral and spiritual temper of the centuries after Constantine the Great, when the church itself became corrupt and became more of an institution than an evangelizing agency. Amillennialism affirms belief in the final triumph of righteousness, the judgment of all men, the destruction of the present earth and heavens, and the creation of a new heavens and a new earth. While this system stands in considerable contrast to the premillennial system, it hinges on the fact that amillennialism believes the "millennium" began when Christ died, and that it applies only to the heavenly estate, not the earth, and that there will be no earthly millennium in a literal sense. While it offers a simplification of the whole scheme of unfulfilled prophecy, and does not cast any doubt on the inspiration of the Scriptures, it leaves unsolved many important passages of Scripture. Any amillennial work in eschatology is notable for the Scriptures it does not use. An interesting example is the work of Floyd E. Hamilton, *The Basis of Millennial Faith* (Grand Rapids: Eerdmans, 1942), which is an attempt to present fairly the amillennial objections to premillennial interpretation. In this work there is no mention at all of the many prophecies of Jeremiah, no mention of 2 Samuel 7, Psalm 72, or Isaiah 11, passages that are among the most important in the Old Testament in relation to the prophesied kingdom. While the work is the result of careful study and is not intentionally unfair to premillennialism, it takes as premillennial truth positions which no intelligent premillennialist holds. It totally neglects the issue that by no principle of hermeneutics can the word "earth" be made to represent heaven in the millennial passages, as it is necessary to interpret the word in the amillennial position.

The consideration of the present subject of the binding of Satan is an important preliminary consideration to premillennial truth in that it determines at once many of the issues. The amillennial position requires the hypothesis that Satan is *now* bound. If it can be demonstrated that Satan is not bound, it will at least leave an important if not insuperable obstacle to the amillennial system of interpretation.

Premillennialism asserts that Christ will return before the millennium and by His own power and presence will institute a period of righteousness and peace on the earth to continue for a thousand years. It offers a satisfactory solution to all the prophetic Word, allows for the literal fulfillment of all God's promises, and honors the Bible as meaning what it appears to mean. Other millennial views have been signally sterile in their prophetic studies. The writer has never heard of those holding either the postmillennial view or the amillennial view conducting a prophetic Bible conference. Many amillennialists and postmillennialists will frankly admit that they have never seriously studied prophecy (though admittedly some have). It is the writer's opinion that anyone coming to the Scriptures without preconceived ideas will naturally assume that the Word of God teaches the premillennial return of Christ.

A fourth millennial view may be merely mentioned. There are some who spiritualize the return of Christ, advancing the theories that Christ returned in the Person of the Spirit at Pentecost, or at the destruction of Jerusalem in A.D. 70, or that He "comes" at the death of saints. While as a class they deny the millennium and are therefore amillennial, they do not attempt to interpret the Scriptures or develop any system, and are always more or less liberal in their theology. This position is easily refuted by the Scriptures themselves. None of the prophesied events to follow the second coming of Christ occurred either at Pentecost or A.D. 70 nor do they occur at the death of saints. The apostle John, writing the Book of Revelation long after A.D. 70, was still looking for the coming of Christ (Rev. 22:20).

The Power of Satan Is Limited

In considering the question of whether Satan is now bound, it is necessary first to establish some of the elements of Satanology. It is after all a matter of tremendous significance whether Satan is bound as indicated in Revelation 20:1–3. The idea that it matters little which view is taken of the millennium is contrary to fact. A full understanding of "the schemes of the devil" (Eph. 6:11) is essential to spiritual victory, and it is unfortunately characteristic of amillennial and postmillennial systems of theology to ignore or minimize the power and activity of Satan, as a survey of their systematic theologies illustrates. Satan is revealed in the Scriptures as a created being of great power, wickedness, and cleverness. The Scriptures never minimize the Adversary. It is essential, then, to know the extent of this power and its nature.

A brief summary of the power of Satan is given in the following quotation:

> According to his own declaration, which Christ did not deny, he [Satan] has power over the kingdoms of this world, which kingdoms he said were delivered unto him, and which power he bestows on whom he will (Luke 4:6). It is said of him that he hath the power of death (Heb. 2:14), but that power has been surrendered to Christ (Rev. 1:18). Satan had the power over sickness in the case of Job (Job 2:7), and was able to sift Peter as wheat in a sieve (Luke 22:31; 1 Cor. 5:5). Likewise, Satan is said to have weakened the nations, to have made the earth to tremble, to have shaken kingdoms, to have made the earth a wilderness, destroying

the cities thereof, and not to have opened the house of his prisoners (Isa. 14:12–17). Against the power of Satan even Michael the archangel durst not contend (Jude 1:9); but there is victory for the child of God through the power of the Spirit and the blood of Christ (Eph. 6:10–12; 1 John 4:4; Rev. 12:11). Satan's power and authority are exercised always and only within the permissive will of God.[2]

The Scriptures present, then, on the one hand the great power of Satan and on the other hand the fact that this power is limited and under the sovereign control of God. It is important to note that the premillennialist, seeking as he does to honor the Word of God, does not for one moment deny that the power of Satan is limited in the present age, in fact, in any age. Strangely, some amillennial writers have attempted to demonstrate that the premillennial view is erroneous by pointing to Scriptures that speak of Satan's limitation. Both the Old and New Testaments bear a clear revelation on this point, and all millennial views must accept what the Scriptures teach. Whether this limitation should be identified with the binding of Satan in Revelation 20:1–3 is quite another issue. While all agree that Satan is limited, all do not agree that Satan is bound.

The Amillennial View of the Binding of Satan

The central passage on the subject of the binding of Satan is, or course, Revelation 20:1–3. "And I saw an angel coming down from heaven, having the key of the abyss and a great chain in his hand. And he laid hold of the dragon, the serpent of old, who is the Devil and Satan, and bound him for a thousand years, and threw him into the abyss, and shut it and sealed it over him, so that he should not deceive the nations any longer, until the thousand years were completed; after those things he must be released for a short time."

Whatever view may be taken of the nature of the millennium, it is obvious from the passage whether taken literally or symbolically that Satan is bound before the millennium. If then the millennium is still future, it follows that Satan is not bound, but if the millennium has already begun and is now in progress, as amillennialists believe, then Satan must be bound now. The usual amillennial approach to this passage points out the fact, which all recognize, that the Book of Revelation uses symbols, that its chronological scheme is that of recapitulation, and that it is therefore difficult to determine dogmatically what the exact meaning of any symbol may be and the exact place in the chronological plan of the book in which to fit each new revelation. It is the opinion of the writer, however, that the events prophesied in Revelation 19 and 20 are progressive and successive and that this is plain in the nature of the narrative, but it is not necessary to assume this in order to determine the meaning of the binding of Satan.

The most obvious fact in Revelation 20 is that the binding of Satan makes the millennium possible, that is, *there is a causal relationship*—the millennium would be impossible without Satan bound. If that is the case, then it is well to ask at the outset, where will the millennium take place, on earth or in heaven? If the millennium has its only fulfillment in heaven, then the binding of Satan applies only to heaven; if the millennium takes place on earth, then Satan is bound in respect to the earth.

Though amillenarians agree that the millennium will take place only in heaven, they have at least four contradictory explanations of the binding of Satan. First and least important is the group, as stated earlier, that spiritualizes the return of Christ, suggesting that He returned at Pentecost or at A.D. 70 or "returns" at the death of each saint. In this view Christ has returned to earth, and the millennium has begun in heaven. They identify the binding of Satan as an act subsequent to the triumph of Christ in His life, death, and resurrection. A second group, in which may be classed the work of William Masselink, *Why a Thousand Years?* (Grand Rapids: Eerdmans, 1930) takes the position that Satan is fully bound in relation to heaven, and partially bound in relation to the earth. This group identifies the binding of Satan with the victory of Christ in His life, death, and resurrection. A third view is advanced by Hamilton, in his work, *The Basis of the Millennial Faith,* in which he seeks to prove that Satan is now bound in relation to the earth. A fourth view to be mentioned—and it is the only one that is logically consistent with the conclusion—was expounded by B. B. Warfield. His view is that the binding of Satan refers only to the freedom of saints in the intermediate state, that is, those in heaven are free from attacks by Satan. Warfield states clearly that the binding of Satan does not refer to the earth.

Amillennialists often refer to difference of opinion among premillennialists in respect to details of prophecy. However, they may well look to their own system. All premillennialists worthy of the name believe that Satan will be bound just before the millennium. Amillennialists offer instead a strange series of interpretations. One group believes Christ has come to earth and produced a millennium in heaven. Another believes Satan is bound in respect to the earth, but that this produces a millennium in heaven. Still another believes that Satan is not bound in respect to earth, but only in heaven. From a standpoint of logic itself, apart from specific revelation of Scripture, it would follow that if Satan is bound only in respect to heaven, the millennium can be only in heaven; if he is partially bound in respect to earth, a partial millennium on earth would follow; if Satan is fully bound in respect to earth, then the millennium must be on earth rather than in heaven. An argument to demonstrate that Satan is now bound in respect to the earth has no logical connection with demonstrating a millennium in heaven, though if proved, would indicate that the millennium has already come to the earth.

In the nature of the case, the issue relative to the binding of Satan leads to two pointed questions: Is Satan bound in respect to heaven? Is Satan bound in respect to earth? In reality it is necessary only to demonstrate the answer to the first question to undo the amillennial position, but inasmuch as many amillennialists also have dealt with the second question, it may well be handled too.

Is Satan Bound in Respect to Heaven?

Warfield, acknowledged by all to be a great theologian, can well be taken as offering the most incisive analysis of the amillennial position.

> The "binding of Satan" is, therefore, in reality, not for a season, but with reference to a sphere; and his "loosing" again is not after a period but in another sphere: it is not subsequence but exteriority that is suggested. There is, indeed, no literal "binding of Satan" to be thought of at all: what happens, happens not to Satan but to the saints, and is only represented as happening to Satan for the purpose of the symbolical picture. What actually happens is that the saints described are removed from the sphere of Satan's assaults. The saints described are free from all access to Satan—he is bound with respect to them: outside of their charmed circle his horrid work goes on. This is indicated, indeed, in the very employment of the two symbols "a thousand years" and "a little time." A "thousand years" is the symbol of heavenly completeness and blessedness; the "little time" of earthly turmoil and evil. Those in the "thousand years" are safe from Satan's assaults: those outside the thousand years are still enduring his attacks.[3]

The amillennial position as stated by Warfield may be summarized as follows. (1) There is no chronological system to the Revelation 20 at all—the millennium is not a millennium and events that are said to occur after the millennium, such as the loosing of Satan, actually occur during the present age. (2) In reality Satan is not bound at all, but saints are merely removed from his power by being taken to heaven. (3) The nations mentioned in Revelation 20:3 are really glorified saints, not nations on earth. (4) Revelation 20:1–3 is not a historic or prophetic event but just a symbolic picture of peace after trial. It will appear to the most casual student that Warfield's interpretation has no basis in the text itself, but that it is superimposed on the text. No one reading Revelation would possibly arrive at such a conclusion unless he were determined to make it harmonize with a preconceived idea. Warfield's view is pure opinion—he offers no proof for his definition of terms worthy of consideration; he makes no attempt at exegesis. If the same principles of hermeneutics used by Warfield in Revelation were applied to the whole Bible, theology would be impossible and there would be no sure foundation for any doctrine.

In the study of prophecy it is absolutely essential to distinguish a revelation in symbolic form from its interpretation. Warfield states that the primary principles of interpretation of prophecy are the principle of recapitulation, the principle of successive visions, the principle of symbolism, and the principle of ethical purpose.[4] It is noteworthy that he omits from his principles that prophecy may be interpreted as factual history prewritten, that prophecy may have a chronological scheme, and that the Bible itself may give the interpretation. His concept seems to be that prophecy is merely ethical—a portrayal of moral purpose rather than a foretelling of a coming event.

Revelation 20:1–3 makes a careful distinction between the vision John saw and its interpretation which was revealed. In fact this is the key to the chapter. John saw an angel bind Satan with a chain, cast him into the abyss, shut him up, and set a seal on him. This was the vision. The interpretation given to John presents facts that in the nature of the case could not be seen. It was revealed to John that Satan was shut up for a thousand years, that the purpose of the act was so that he would not deceive the nations, and that he would be loosed again for a short time after the thousand years. If John had merely recorded what he saw, there would be room for varied interpretation, but he was guided by the Spirit in also writing the interpretation of the vision. this interpretation must be taken in the same degree of authority as any doctrinal portion or historical portion of the Scriptures. When John wrote of a thousand years or of Satan not deceiving the nations, he was revealing a doctrine, not a vision.

Warfield's position concerning the binding of Satan is that saints in glory are free from his attacks. To this all must agree, even those who believe that Satan is not cast out of heaven until the time of the tribulation (Rev. 12:9). It is inconceivable that saints in heaven are even open to attacks from Satan, and if the binding of Satan means only that, it is merely a reaffirmation of Satan's limitations and gives no new revelation. The millennium then is simply identical with the glorified state.

The binding of Satan is not, however, in reference to attacks on glorified saints. The only statement in Revelation 20:1–3 about the purpose of the binding of Satan is that he is no longer permitted to deceive the nations. Was Satan ever permitted to deceive the glorified saints? While it is clear from the Scripture that Satan is the accuser of saints and is permitted access to heaven, it can hardly be said that at any time Satan could attack saints in heaven or even deceive them.

In the final analysis one must choose between two alternatives: either Revelation 20 reveals nothing more than what has already been made clear in other Scriptures (viz., that the saints in heaven are safe from all his evil work), or the binding of Satan must have reference to the earth and consists in a total end to his work of deceiving the nations. Facing this obvious alternative, Masselink and Hamilton in their defense of the amillennial position say the binding of Satan is related to the earth, not simply to heaven.

A fact apparently overlooked by the amillennial interpretation is that the binding of Satan is not the extent of his being limited. According to Revelation 20:3, Satan is not only bound but also an angel "threw him into the abyss, and shut it and sealed it over him." This is not a picture of partial limitation; it describes total limitation. Only the premillennial interpretation can fit such a description. According to the Scriptures Satan is far from being totally inactive either in heaven or in earth. While it is true that the victory of the disciples in performing great miracles is connected by Christ to Satan falling as lightning from heaven (Luke 10:18), which is a sign pointing to his ultimate downfall, and it is also said that Satan is now judged through the work of Christ on the cross (John 16:11), and the actual dismissal of Satan from access to heaven will not occur until the time of the great tribulation

(Rev. 12:9). That Satan does have access to heaven is the clear implication of the Scriptures (Job. 1:6; 2:1–2; Rev. 12:7–13). Obviously Satan cannot be cast out of heaven unless he once was in heaven. The terrible conditions on earth during the tribulation period are traced to the fact that Satan knows he has only a short time (12:12). If the binding of Satan and his being shut up in the abyss occur at the same time, then it is inaccurate and misleading to say that Satan is now bound. While his power is limited and always has been, and while glorified saints in heaven are free from his assaults, it is not proper to refer to this limitation as the binding of Satan. One can conclude, therefore, that Satan is not "bound" now in respect to heaven. If this conclusion is accepted, obviously there is no ground for the amillennial position that there is now a millennium in heaven following the binding of Satan.

Is Satan Bound in Respect to the Earth?

As has been previously stated, one of the peculiarities of the amillennial position is that amillennialists cannot agree among themselves as to the extent of the binding of Satan. Warfield denies that the binding of Satan has any reference to the earth now, as indicated in his statement, "Outside of their charmed circle [the saints in glory] his horrid work goes on."[5] Other amillennialists are more prone to attempt to meet the premillennial arguments that the Old Testament demands a kingdom of righteousness *on earth,* if prophecy is to be fulfilled. After amillennialists have referred all the passages to heaven which can possibly be made to refer to a heavenly kingdom, there remains a great number of passages which cannot be explained away. If words mean anything, Isaiah 11 refers to the earth, not heaven. Psalm 72 could not possibly be twisted to apply to heaven, and the same is true of several other passages as well. In an attempt to meet this problem of the amillennial interpretation, the binding of Satan has also been referred to the earth, even though logically it would have nothing to do with a heavenly kingdom. The question is then, Is Satan now bound in respect to the earth? If he is, one must find some explanation for this present evil world, for apostasy in the church, for the rapid growth of non-Christian religions. One must be able to explain all references in the New Testament to the present activity of Satan. Since this is impossible, then Satan is not bound in respect to the earth, amillennialists must find some other explanation for passages that refer to a period of righteousness on earth and universal peace and knowledge of the Lord.

What is the testimony of the Scriptures? Can Satan deceive the nations now? Is he totally inactive? Numerous Scripture passages clearly present a negative answer. "But Peter said, Ananias, why has Satan filled your heart to lie to the Holy Spirit, and to keep back some of the price of the land?" (Acts 5:3). "Stop depriving one another, except by agreement for a time that you may devote yourselves to prayer, and come together again lest Satan tempt you because of your lack of self-control" (1 Cor. 7:5). "And even if our gospel is veiled, it is veiled to those who are perishing, in whose case the god of this world has blinded the minds of the unbelieving, that they might not see the light of the gospel of the glory of Christ, who is the image of God" (2 Cor. 4:3–4). "And no wonder, for even Satan disguises himself as an angel of light" (2 Cor. 11:14). "And because of the surpassing greatness of the revelation, for this reason, to keep me from exalting myself, there was given me a thorn in the flesh, a messenger of Satan to buffet me—to keep me from exalting myself!" (2 Cor. 12:7). "For we wanted to come to you—I, Paul, more than once—and yet Satan thwarted us" (1 Thess. 2:18). "And then that lawless one will be revealed whom the Lord will slay with the breath of His mouth and bring to an end by the appearance of His coming; that is, the one whose coming is in accord with the activity of Satan, with all power and signs and false wonders" (2 Thess. 2:8–9). "Among these are Hymenaeus and Alexander, whom I delivered over to Satan, so that they may be taught not to blaspheme" (1 Tim. 1:20). "Be of sober spirit, be on the alert. Your adversary, the devil, prowls about like a roaring lion, seeking someone to devour" (1 Peter 5:8). "The one who practices sin is of the devil; for the devil has sinned from the beginning. The Son of God appeared for this purpose, that He might destroy the works of the devil" (1 John 3:8). "By this the children of God and the children of the devil are obvious" (1 John 3:10a).

Satan is seen to tempt, to deceive, to blind, to buffet, to hinder, to work signs and lying wonders, to influence unbelievers, to seek to devour individuals. Is this a picture of Satan bound? Is this in harmony with the amillennial interpretation of Revelation 20:1–3? The obvious answer is that Satan is not bound, that he still deceives, that he still has great power, and that in respect to the earth he can severely attack both Christians and the unsaved—howbeit in the will of God.

Compare these Scriptures with the following statement by amillennialist Masselink:

> The binding of Satan for a thousand years is the symbolical figure used to teach us that his power is completely broken for a season. . . . From this passage in Revelation we learn that Satan is bound in a twofold sense: in the relative sense and in the absolute sense. With respect to the nations he is not bound completely. The result of this binding is that he can deceive the nations no more. In regard to the saints he is bound in the absolute sense. The glorified souls are entirely beyond his dominion.[6]

In contrast to this view Revelation 20:1–3 teaches that Satan will be completely bound, that he will be totally inactive. At the present time, the Scriptures themselves indicate the continued activity of Satan, his attacks on saints in the earth, and his deceiving of individuals.

Hamilton's argument from Matthew 12:24–29 that Satan was already bound at that time is refuted by the plain facts of the context. In the first place Christ did not say that Satan is bound—He used the word only in the illustration. Obviously because demon possession abounded then, Satan was not bound in the sense of the statement in Revelation 20:1–3. Even Hamilton would be loathe to state that the Jews who demanded the crucifixion of Christ were not deceived by Satan. Yet his hypothesis demands that Satan can no longer deceive the nations. He states, "The way of salvation has been opened to all nations and there is nothing that Satan can do to block that way."[7] Do not the Scriptures reveal that the reason for the unbelief of the world in relation to the Gospel is due to Satan's deceptive and blinding work (2 Cor. 4:3–4)? How is it that after 19 centuries of proclamation, the Gospel has yet to win even a majority of those who have heard it? How is it that in contrast to the Christian faith with its spiritual power the heathen religions such as Islam are actually gaining converts more quickly than is Christianity? How is it that apostasy has overtaken the church today? There can be only one answer, namely, that Satan is working, deceiving, hindering, blinding, devouring. Therefore Satan is not bound, nor is he shut up where he cannot deceive the nations. And since he is not bound, the millennium is yet future and the believer's hope is for the coming of the Lord.

Conclusion

A study of all the factors involved in the interpretation of Revelation 20:1–3 leads to three conclusions. First, Satan is not now bound and shut up in the abyss in relation to heaven, though his power has always been limited. Second, Satan is not now bound and shut up in the abyss in relation to the earth, though here too his power is limited; Satan stands judged and defeated and Christ is victorious. Third, the binding of Satan and his period of total inactivity are still future and will constitute a major feature of the future millennium on earth. There is not now nor ever will be a fulfillment of the prophecies of Christ's righteous rule on earth until Satan is bound—an event coincident with the return of Christ to establish His earthly kingdom.

CHAPTER 8

An Evaluation of Theonomic Neopostmillennialism

Thomas D. Ice

T oday Christians are witnessing "the most rapid cultural realignment in history."[1] One Christian writer describes the last twenty-five years as "The Great Rebellion," which has resulted in a whole new culture replacing the more traditional Christian-influenced American culture.[2] Is the light flickering and about to go out? Is this a part of the further development of the apostasy that many premillennialists say is taught in the Bible? Or is this "*post*-Christian" culture[3] one of the periodic visitations of a judgment/salvation[4] which is furthering the coming of a *post*millennial kingdom? Leaders of the Christian Reconstruction Movement (hereafter referred to as CRM) clearly state how Christians should respond to these times. But what is the CRM? How did it begin? Who are its leaders and what are its goals? How should believers view this movement? This chapter seeks to answer these questions in an introductory and survey manner, as a means of stimulating further evaluation in light of God's Word.

History and Background

"Twenty years ago, the Christian Reconstruction movement did not exist."[5] However, today the movement has grown rapidly and is exerting great influence within Christianity. The patriarch of the movement is R. J. Rushdoony, son of Armenian emigrants to New York City. "Rush," as he is often known to his friends, is the latest in "an unbroken succession of fathers and sons or nephews who were pastors from the early 4th century until the present."[6] He holds B.A. and M.A. degrees from the University of California and received his theological training at the Pacific School of Religion. His Ph.D. degree from Valley Christian University in Clovis, California, is in educational philosophy.

Rushdoony worked with Chinese youth in San Francisco and was a missionary to the Paiute and Shoshone Indians for about nine years. He then served as pastor of several Presbyterian churches.[7] He founded the Chalcedon Foundation in 1965 to promote "Christian Reconstruction."[8] Rushdoony's first book, *By What Standard* (1959), was the fountainhead of a steady stream of publications to come from his pen. In 1973 the Presbyterian and Reformed Publishing Company published his controversial and influential book *The Institutes of Biblical Law*, which, because of its theonomic appeal to the Bible,[9] drew fire from the establishment Reformed community. Because of the movement's influence *Newsweek* labeled Chalcedon "the think tank for the religious right."[10] CRM Books are being published by major Christian presses, and their ideas have influenced mainstream Christian thinkers including Francis Schaeffer.[11]

Gary North and Greg Bahnsen are the other major players in the movement. North, Rushdoony's son-in-law, considers himself a Christian economist. His major association with Rushdoony was in editing Chalcedon's *Journal of Christian Reconstruction* from 1974 until they had a falling out in 1981. North moved to Tyler, Texas,[12] in the early 1980s and launched what many call "the Tyler group."[13] The ICE (Institute for Christian Economics)[14] was established there, and the sister organization Geneva Ministries[15] followed.

Other players under the North/Tyler umbrella include Ray Sutton, the pastor of Westminster Presbyterian Church, Tyler, Texas, and James Jordan, a "scholar-in-residence" who teaches at the Geneva Divinity School. David Chilton, who worked with North for about four years in Tyler, has written books on economics and eschatology.[16] Chilton, now a pastor in California, was groomed by North to promote theonomy in relation to eschatology. Another rising star who is aligned with the Tyler group is George Grant, pastor of Believers Fellowship in Humble, Texas. Grant has developed Reconstructionist views on welfare, the poor, and literature. Others at Geneva Ministries include Michael Gilstrap, James Michael Peters, and Lewis E. Bulkeley.

The brilliant Greg Bahnsen, who read some of Rushdoony's works when just a boy, has emerged as the pointman on the theonomy issue. Unlike the other two leaders, he has not developed an organization but "currently pastors a small Orthodox

Presbyterian Church in Orange County, California, and is dean of the graduate school at an area teachers college."[17]

Atlanta, Georgia, is another center of the CRM. Chalcedon Presbyterian Church in Dunwoody, Georgia, voted on February 20, 1983 to withdraw from the PCA, with which it had been affiliated since its founding nine years before. The church cited many reasons for withdrawal, but the most serious seems to be its charge that the PCA was not in keeping with the Westminster Standards because they were not interpreting the Standards according to theonomy and postmillennialism.[18] Joseph C. Morecraft III is their Reconstructionist pastor. He ran for Larry McDonald's Congressional seat in the 1986 election, losing by a ratio of two to one. Morecraft differs from other Reconstructionists in that he has never written a book; however, he does have a monthly publication.[19] He even bemoans the fact that while believing that the preaching of the Gospel will be the key instrument for bringing in the kingdom, the CRM does not practice evangelism and the high standards of personal godly living which he sees consistent with their high calling.[20]

Another of Bahnsen's students at Reformed Theological Seminary was Gary DeMar, who in Atlanta heads up the Institute of Christian Government. DeMar leads conferences using his three workbooks on *God and Government*, from the Reconstructionist perspective.[21]

Others in the movement include the South African Francis Nigel Lee, who has been associated with the Christian Studies Center in Memphis, Tennessee, and Joe Kickasola, professor of International Affairs at CBN University, Virginia Beach, Virginia. A graduate of Westminster Seminary, he teaches CRM views in his classes.[22]

Gary North is certainly correct in saying that the Reconstructionist position cannot be ignored[23] by those who do not fall in line with its perspective. What are the main beliefs that distinguish the CRM from many other theologies?

Beliefs and Theology

The relationship of Christian Reconstructionists to Meredith Kline seems to epitomize the way they view their theology. On the one hand Kline is the source of much inspiration and support[24] for their ideas, but on the other hand he attacks them as being involved in "an old-new error."[25] The CRM has grouped old ideas along with revived Puritanism.[26]

The CRM criticizes dispensationalism for being a relatively recent development and claims that the CRM is the historically orthodox position of the church.[27] CRM leaders certainly claim an old foundation for much of their theology. This is seen in Rushdoony's alignment with the Council of Chalcedon, his love for medieval culture and government, as well as the movement's overall claim to be modern Puritans[28] loyal to the Westminster Confession. However, they often speak of innovation and "breakthroughs" in their theology.[29] They seem to suggest that the basic categories of theology have been with the church since the Reformation, but that they need further development, arrangement, and perseverance, which their movement is giving. Then when that is supplied, the knowledge of the Lord will cover the earth as the waters cover the sea.

It is inconsistent for them to advocate legitimate "development" of their theology, but to disallow it for their opponents. Their "developments" presumably allow them to disassociate with the failures and shortcomings of their theological fathers,[30] while on the other hand associating with their predecessors' strengths.

North cites five fundamental points on which the CRM rests:[31] the sovereignty of God, biblical law, Cornelius Van Til's biblical presuppositionalism, biblical optimism, and the covenant.[32] North and Chilton hold that these elements have to be blended together as a system to be effective. They "too often have been missing *as a unit*, from the days of the early church fathers until the 1960's."[33] This is a bold claim. The two major areas that seem to drive the system of the CRM are theonomy and postmillennialism. Since there has been considerably more attention given to their view of theonomy,[34] the remainder of this chapter concentrates on their eschatology.

POSTMILLENNIALISM

Optimism. Postmillennialism almost died out after the two world wars left only a handful of advocates. However, the last ten to fifteen years have witnessed a renewed emphasis on postmillennialism.[35] The eschatology of the CRM may be called *neo*postmillennialism. Its proponents say it is similar to amillennialism.[36] "Indeed, it is no accident," declares a Reformed writer explaining the recent rise of postmillennialism, "that both postmillennialism and theonomy . . . have sprouted in the soil of a strong Reformed revival."[37] This may explain the initial spark;

however, the recent spread into other circles, especially into the "positive-confession" charismatic realm, is better explained by the word "optimism." North notes the spread of postmillennial optimism into this branch of the charismatic movement as he critiques this same observation made by David Hunt in *The Seduction of Christianity.*

> He [Hunt] implicitly associates New Age optimism with an optimistic eschatology. He recognizes (as few of the "positive confession" leaders have recognized) that they have become operational postmillennialists. . . . He sees clearly that a new eschatology is involved in "positive confession," a *dominion eschatology.*[38]

North later boasts of a specific inroad of their views into the ministry of "positive confession" minister Robert Tilton.

> Mr. Hunt understands far better than most observers what is *really* taking place. Indeed, it has already begun: bringing together the postmillennial Christian reconstructionists and the "positive confession" charismatics. . . . It began when Robert Tilton's wife read Gary DeMar's *God and Government* in late 1983, and then persuaded her husband to invite a group of reconstructionists to speak before 1,000 "positive confession" pastors and their wives at a January 1984 rally sponsored by Rev. Tilton's church. The all-day panel was very well received. . . .
> Mr. Hunt sees that if this fusion of theological interests takes place, then the day of unchallenged dominance by the old-timed dispensational eschatology is about to come to an end. A new fundamentalism is appearing.[39]

More recently, North admits to some potential problems with misdirected optimism.

> If all a person gains from the Christian Reconstruction movement in general is its optimistic eschatology, then he is skating on thin ice. Optimism is not enough. In fact, optimism alone is highly dangerous. The Communists have a doctrine of inevitable victory; so do radical Muslims. So did a group of revolutionary communist murderers and polygamists, the Anabaptists who captured the German city of Munster from 1525–35, before they were defeated militarily by Christian forces. Optimism in the wrong hands is a dangerous weapon.[40]

This misguided optimism is a major error in neopostmillennialism. In the last century postmillennialism provided the optimistic climate in which the social gospel grew. Smith has argued that evangelicals were perhaps the leading force in many of the social gospel issues.

> Evangelical Christians provided the example, inspiration, and principles for much of the Social Gospel. . . . the evangelical ideology of the millennium merged without a break into what came to be called the

social gospel in the years after 1870. . . . these evangelicals worked as
vigorously for social betterment as did the Social Gospel leaders.[41]

Evangelical postmillennialism is to be distinguished from the liberal form. However, one cannot overlook the role that postmillennialism in general played in the rise and development of the "social gospel." Postmillenarians blame dispensationalism for creating a climate of retreat from social and political issues. Are they denying that postmillennialism, an eschatology which they say has had great effect on Western culture, contributed to the optimism of the 1800s? Chilton does admit to some postmillennial heresy. "Examples of the Postmillenarian heresy would be easy to name as well: the Munster Revolt of 1534, Nazism, and Marxism (whether 'Christian' or otherwise)."[42] Nazism and Marxism are undesirable movements. Why then does Chilton not admit the relationship of postmillennialism to the "social gospel" movement?[43]

The wedding between certain errant charismatic theologies and current neopostmillennialism may be similar to the deterioration of Puritan postmillennialism into the social gospel movement. If this is happening, then one may expect to see the spread of optimistic eschatology at the expense of historic orthodoxy. And again the tendency of postmillennialism to raise false hopes will have occurred.

Common grace. North and the "Tyler group" have taken an aggressive stand regarding their eschatology.[44] They feel they can work with various groups, even though they admit those groups are wrong in many areas of theology.[45] This is because theonomists believe common grace is increasing as the age progresses. They do not believe that apostasy will increase (as common grace decreases).[46] They say God is gradually developing various tools in the church for bringing in the kingdom. Some examples are the development of a consistent biblical epistemology by Van Til;[47] Sutton's view on the covenant;[48] Rushdoony's innovation of law as the tool or blueprint for bringing in dominion;[49] and North's interpretation that modern technology leads to decentralization (rather than centralization and one world government).

This enlightenment/breakthrough attitude is producing the opposite effect for this movement which seeks to provide the tools for furthering the kingdom.[50] Rather than protecting CRMers from errors of the past, their overestimation of their own historical importance causes them to be closed to outside criticism. Therefore Rushdoony does not read reviews of his work, according to Joe Kickasola.[51] North and others repeatedly say that everyone in one hundred or two hundred years will look back to developments in the CRM theology as a turning point in bringing in the kingdom.[52] This may explain why the tone, especially of Rushdoony and North is more like that of a communist propaganda assault than marketplace persuasion. One wonders if they believe God's grace will give them success or if they think success will come from their own development, defense, and proclamation of their views?

HERMENEUTICS

Theological presuppositions. The CRM makes much of theological presuppositions. As Taylor says,

> The fatal weakness of the new postmillennialism is that its Scriptural support is derived precisely from those very passages which also form the backbone of the other views of what can be expected to happen before Christ returns.
> When opposing views use precisely the same text for support against each other, it isn't the text which has produced the contrast; it probably was something else—"newspaper exegesis," if you will, or *theological presuppositions.*[53]

However, theological presuppositions should be tested by the "exegetical spiral," as Packer suggests.

> Exegesis presupposes a hermeneutic which in turn is drawn from an overall theology, which theology in its turn rests on exegesis. The circle is not, of course, logically vicious; it is not the circle of presupposing what you ought to prove, but the circle, or rather the ascending spiral, of successive approximation. . . . The circle thus appears as a one-way system: from texts to doctrine, from doctrine to hermeneutic, from hermeneutic to texts again.[54]

This method of "checking your math" certainly fits into the Van Tilian tradition, which the CRM claims to have as its epistemological foundation, since the essay appeared in Van Til's *Festschrift.* While the CRM proponents do not spend much time discussing hermeneutical theory, they generally try to use their "Trinitarian epistemology" as their guide.[55] Jordan has said many times at conferences that in all of life the one and the many are necessary. To stress one over the other makes one a rationalist. There is no conflict, as in humanistic, dialectical thinking, he says, between the one (interpretation/meaning/theology) and the many (data/exegesis of the biblical texts). Hermeneutically this means if a person comes up with theological presuppositions, he should be able to explain them from specific texts of Scripture. In other words an issue can be approached from either direction of the exegetical circle, from the one or the many, since they should not conflict.

Chilton says that the Great Commission of Matthew 28:19–20

> does not end with simply *witnessing* to the nations. Christ's command is that we *disciple* the nations—*all* the nations. The kingdoms of the world are to become the kingdoms of Christ. They are to be discipled, made obedient to the faith. This means that every aspect of life throughout the world is to be brought under the lordship of Jesus Christ: families, individuals, business, science, agriculture, the arts, law, education, economics, psychology, philosophy, and every other sphere of human activity.[56]

However, this passage does not say what Chilton wants it to say, unless a priori assumptions are carried into it. He is reading his theology into the passage and then citing it as proof for his theology. Why is this passage not talking about evangelism, as most understand it? Premillennialists certainly believe that all those things Chilton mentioned will occur, but they disagree with the postmillennialists on *timing* (these changes will occur after Christ returns, not before) and *agency* (just as in creation, the Flood, the Exodus, and salvation, Christ will accomplish this directly, not through secondary means). The rest of the New Testament contains the theology that the church is to teach the disciples to observe. But the New Testament does not give the agenda Chilton suggests. He lists two checks he thinks keep the interpreter from lapsing into speculation.

> First, he must be faithful to the *system of doctrine* taught in the Bible. . . . Second, the interpreter must keep in mind that the symbols in the Bible are not isolated; rather, they are part of a *system of symbolism* given in the Bible, an architecture of images in which all the parts fit together. If we honestly and carefully read the Bible theologically and with respect to the Bible's own literary structure, we will not go very far astray.[57]

A major problem with these two rules is that they are both *subjective*. This is like telling a child to stop eating ice cream when he thinks he has had enough. Children need a rule or "law" that says, "You have had enough when you finish one scoop." A good Van Tilian should know that a *system* (the "one" or interpretation) should be checked by *exegesis* (the "many" or data in the text).

CRM leaders are long on interpretation and theological presuppositions but short on exegesis of specific passages to support their theology. North is sensitive to this charge when he says, "For over two decades, critics chided the Christian Reconstructionists with this refrain: 'You people just haven't produced any Biblical exegesis to prove your case for eschatological optimism.'"[58]

Spiritualization. The hermeneutical approach of neopostmillennialism is rightly said to be a blend of the literal and nonliteral approach to Scripture.[59] Walvoord's criticism of classical postmillennialism still stands in relation to neopostmillennialism.

> Postmillennialism is based on the figurative interpretation of prophecy which permits wide freedom in finding the meaning of difficult passages. . . . As a system of theology based upon a subjective spiritualizing of Scripture, postmillennialism lacks the central principles necessary for coherence. Each postmillennialist is left more or less to his own ingenuity in solving the problem of what to do with prophecies of a millennium on earth. . . . The result is that postmillennialism has no unified front to protect itself from the inroads of other interpretations. At best postmillennialism is superimposed upon systems of theology which were developed without its aid.[60]

It appears to this writer that the particular brand of spiritualization used by those in the CRM to justify their eschatology is that of "statement." In discussing a passage they merely *state* their theology rather than developing it *from* the text. Examples are found in James Jordan's lecture series on Matthew 24.[61] His point is that the coming of Christ will not be at the end of history for it already occurred in A.D. 70.

In interpreting Matthew 24:30, "They will see the Son of Man coming on the clouds of the sky with power and great glory," Jordan refers to Daniel 7:13. Since "one like a son of man" does not go to the earth, but rather approaches the throne of "the Ancient of Days," Jordan reasons that Matthew was not referring to the second coming of Christ to the earth. Jordan transports the context of Daniel 7, which is heavenly and not earthly, into the context of Matthew 24 without comparing and contrasting the two. He simply declares that is the meaning and then develops his theology on the basis of that statement.

He fails to take into account the fact that Matthew 24 refers to the reaction of people on earth when they see the Messiah return in the physical sky "with power and great glory." Power and glory are the language of a physical display by God, as seen, for example, in the Exodus (Ex. 7:3; 14:30; 15:1–18). As Carson explains,

> We may imagine Jesus the Son of Man receiving the kingdom through his resurrection and ascension, his divine vindication, so that now all authority is his (28:18). Yet it is equally possible to think of him receiving the kingdom at the consummation, when his reign or kingdom becomes direct and immediate, uncontested and universal.[62]

Jordan and Chilton try to justify their approach with a dialectic they call "sense" and "referent." Chilton explains,

> While the sense of a symbol remains the same (the words "white house" always mean "white house"), it can have numerous referents (White House in Washington, D.C.; the white house across the street; the green house that belongs to Fred White; etc.). St. John's images do not mean anything you like; their sense can be determined. But they still have an astonishing multiplicity of reference.[63]

Chilton cites examples from Isaiah 65:22; Amos 2:9; and Psalm 114 and concludes, "It includes the use of huge figures; a reign of forty years means a good long reign, and a kingdom of a thousand years means a good long kingdom."[64]

It is wrong, however, to argue against literalness simply because there is a symbolic aspect in some sentences. True, the serpent is a symbol of evil throughout history, but this does not rule out the presence of a literal serpent in the Garden of Eden. Forty connotes the idea of testing, but this does not rule out the fact that Christ was literally tempted in the wilderness for forty literal days. Mountains often symbolically suggest rulership, but that does not mean the mountains mentioned in connection with rule in Scripture are not literal (e.g., Mount Zion is a real mountain, even though there is much theology attached to this theme). Therefore the one thousand years of Revelation 20 can rightly be taken as literal (which some postmillenarians have held).

In relation to the interpretation of symbols, Chilton quotes Herman Bavinck's *The Doctrine of God* to establish two points. "First, *all creation is primarily symbolic.* . . . The *central* value of anything is that it is a symbol of God. All other values and relationships are secondary. . . . Second, *symbolism is analogical, not realistic.* . . . The symbolism is analogical, not metaphysical."[65]

Chilton is right in saying that the analogy of marriage used in the Bible to speak of God's relationship with His people does not mean believers have physical sexual relations with God. But to carry that thinking over to days or years, as do CRMers in relation to the millennium is to add too much fluidity to symbolism.

It is inconsistent for CRMers to be so "literal" in applying every detail of the Old Testament Law, but to be so fluid and flexible when it comes to interpreting prophecy. This is the type of philosophical idealism which is at the heart of the movement, rather than a correct application of biblical symbolism. As Johnson states, "The concept of 'literal interpretation' affirms that the meaning of a symbol is determined by textual and contextual considerations. It may appear that such a method would exclude figures and symbols altogether,"[66] but it does not.

Literal interpretation includes the development of symbols and themes which yield a rich premillennial theology. The darkness/light motif begun in Genesis 1 grows into a major theme as Scripture unfolds. The pattern of God separating light from darkness sets the precedent for how He views the makeup of a day and for the holiness/commonality theme. God's day includes evening (darkness) and then morning (light). This was a preview of how God would bring individuals out of the darkness of sin into the light of His salvation.

This theme of darkness and light shows up in many ways throughout the Bible. The ninth plague brought darkness on the Egyptians but not on the houses of the Israelites. The darkness symbolized blindness and sin, while light showed the favor and blessing of God. This theological meaning is based on the literal, actual event. This is also seen in Judas' betrayal of Christ. As John wrote, "[Judas] went out immediately; and it was night" (John 13:30). Judas left the light of the world, Jesus, and went into the darkness of sin, but it was also literally night. God sovereignly coordinates the theology with the actual circumstances and events.

Paul further developed the darkness/light motif in 1 Thessalonians 5:1–11. He wrote, "The day of the Lord will come just like a thief in the night" (v. 2). The passage then develops the implications of that statement. "Day" refers to "the day of the Lord," and this present age is compared to "night."[67] Therefore since believers are "sons of light" (those who will inherit the kingdom), even though they are living in the night (the period before the coming in of the kingdom, the day of the Lord), their behavior is to reflect their future. Therefore believers in the church age are working the "night shift." Even Daniel was not commissioned to bring in the kingdom, especially since the New Covenant had not unfolded.

To the pagans in Babylon he was to be a faithful testimony of his God, even though the nation was largely faithless. Christ will bring in the "day" at the second coming; this is why He is called the "morning star" (2 Peter 1:19), which accompanies the dawning of the day (the millennium). The job of believers on the night shift is further clarified by Paul (Eph. 5:7–14), who wrote that they are to *expose* (bring to light) evil, not *conquer* it, as the CRMers insist. Christ will do that at His coming. Kline speaks of differences between this age, in which common grace is functioning, and what the present age would be like if the church's mission is to bring in the theocratic kingdom.

> To accept the Chalcedon theory, one would have to read the biblical record as though it were not the history of the particular kingdom of Israel but an historicized myth about Everynation. . . . Chalcedon's mistake is that of sacralizing the other nations. . . . And inevitably Chalcedon does the same to the concept of the nonholy, or common. It renders pointless and meaningless the biblical distinction between the holy and the common. [68]

Dispensationalism teaches that after the rapture God will resume His plans for Israel. The millennial reign of Christ is a better explanation of the consummation of history than what the neopostmillennialists set forth.

Other hermeneutical issues. Other issues can be raised against neopostmillennialism, such as the following: At what point in the present age (the kingdom, according to CRMers) will the curse be removed? When will the lamb lie down with the wolf (Isa. 11:6) and the human life span be more than one hundred years (Isa. 65:20)? How can one say progress is being made when the killer disease AIDS is increasing? CRMers say progress is gradual, but Romans 8:18–25 uses catastrophic/interventionist language. One dispensationalist raised two major objections to equating this current age with the millennium.

> (1) The interaction between group, individual and environment evidently is a lot more profound than even sociologists are willing to admit, so profound in fact that a catastrophic alteration is required for the "perfect" social order. (2) This being the case, even total regeneration of the human race would not be far reaching enough to establish the "millennial vision." The physical environment must be totally changed (Rom. 8:19–22).[69]

How can CRMers say the Gospel is conquering the world, since at the end of the millennium the Gog and Magog battle will take place in which Christ will directly intervene to rescue believers

(Rev. 20:7–10).[70] During the tribulation many will turn to Christ, and perhaps a majority of the world will be converted during the millennium. The Gospel will penetrate the world, but not in the way CRMers envision. They cannot argue against the premillenarian schedule of events in *principle* (or as Bahnsen would say, *prima facie*), since they see a similar outline. The difference is one of timing.

Dispensationalism and social involvement. North accuses dispensationalists of being defeatists, sitting around waiting for the rapture.[71] However, social and cultural impotence is not endemic to dispensationalism. As already stated, believers are called to expose evil during the night. They are to be the light of the world shining in the current darkness, testifying to those in the night as to what the day will be like. However, this does not mean Christians are in the kingdom during this age. Their primary mission is evangelism, while looking for the coming of Christ. Believers are to be like a steward left with a job to do during the absence of the owner of the house. They are motivated by the future event—the desire to be found faithful when the householder returns. The future motivates the steward in the present.

This is the same basic philosophy North preaches in economics. He says one must be future-oriented to be productive in the present. Because a person's hopes and aspirations are ahead, he sacrifices in the present for the sake of future goals.[72]

A dispensational theory of the current social order has been proposed by Clough.

> A major insight of dispensational premillennialism is the picture it gives of the dynamics of evil. There are three factors involved: (1) the impact of regenerated and spiritually active people relative to the impact of the remainder; (2) the restraining ministry of the Spirit during the Church Age in suppressing total evil domination of basic social structures; (3) all-pervading domain of Satan over both the social order and its physical environment. Factor (2) is relatively stable, and factor (3) in the realm of the social order appears to vary approximately inversely with factor (1). As is commonly recognized, then, the basic variable is the impact of the church.
>
> But the unique contribution of this eschatology is how it establishes realistic upper and lower limits on the variation of Satanic domination in the present social order. The upper limit *of which the pretribulational rapture is an integral part* states, in effect, that no matter how small the church is in the world the general social order of the world will be graciously kept from total Satanic control until the rapture. Satan's plans are held in temporary suspension while the human race is given

opportunity to trust Christ (2 Peter 3:9). The lower limit *of which Satan's reign over physical creation is an integral part* states, in effect, that no matter how many are won to Christ in the world the general social order of the world will still remain under the influence of a corrupt physical environment. Christ must return and redeem physical creation for elimination of this influence. . . . Thus dispensational premillennialism sets forth data from which it is possible to deduce a realistic picture of the working of evil in the social order today and why the "perfect" social order must be future to a supernatural realignment of the basic factors.[73]

This view leads to a certain degree of present social and political involvement during the church age. Because the rapture could occur at any moment, the Lord's stewards are to be doing His business faithfully every day. If dispensationalists are not properly involved in issues today, they are unfaithful to their calling.

Dispensationalists believe in victory in history in every sphere of life. In fact they believe, in one sense, in dominion theology! Just as salvation is accomplished immediately by Christ's work, so will the consummation of the age be immediate, not mediate as the CRM preaches. McClain also notes that many accomplishments during the church age will be carried over into the kingdom.

The premillennial philosophy of history makes sense. It lays a biblical and rational basis for a truly optimistic view of human history. Furthermore, rightly apprehended, it has practical effects. It says that life here and now, in spite of the tragedy of sin, is nevertheless something worthwhile; and therefore all efforts to make it better are also worthwhile. All the true values of human life will be preserved and carried over into the coming kingdom; nothing worthwhile will be lost. Furthermore, we are encouraged in the midst of opposition and reverses by the assurance that help is on the way, help from above, supernatural help—"Give the king thy judgments, O God. . . . In his days shall the righteous flourish. . . . all nations shall call him blessed" (Ps. 72:1, 7, 17).[74]

Conclusion

The CRM, like most movements within orthodox Christianity, has some healthy aspects to it. It is causing believers to think through what the Bible says should be their view on many social and political issues. It shows that Christians must take Scripture and Scripture alone as the basis for formulating views on all of life. The CRMers have shown that one can be both intellectual and practical. They have made contributions to the study of biblical theology and philosophy. They have sparked a renewed interest in eschatology.

The major dangers of the CRM are theonomy and neopostmillennialism. The application of Old Testament law advocated by the CRM is a new phariseeism. Christians are not to insist on a militant working for and enforcement of the Mosaic Law. The eschatology of the CRM produces a misplaced perspective on history and God's timing of future events. In theory CRMers strongly believe in evangelism; however, in practice it is ignored. They are working to build a society that God has not purposed. There is the danger that they will become wrongly involved in this world's system in their zeal to make the kingdoms of this world the kingdom of the Lord Jesus Christ.

CHAPTER 9

The Kingdom of God in the Old Testament

John F. Walvoord

The masterful chapter on "The Kingdom Concept in the Old Testament" by J. Dwight Pentecost in his work, *Things to Come*,[1] sets forth in a comprehensive way the doctrine of the kingdom of God in the Old Testament. Unfortunately, in spite of the comprehensive presentation in this chapter, as well as numerous other books that set forth the doctrine of the kingdom in the Old Testament, amillenarians have repeatedly stated that the Bible nowhere teaches a future kingdom on earth.[2] Rather than leave such statements unchallenged, it seems best to review briefly the specific contribution of the Old Testament to the premillennial interpretation of a future kingdom on earth.

The problem is by no means simplistic. Many varying definitions of the kingdom of God are given. As Pentecost states, "Through this maze of interpretations it is almost impossible to make one's way."[3]

Pentecost divides these confusing aspects of the kingdom of God into two categories, the eternal kingdom and the theocratic kingdom.[4] As Pentecost and others have noted, the theme of the theocratic kingdom can be traced from the Garden of Eden through the period of human government initiated by Noah, the period of the patriarchs initiated by Abraham, the kingdom under the judges, the kingdom under the kings, and finally the kingdom under the prophets.[5] Although interpretations of these aspects of the kingdom of God vary in differing systems of eschatology, the primary problem of interpretation is found in the theocratic kingdom under the prophets. Usually it is conceded that the kingdom was in theocratic form in Israel under Saul, David, Solomon, and their successors. The question remains whether there is a future form of the kingdom that will also be theocratic, political, and on earth. This is the point of tension between premillennial and amillennial interpretation. Obviously for an amillenarian to say summarily that no verse in the Bible teaches a future earthly kingdom is a dogmatic statement that needs to be examined. The purpose of this discussion is to refer primarily to what the Scriptures actually state and then raise the question as to the proper interpretation of these passages.

The Prophecies of Isaiah

As a casual reading of the Book of Isaiah demonstrates, the prophet Isaiah speaks repeatedly on the subject of a future earthly kingdom. In his book he predicts a future kingdom with Jerusalem as its capital and involving the tribe of Judah.

> In the last days, the mountain of the house of the LORD will be established as the chief of the mountains, and will be raised above the hills; and all the nations will stream to it. And many peoples will come and say, Come, let us go up to the mountain of the LORD, to the house of the God of Jacob; that He may teach us concerning His ways, and that we may walk in His paths. For the law will go forth from Zion, and the word of the LORD from Jerusalem. And He will judge between the nations, and will render decisions for many peoples, and they will hammer their swords into plowshares, and their spears into pruning hooks. Nation will not lift up sword against nation, and never again will they learn war (Isa. 2:2–4).

This prophecy has had no literal fulfillment in the past, but a future kingdom on earth could fulfill precisely these predictions of Isaiah.

One of the better known of Isaiah's pronouncements concerning the future kingdom is his prediction of Christ's birth.

> For a child will be born to us, a son will be given to us; and the government will rest on His shoulders; and His name will be called Wonderful Counselor, Mighty God, Eternal Father, Prince of Peace. There will be no end to the increase of His government or of peace, on the throne of David and over his kingdom, to establish it and to uphold it with justice and righteousness from then on and forevermore. The zeal of the LORD of hosts will accomplish this (9:6–7).

Again this passage refers to an earthly government. The child will be born on earth; the throne will be that of David; rule will be characterized by justice and righteousness; and it will be accomplished by the power of God rather than the power of men. His birth has been fulfilled, but the establishment of His earthly government has not.

One of the most extensive passages by Isaiah refers to Christ's coming and the characteristics of His reign on the earth.

> Then a shoot will spring from the stem of Jesse, and a branch from his roots will bear fruit. And the Spirit of the LORD will rest on Him, the spirit of wisdom and understanding, the spirit of counsel and strength, the spirit of knowledge and the fear of the LORD. And He will delight in the fear of the LORD, and He will not judge by what His eyes see, nor make a decision by what His ears hear; but with righteousness He will judge the poor, and decide with fairness for the afflicted of the earth; and He will strike the earth with the rod of His mouth, and with the breath of His lips He will slay the wicked. Also righteousness will be the belt about His loins, and faithfulness the belt about His waist. And the wolf will dwell with the lamb, and the leopard will lie down with the kid, and the calf and the young lion and the fatling together; and a little boy will lead them. Also the cow and the bear will graze; their young will lie down together; and the lion will eat straw like the ox. And the nursing child will play by the hole of the cobra, and the weaned child will put his hand on the viper's den. They will not hurt or destroy in all My holy mountain, for the earth will be full of the knowledge of the LORD as the waters cover the sea (11:1–9).

These characteristics of Christ's reign obviously refer to the earth. The righteousness of His rule, the destruction of the wicked, the accompanying tranquillity in nature does not correspond to anything in history nor anything in the future in heaven, but refers to the earth. Verse 9 refers to "My holy mountain" and "the earth" being "full of the knowledge of the LORD." To these prophecies Isaiah added the graphic picture of judgment on earth in chapter 24 in connection with His earthly reign, He concluded, "Then the moon will be abashed and the sun ashamed, for the LORD of hosts will reign on Mount Zion and in Jerusalem, and His glory will be before His elders" (24:23).

To this Isaiah added another point in Isaiah 32:1, "Behold a king will reign righteously, and princes will rule justly." And in 33:20, he described Zion: "Look upon Zion, the city of our appointed feasts, your eyes shall see Jerusalem an undisturbed habitation, a tent which shall not be folded, its stakes shall never be pulled up nor any of its cords be torn apart." Again, this prophecy has never been fulfilled in any way in the past; thus it requires a future fulfillment.

All of Isaiah 35 is in poetic form expressing in detail the wonders of the future kingdom on earth.

In Isaiah 40:1–5, a frequently quoted passage, the earth is described as receiving her king, and Jerusalem is pictured as completely restored spiritually when all men will see the glory of the Lord revealed.

> Comfort, O comfort My people, says your God. Speak kindly to Jerusalem; and call out to her, that her warfare has ended, that her iniquity has been removed, that she has received of the LORD's hand double for all her sins. A voice is calling, Clear the way for the LORD in the wilderness; make smooth in the desert a highway for our God. Let every valley be lifted up, and every mountain and hill be made low; and let the rough ground become a plain, and the rugged terrain a broad valley; then the glory of the LORD will be revealed, and all flesh will see it together; for the mouth of the LORD has spoken.

Isaiah 42 gives a dramatic picture of the justice and reign of Christ on earth. Reference is made to the future time when the Messiah King will have "established justice in the earth" (42:4).

The beauty of the reign of the Lord in Jerusalem is described in Isaiah 52:7–10. In chapter 60 is revealed the mingled picture of the glory of the Lord in the millennial kingdom and its later display in the eternal new earth. This does not justify confusing the millennial earth with the eternal new earth any more than the mingled prophecies of His first and second coming (e.g., 9:6–7; 61:1–2) make them the same event.

The rebuilding of Israel and Zion is described in Isaiah 61:4–7.

> Then they will rebuild the ancient ruins, they will raise up the former devastations, and they will repair the ruined cities, the desolations of many generations. And strangers will stand and pasture your flocks, and foreigners will be your farmers and your vinedressers. But you will be called the priests of the LORD; you will be spoken of as ministers of our God. You will eat the wealth of nations, and in their riches you will boast. Instead of your shame you will have a double portion, and instead of humiliation they will shout for joy over their portion. Therefore they will possess a double portion in their land, everlasting joy will be theirs.

In Isaiah 65, another mingled picture of the millennial earth and the new heaven and new earth is presented.

> For behold, I create new heavens and a new earth; and the former things shall not be remembered or come to mind. But be glad and rejoice forever in what I create; for behold, I create Jerusalem for rejoicing, and her people for gladness. I will also rejoice in Jerusalem, and be glad in My people; and there will no longer be heard in her the voice of weeping and the sound of crying. No longer will there be in it an infant who lives but a few days, or an old man who does not live out his days; for the youth will die at the age of one hundred and the one who does not reach the age of one hundred shall be thought accursed. And they shall build houses and inhabit them; they shall also plant vineyards and eat their fruit. They shall not build, and another inhabit, they shall not plant, and another eat; for as the lifetime of a tree, so shall be the days of My people, and My chosen ones shall wear out the

work of their hands. They shall not labor in vain, or bear children for calamity; for they are the offspring of those blessed by the LORD, and their descendants with them. It will also come to pass that before they call, I will answer; and while they are still speaking, I will hear. The wolf and the lamb shall graze together, and the lion shall eat straw like the ox; and dust shall be the serpent's food. They shall do no evil or harm in all My holy mountain, says the LORD (65:17–25).

This passage is most interesting because it combines the hope of the millennium and the hope of the eternal earth. But the two are distinct. In the millennial earth there will be death and birth, the building of houses and the planting of vineyards. The peaceful coexistence of animals is also described—a situation foreign to the new earth in eternity. The millennium will serve as an introduction to the eternal state when the new heavens and the new earth will be brought into being. The passage clearly teaches primarily about the earth and its functions in the earthly reign of Christ.

To these prophecies, other prophets added their voice.

The Prophecies of Jeremiah

Jeremiah, who lived before and at the beginning of the Babylonian Captivity, also prophesied of Israel's restoration. Not only did he predict the end of the Babylonian Captivity after seventy years (Jer. 29:10), but he also anticipated the future complete restoration of Israel.

Behold, the days are coming, declares the LORD, when I shall raise up for David a righteous Branch; and He will reign as king and act wisely and do justice and righteousness in the land. In His days Judah will be saved, and Israel will dwell securely; and this is His name by which He will be called, "The LORD our righteousness." Therefore behold, the days are coming, declares the LORD, when they will no longer say, "As the LORD lives, who brought up the sons of Israel from the land of Egypt," but, "As the LORD lives, who brought up and led back the descendants of the household of Israel from the north land and from all the countries where I had driven them." Then they will live on their own soil (Jer. 23:5–8).

It should be noted that this prophecy will be fulfilled by the regathering of Israel to her ancient land, the establishment of justice and righteousness in the land by the same Lord who had brought the children of Israel from the land of Egypt years before. The passage concludes decisively, "Then they will live on their own soil" (23:8). Obviously this cannot refer to the new heavens or the new earth.

Jeremiah also wrote in eloquent language concerning Israel's future time of trouble preceding the earthly kingdom and her deliverance from that time of trouble by the Lord who will reign over them.

> Now these are the words which the LORD spoke concerning Israel and concerning Judah, For thus says the LORD, I have heard a sound of terror, of dread, and there is no peace. Ask now, and see, if a male can give birth. Why do I see every man with his hands on his loins, as a woman in childbirth? And why have all faces turned pale? Alas! for that day is great, there is none like it; and it is the time of Jacob's distress, but he will be saved from it. And it shall come about on that day, declares the LORD of hosts, that I will break his yoke from off their neck, and will tear off their bonds; and strangers shall no longer make them their slaves. But they shall serve the LORD their God, and David their king, whom I will raise up for them. And fear not, O Jacob My servant, declares the LORD, and do not be dismayed, O Israel; for behold, I will save you from afar, and your offspring from the land of their captivity. And Jacob shall return, and shall be quiet and at ease, and no one shall make him afraid. For I am with you, declares the LORD, to save you; for I will destroy completely all the nations where I have scattered you, only I will not destroy you completely. But I will chasten you justly, and will by no means leave you unpunished (30:4–11).

This passage predicts that the great tribulation will occur on earth before Christ's second coming, which will be followed by His reign on earth. David will be resurrected to share as a prince under Christ in reigning over Israel (cf. Isa. 55:3–5; Ezek. 34:24–25, 37:25, Hos. 3:5). The regathering of Israel, which characterizes the formation of the kingdom, is described graphically in Jeremiah 31:8, "Behold, I am bringing them from the north country, and I will gather them from the remote parts of the earth, among them the blind and the lame, the woman with child and she who is in labor with child, together; a great company, they shall return here."

The New Covenant which God will make with the house of Israel and the house of Judah to replace the Mosaic Covenant is described in Jeremiah 31:31–37. The New Covenant was established in grace by the death of Christ on the cross. This makes possible the relationship of the church in grace which the church experiences in the present age. In the future, however, the New Covenant will be manifested primarily by the renewal of Israel spiritually and nationally, and her regathering to her ancient land. Jeremiah called the heavens to witness—with the continued existence of the moon, the stars, and the sun as confirmations.

> If this fixed order departs from before Me, declares the LORD, then the
> offspring of Israel also shall cease from being a nation before Me forever.
> Thus says the LORD, If the heavens above can be measured, and the
> foundations of the earth searched out below, then I will also cast off all
> the offspring of Israel for all that they have done, declares the LORD
> (31:36–37).

While both the church in the present age and Israel in the future
age will experience the New Covenant brought in by Jesus Christ,
the fulfillment of the covenant in respect to Israel differs from its
fulfillment for the church, as this passage makes clear. For Israel
as a nation the New Covenant is not being fulfilled in the present
age; that will occur after Christ's second coming. Hebrews 8:7–
13, quoting Jeremiah 31:31–34, does not contradict this as is so
often erroneously stated.

Jeremiah 33:14–22 predicts the Messiah's righteous reign.

> Behold, days are coming, declares the LORD, when I will fulfill the good
> word which I have spoken concerning the house of Israel and the house
> of Judah. In those days and at that time I will cause a righteous Branch of
> David to spring forth; and He shall execute justice and righteousness on
> the earth. In those days Judah shall be saved, and Jerusalem shall dwell
> in safety; and this is the name by which she shall be called: The LORD is
> our righteousness. For thus says the LORD, David shall never lack a man
> to sit on the throne of the house of Israel; and the Levitical priests shall
> never lack a man before Me to offer burnt offerings, to burn grain
> offerings, and to prepare sacrifices continually. And the word of the
> LORD came to Jeremiah, saying, Thus says the LORD, if you can break
> My covenant for the day, and My covenant for the night, so that day and
> night will not be at their appointed time, then My covenant may also be
> broken with David My servant that he shall not have a son to reign on his
> throne, and with the Levitical priests, My ministers. As the host of heaven
> cannot be counted, and the sand of the sea cannot be measured, so I will
> multiply the descendants of David My servant and the Levites who
> minister to Me.

As in the previous reference to the New Covenant in Jeremiah
31, so here again God puts His own integrity behind the fulfillment
of the promise of the restoration of Israel to their land, referred to
as "the earth."

The Prophecies of Ezekiel

To these graphic prophecies by Isaiah and Jeremiah, Ezekiel
added his own. In Ezekiel 20:34–38 he pictured the judgment on
Israel at the time of Christ's return. Regathered Israel will be
severely judged, and only the godly remnant will be allowed to

enter the land. "And you will know that I am the LORD, when I bring you into the land of Israel, into the land which I swore to give to your forefathers" (20:42).

Ezekiel wrote eloquently about the future kingdom.

> Then I will set over them one shepherd, My servant David, and he will feed them; he will feed them himself and be their shepherd. And I, the LORD, will be their God, and My servant David will be prince among them; I, the LORD, have spoken. And I will make a covenant of peace with them and eliminate harmful beasts from the land, so that they may live securely in the wilderness and sleep in the woods. And I will make them and the places around My hill a blessing. And I will cause showers to come down in their season; they will be showers of blessing. Also the tree of the field will yield its fruit, and the earth will yield its increase, and they will be secure on their land. Then they will know that I am the LORD, when I have broken the bars of their yoke and have delivered them from the hand of those who enslaved them. And they will no longer be a prey to the nations, and the beasts of the earth will not devour them; but they will live securely, and no one will make them afraid. And I will establish for them a renowned planting place, and they will not again be victims of famine in the land, and they will not endure the insults of the nations anymore. Then they will know that I, the LORD their God, am with them, and that they, the house of Israel, are My people, declares the Lord GOD. As for you, My sheep, the sheep of My pasture, you are men, and I am your God, declares the Lord GOD (34:23–31).

As in previous passages, this can hardly refer to heaven or the eternal earth; instead, it refers to the earth in its millennial form. A future earthly kingdom is absolutely necessary to fulfill these prophecies.

The spiritual restoration that will occur in the millennial kingdom is pictured in Ezekiel 36:23–27.

> And I will vindicate the holiness of My great name which has been profaned among the nations, which you have profaned in their midst. Then the nations will know that I am the LORD, declares the Lord GOD, when I prove Myself holy among you in their sight. For I will take you from the nations, gather you from all the lands, and bring you into your own land. Then I will sprinkle clean water on you, and you will be clean; I will cleanse you from all your filthiness and from all your idols. Moreover, I will give you a new heart and put a new spirit within you; and I will remove the heart of stone from your flesh and give you a heart of flesh. And I will put My Spirit within you and cause you to walk in My statutes, and you will be careful to observe My ordinances.

This passage, like others quoted, refers to restoration in the earth and the regathering of Israel from the nations. At that time Israel "will live in the land that I gave to your forefathers" (36:28).

Ezekiel 37 speaks of Israel's restoration under the symbolism of a resurrected body. While literal bodily resurrection will occur when Christ returns, Ezekiel 37 refers to the spiritual restoration of Israel.

> And My servant David will be king over them, and they will all have one shepherd: and they will walk in My ordinances, and keep My statutes, and observe them. And they shall live on the land that I gave to Jacob My servant, in which your fathers lived; and they will live on it, they, and their sons, and their sons' sons, forever; and David My servant shall be their prince forever. And I will make a covenant of peace with them; it will be an everlasting covenant with them. And I will place them and multiply them, and will set My sanctuary in their midst forever. My dwelling place also will be with them; and I will be their God, and they will be My people. And the nations will know that I am the LORD who sanctifies Israel, when My sanctuary is in their midst forever (37:24–28).

The ultimate regathering of Israel to her land is described in Ezekiel 39:25–29.

> Therefore thus says the Lord GOD, Now I shall restore the fortunes of Jacob, and have mercy on the whole house of Israel; and I shall be jealous for My holy name. And they shall forget their disgrace and all their treachery which they perpetrated against Me, when they live securely on their own land with no one to make them afraid. When I bring them back from the peoples and gather them from the lands of their enemies, then I shall be sanctified through them in the sight of the many nations. Then they will know that I am the LORD their God because I made them go into exile among the nations, and then gathered them again to their own land; and I will leave none of them there any longer. And I will not hide My face from them any longer, for I shall have poured out My Spirit on the house of Israel, declares the Lord GOD.

Emphasis here is again on Israel's regathering to her "own land.

The closing chapters of Ezekiel (40–48) likewise deal with the millennial earth, the millennial kingdom, and the sacrificial system that will commemorate the death of Christ much as the sacrifices of the Mosaic Law anticipated Christ's death, The division of the land among the tribes of Israel and other related prophecies confirm that the scene is the kingdom on earth preceding the eternal state. Obviously these prophecies have not been fulfilled in the past, nor can they be fulfilled in the eternal new earth. They require a kingdom on earth following the second coming of Christ.

The Prophecies of Daniel

The prophecies of Daniel deal not primarily with the millennial kingdom but with the movement of the nations and of Israel leading up to the Second Advent. Nevertheless the book does include some references by Daniel to this future kingdom. He predicted in Daniel 2:35 (as interpreted in 2:44–45) that in a future divine kingdom, Gentile world power will be crushed and replaced by the kingdom of God. Daniel 7 concentrates on the Gentile world power preceding the Second Coming, which power will be destroyed by the coming of the Son of Man whose reign will never be terminated.

> I kept looking in the night visions, and behold, with the clouds of heaven one like a Son of Man was coming, and He came up to the Ancient of Days and was presented before Him. And to Him was given dominion, glory and a kingdom, that all the peoples, nations, and men of every language might serve Him. His dominion is an everlasting dominion which will not pass away; and His kingdom is one which will not be destroyed (7:13–14).

In brief, the millennial reign of Christ will never be superseded by another kingdom but will continue in different form throughout eternity.

The Prophecies of the Minor Prophets

The theme of a coming kingdom of God on earth to be established by the returning Son of God from heaven is continued in the Minor Prophets. Hosea predicted that David will rule in the last days: "For the sons of Israel will remain for many days without king or prince, without sacrifice or sacred pillar, and without ephod or household idols. Afterward the sons of Israel will return and seek the LORD their God and David their king, and they will come trembling to the LORD and to His goodness in the last days" (3:4–5),

Hosea, though he lived years after the death of David the king of Israel, predicted that David would return. This resurrection of David is promised by several other prophets and is related to the second coming of Christ. That is when David will live and reign with Christ. The kingdom of God, over which David will reign after the second coming of Christ, was predicted by Ezekiel. "And I, the LORD, will be their God, and My servant David will be prince among them; I, the LORD, have spoken" (34:24).

Ezekiel confirmed this again with these words: "And My servant David will be king over them, and they will all have one shepherd; and they will walk in My ordinances, and keep My statutes, and observe them" (37:24).

Jeremiah added his confirming word. "But they shall serve the LORD their God, and David their king, whom I will raise up for them" (Jer. 30:9).

In these passages it is clear that David is not Christ. The resurrected David who once reigned on the throne of Israel will serve as a prince under Christ, the King of Kings.

The revival of the Davidic kingdom and the restoration of the cities and vineyards of Israel is graphically prophesied by Amos. "In that day I will raise up the fallen booth of David, and wall up its breaches; I will also raise up its ruins, and rebuild it as in the days of old" (Amos 9:11). The prophecy concludes:

> Also I will restore the captivity of My people Israel, and they will rebuild the ruined cities and live in them, they will also plant vineyards and drink their wine, and make gardens and eat their fruit. I will also plant them on their land, and they will not again be rooted out from their land which I have given them, says the LORD your God (9:14–15).

This does not describe a spiritual kingdom in the hearts of the followers of Christ, nor does it refer to the eternal new earth. Instead Amos was writing about a literal kingdom on earth with cities and vineyards. This will be a literal Davidic kingdom.

A major prophecy is given in Micah 4:1–5:5, the early portion of which parallels Isaiah 2:1–5. Zion is declared to be the source of the Law (Mic. 4:2). Peace will characterize world government (4:3). This will be when "the LORD will reign over them in Mount Zion from now on and forever" (4:7). As in many other promises of the coming kingdom, nothing in history or in the contemporary spiritual situation parallels these prophecies, or in any sense provides a reasonable fulfillment.

Zechariah 2:10–12 adds its testimony to the future joy and blessing of the kingdom.

> Sing for joy and be glad, O daughter of Zion; for behold I am coming and I will dwell in your midst, declares the LORD. And many nations will join themselves to the LORD in that day and will become My people. Then I will dwell in your midst, and you will know that the LORD of hosts has sent Me to you. And the LORD will possess Judah as His portion in the holy land, and will again choose Jerusalem.

As in other prophecies, the center of the government will be Jerusalem and the central fact of the kingdom will be the abiding presence of the Lord on the earth.

Another confirming word is found in Zechariah 8:1–8.

> Then the word of the LORD of hosts came saying, Thus says the LORD of hosts, I am exceedingly jealous for Zion, yes, with great wrath I am jealous for her. Thus says the LORD, I will return to Zion and will dwell in the midst of Jerusalem. Then Jerusalem will be called the City of Truth, and the mountain of the LORD of hosts will be called the Holy Mountain. Thus says the LORD of hosts, Old men and old women will again sit in the streets of Jerusalem, each man with his staff in his hand because of age. And the streets of the city will be filled with boys and girls playing in its streets, Thus says the LORD Of hosts, If it is too difficult in the sight of the remnant of this people in those days, will it also be too difficult in My sight? declares the LORD of hosts. Thus says the LORD of hosts, Behold, I am going to save My people from the land of the east and from the land of the west; and I will bring them back, and they will live in the midst of Jerusalem, and they will be My people and I will be their God in truth and righteousness.

Familiar predictions of Jerusalem as the center of God's kingdom and the presence of the Lord and His blessing on His people are again emphasized in this prophecy. Zechariah 9:9–10 adds:

> Rejoice greatly, O daughter of Zion! Shout in triumph, O daughter of Jerusalem! Behold, your king is coming to you; He is just and endowed with salvation, humble, and mounted on a donkey, even on a colt, the foal of a donkey. And I will cut off the chariot from Ephraim, and the horse from Jerusalem; and the bow of war will be cut off. And He will speak peace to the nations; and His dominion will be from sea to sea, and from the River to the ends of the earth.

This passage, like Isaiah 9:6–7, views both advents of Christ together. At His first coming, the nation welcomed Him as her King. But His crucifixion followed. Christ will nevertheless reign over Jerusalem when He returns again, "and His dominion will be from sea to sea" (9:10). Zechariah 14 describes in detail the return of the Lord, the battle of Jerusalem, the establishment of the kingdom, the change in the typography of the land, and the ultimate victory of Christ as King of Kings and Lord of Lords. As in other millennial passages, nothing in history, in the present age, nor in the eternal new earth corresponds to these events. Many other Old Testament passages bring confirming evidence to these passages that have been quoted. The kingdom of God, brought to the world by Christ in His second coming, is not taught merely by an isolated passage here and there; it is a major theme of Old Testament prophetic revelation.

Prophecies in the Psalms

Frequently in the Psalms as in the Prophets, references are made to God's future theocratic kingdom. Psalm 2:6 predicts that

Christ will be "installed [as] My King upon Zion, My holy mountain." While Psalm 22 prophesies the crucifixion of Christ, Psalm 24 predicts His reign on earth.

> Lift up your heads, O gates, and be lifted up, O ancient doors, that the King of glory may come in! Who is the King of glory? The LORD strong and mighty, the LORD mighty in battle. Lift up your heads, O gates, and lift them up, O ancient doors, that the King of glory may come in! Who is this King of glory? The LORD of hosts, He is the King of glory (24:7– 10).

Many understand Psalms 45 and 46 to refer to the reign of Christ. Psalm 48 speaks of the future glory of Zion.

One of the clearest passages is Psalm 72. Although given in the form of a prayer, it will surely be fulfilled, as is evident for instance, in verses 7–8. "In his days may the righteous flourish, and abundance of peace till the moon is no more. May he also rule from sea to sea, and from the River to the ends of the earth." The universal submission of the kings of the world in the future theocratic kingdom is described in verses 10–11, "Let the kings of Tarshish and of the islands bring presents, the kings of Sheba and Seba offer gifts. And let all kings bow down before him, all nations serve him." The psalm closes with the prayer, "And blessed be His glorious name forever; and may the whole earth be filled with His glory. Amen, and Amen" (v. 19). It should be noted that this prophecy relates to earth, not heaven.

The certainty of the fulfillment of God's covenant with David that his throne would continue forever is presented in Psalm 89. "I have made a covenant with My chosen; I have sworn to David My servant, I will establish your seed forever, and build up your throne to all generations" (vv. 3–4). David's throne is an earthly throne, not the Father's throne in heaven.

The unconditional character of this covenant and its certain fulfillment is stated in Psalm 89:28–37.

> My lovingkindness I will keep for him forever, and My covenant shall be confirmed to him. So I will establish his descendants forever, and his throne as the days of heaven. If his sons forsake My law, and do not walk in My judgments, if they violate My statutes, and do not keep My commandments, then I will visit their transgression with the rod, and their iniquity with stripes. But I will not break off My lovingkindness from him, nor deal falsely in My faithfulness. My covenant I will not violate, nor will I alter the utterance of My lips. Once I have sworn by My holiness; I will not lie to David. His descendants shall endure forever, and his throne as the sun before Me. It shall be established forever like the moon, and the witness in the sky is faithful.

The universal worship of Christ in the theocratic kingdom on earth is the subject of Psalm 96. Likewise Psalm 98 describes the future righteous reign of Christ as seen in verse 9, "He is coming to judge the earth, He will judge the world with righteousness, and the peoples with equity." In Psalm 110:1 Christ is instructed to sit at the right hand of the Father until the time for his earthly rule comes.

All major sections of the Old Testament that deal with the prophetic future speak frequently of this earthly kingdom which on the one hand is distinguished from the present age, and on the other, from the eternal new earth.

Major Features of the Kingdom of God on Earth

Detailed again and again in these messianic prophecies of the coming kingdom are major features which could be fulfilled only by Christ ruling on earth after His second coming. These items are repeated again and again:

1. The theocratic kingdom of God will be an earthly kingdom.
2. Jesus Christ will be the King of Kings and Lord of Lords.
3. David will be resurrected to serve as a prince under Christ.
4. The kingdom will be over the entire earth, not simply the land once conquered by Solomon.
5. The kingdom will be characterized by righteousness, justice, and peace.
6. Israel will be regathered to her own land.
7. Jerusalem will be the capital of the world, in the center of God's dealings with the world.
8. Gentiles will also be blessed in the kingdom period.
9. The kingdom, while political, will also foster and support a high level of spiritual life with the Holy Spirit in much evidence.
10. Christ will be visibly present on His earthly throne.
11. The whole earth will know about the Lord, and missionary activity will thus be unnecessary.
12. The earth will be at least partially relieved from the curse and will once again display Edenic splendor.
13. Society in general will prosper, with justice making possible a perfect society.

14. Many changes will occur in the earth with the topography of Israel changed, Jerusalem elevated as a city, and desolate areas made productive.

Alternative Interpretations of Millennial Passages

Two divergent interpretations of the millennial passages have been offered as a substitute for the literal, premillennial coming of Christ and the kingdom of God to follow. The most recent of these is postmillennialism. Existing in various forms, it contends in general that the conditions described in this kingdom on earth will be brought about through preaching the Gospel. Actually nothing is further from the truth. it would be impossible to produce the detailed fulfillment of these prophecies by any man-made program or human effort in preaching the Gospel. It requires the power of God and the return of the Lord from heaven. A more complete study of postmillennialism has already been offered by this writer in a previous publication.[6]

A second major alternative interpretation is that of amillennialism, which exists in three forms: (1) the historic Augustinian type of amillennialism, which says these prophecies are fulfilled in the present age before the second coming of Christ; (2) a more recent form of amillennialism, which says the prophecies are fulfilled in a nonliteral way for the believer in heaven (in the intermediate state) before the creation of the new heavens and the new earth; (3) a combination of the other two forms, that interprets some kingdom passages as being fulfilled in the present age, some fulfilled in their intermediate state during the present period, and others yet to be fulfilled in the eternal state in the new heavens and the new earth.

The variety of approaches of the amillennial view, which is essentially a denial of a literal millennium on earth, is its own commentary. None of these views provides any reasonable literal fulfillment of the passages. Amillennial writings, which sometimes boldly state that not a single verse in the Bible teaches a kingdom of God on earth following the second coming of Christ, usually avoid the many Scriptures that have been cited in this chapter. Amillennialism nevertheless has appealed to many scholars in the past as well as the present. But that theory does not provide an adequate explanation of these passages. Amillenarians often simply avoid passages that would contradict their conclusions or dismiss them by asserting dogmatically that the premillennial interpretation is wrong.

An illustration of this is the discussion by Jay Adams in his work, *The Time Is at Hand*. This book does mention some passages that seem to teach premillennialism but often his references are only a sentence or two, a footnote here and there, or a strong assertion that the premillennial view is wrong. Of fourteen references to Isaiah, nine are simply references in footnotes. In two sentences in a footnote he dismisses eleven passages in Isaiah as being already fulfilled, and he claims that his interpretation "can hardly be questioned."[7]

Amillenarians in their interpretation of millennial passages have several alternative explanations: (1) they declare them conditional and therefore never to be fulfilled; (2) they declare them historical and already fulfilled; or (3) when historical fulfillment is doubtful, they say they will be fulfilled in the new earth. But with one voice they declare that it is impossible to find their fulfillment in an earthly millennial kingdom. There is a growing tendency among amillenarians to refer millennial passages to the new earth as this eliminates the difficulty of finding historic fulfillment for many such prophecies.

Adams provides another illustration. Regarding the numerous passages on the millennial Jerusalem he writes, "Was Christ to rule in Jerusalem? Of course! And that is precisely what he does. Today he reigns and rules from that 'Jerusalem which is above' (Gal. 4:26); from that heavenly 'Mount Zion' to which the writer of Hebrews says that believers 'have come' (Heb. 12:22)."[8]

Certainly all recognize that Hebrews 12:22 refers to the new Jerusalem in the eternal state (and it could conceivably be in existence now). But does this satisfy the many references to a millennial Jerusalem? Again Adams writes, "Come to a millennial city? Come up to a literal mountain? A physical throne? An earthly temple? Of course not."[9] Why does he say, "Of course not"? The answer is that it would teach a millennial kingdom, which he is unwilling to accept.

All of Adams's references to the millennium in Jeremiah, Ezekiel, Hosea, Joel, Nahum, and Malachi are discussed in footnotes. He avoids giving a detailed exegesis of pertinent passages. A reading of the many Old Testament passages previously quoted reveals that they do not disappear simply because a footnote says a literal interpretation is impossible and a nonliteral interpretation is "of course" the only proper one. Even his claim that the amillennial interpretation is transparently the only possible one is supported by too scanty a New Testament confirmation.

In defense of Adams, it may be pointed out that he is attempting only a relatively small paperback discussion of a large problem. But the sweeping dismissal of alternative views and the failure to recognize that there is a variety of contradictory amillennial interpretations are all too characteristic of amillenarians' discussions. The fact is that the many allusions to an earthly kingdom yet to be fulfilled in the future are too detailed to dismiss them that easily.

It is not the purpose of this article to provide a detailed refutation of amillennialism. The writer has sought to do that in his work, *The Millennial Kingdom*, which is confirmed by the extensive work of J. Dwight Pentecost, *Things to Come*, both of which have been mentioned earlier. The goal of this discussion is to call attention to the many detailed prophecies related to the millennium which premillenarians feel have never been satisfactorily explained by the amillennial approach. Premillenarians believe that it is honoring to Scripture to allow it to mean what it appears to mean when taken literally and that it is just as wrong to explain away prophetic passages about the millennium as it is to explain away historic passages referring to the Virgin Birth, the resurrection of Christ, and other central doctrines of biblical faith.

The familiar cry of amillenarians is that the New Testament confirms their interpretation of the Old Testament. The next chapter discusses the New Testament doctrine of the kingdom of God.

CHAPTER 10

The New Testament Doctrine of the Kingdom

John F. Walvoord

The Old Testament Background

Like with many other doctrines, the doctrine of the kingdom in the New Testament builds on the concepts already revealed in the Old Testament. In summarizing the Old Testament doctrine, it was noted in the previous chapter that the Old Testament concept of the kingdom includes fourteen major features. These can be summarized under three headings.

THE THEOCRATIC KINGDOM OF DAVID

Prophecies of a theocratic kingdom on earth in which David would reign as king were partially fulfilled in David's day. God also promised him that his throne and his kingdom would endure forever (2 Sam. 7:16).

THE KINGDOM OF THE FUTURE PROPHESIED

Details of the future theocratic kingdom on earth include the factors that it will be an earthly kingdom, that David will be resurrected to serve as a prince under Christ, that Christ Himself will be the King of Kings and Lord of Lords ruling over the entire earth, not simply the land conquered by Solomon. In the kingdom, Jerusalem will be its capital, Israel will be regathered to her land with the kingdom extending to the whole earth with blessing to the Gentiles as well as to Jews, and Christ's rule will be characterized by righteousness, justice, and peace. In addition to its political and theocratic character, the kingdom will have a high level of spiritual life in which the ministry and presence of the Holy Spirit will be much in evidence.

In view of occasional sweeping statements on the part of amillenarians that the Bible nowhere teaches a premillennial kingdom of Christ on earth, it should be noted that the Old Testament has abundant evidence which, interpreted normally and literally, clearly teaches the kingdom on earth in no sense can be fulfilled either (a) in the present age by the church in heaven, or (b) by the saints who are in the intermediate state, or in the new earth (Rev. 21–22).

THE KINGDOM AS A SPIRITUAL ENTITY

Many Old Testament passages speak of the high level of spiritual life in the future kingdom on earth referred to as "a new covenant with the house of Israel and with the house of Judah" (Jer. 31:31). This New Covenant is described in Jeremiah 31:32–37 with many other Scripture passages supplying additional details. As many have pointed out, the New Testament emphasizes this spiritual character of the kingdom without contradicting its political and earthly character.

New Testament Emphasis on the Kingdom

Interpretations of the kingdom in the New Testament may be divided into four types, with some overlapping. (1) Premillennial interpreters have found confirmation in the New Testament of a kingdom on earth, as will be supported in the discussion to follow. (2) The amillennial interpretation of the New Testament, however, building on the spiritual characteristics of the kingdom, denies that the earthly kingdom will ever be literally fulfilled, and denies a literal thousand-year reign of Christ on earth. Conservative amillenarians usually follow Augustine in holding that the kingdom is on earth now in the hearts of the people of God and that at Christ's second coming the new heavens and the new earth are immediately introduced. However, some do believe that the millennium is fulfilled in heaven or in the intermediate state. Allis traces this view to Duesterdieck (1859) and Kliefoth (1874).[1] Currently some amillenarians combine the two concepts and find some prophecies fulfilled in the present age and some prophecies fulfilled in heaven. Another alternative has the prophecies fulfilled in the new heavens and the new earth.

(3) Postmillennialism, while appearing in embryo form early in the church, is usually attributed to Daniel Whitby, as noted by Strong,[2] although some trace it to Joachim of Floris, a twelfth-century Roman Catholic, as is pointed out by Kromminga.[3] Postmillennialism claims that the millennium will either be the

entire present age or the last thousand years of the present age and that Christ will return after His "reign" on earth rather than before the millennium. In many respects it is similar to amillennialism, and some writers confuse the two terms because they are similar. Postmillennialism usually is more optimistic about progress for good in the church. In contrast, Augustinian amillennialism traces a dual track of good and evil in the church until the second coming of Christ and also includes a brief time of tribulation and final conflict before the Second Coming.

(4) A fourth approach to the New Testament doctrine of the kingdom is that of modern liberals who say the kingdom refers to social structures. This view is the basis of what they sometimes call the social gospel. Obviously a great variety of particulars exists in all these four areas of interpretation of the doctrine of the kingdom in the New Testament. Accordingly, as various passages are examined, the question constantly before the interpreter is, Which of these views is supported by the text? Hermeneutics becomes a major factor in determining the New Testament doctrine. A literal and grammatical form of interpretation confirms the Old Testament teaching of a literal kingdom on earth following the second advent of Christ.

All agree that there is an emphasis on the spiritual aspects of the kingdom in the New Testament. This is seen in the teachings of Christ in the Sermon on the Mount (Matt. 5–7). Also most expositors see the concept of a spiritual kingdom in which Christ rules in the hearts of His followers. While premillenarians continue to insist that Old Testament prophecies concerning a kingdom on earth will be fulfilled literally, most premillenarians recognize that there is a present form of the kingdom which is spiritual. In a sense God is presently reigning, but that is not fulfilling the Old Testament prophecies.

The phrase "the kingdom of God" is used throughout much of the New Testament, whereas "the kingdom of heaven" is used only by Matthew. Most scholars, whether premillennial, amillennial, or postmillennial, feel that these two designations refer to the same entity, but some like Miller point out certain proper distinctions.[4] In the discussion which follows in this chapter the New Testament passages that relate to the doctrine of the kingdom will be examined. Without reviewing all the prolific literature that has been written on all sides of the question concerning the nature of the kingdom, the question constantly before the interpreter is whether the New Testament supports the premillennial, amillennial, postmillennial, or liberal interpretation.

The Kingdom in the Gospel of Matthew

Pentecost has written an excellent discussion on "The Kingdom Program in the New Testament."[5] He cites Peters in support of the concept that the Jews expected the Messiah, when He came, to bring in a literal fulfillment of the Old Testament prophecies. Peters states:

> It is universally admitted by writers of prominence (e.g., Neander, Hagenbach, Schaff, Kurtz, etc.), whatever their respective views concerning the Kingdom itself, that the Jews, including the pious, held to a personal coming of the Messiah, the literal restoration of the Davidic throne and kingdom, the personal reign of Messiah on David's throne, the resultant exaltation of Jerusalem and the Jewish nation, and the fulfillment of the Millennial descriptions of that reign. It is also acknowledged that the utterances of Luke 1:71: Acts 1:6; Luke 2:26, 30, etc., include the above belief, and that down, at least to the day of Pentecost, the Jews, the disciples, and even the apostles held to such a view. . . . they regarded the prophecies and covenanted promises as literal (i.e., in their naked grammatical sense); and, believing in their fulfillment, looked for such a restoration of the Davidic Kingdom under the Messiah, with an increased power and glory befitting the majesty of the predicted King; and also that the pious of former ages would be raised up from the dead to enjoy the same.[8]

Amillennial and postmillennial refutation of this premillennial concept usually follows one of four patterns: (a) that the promises of the Old Testament were literal but were forfeited by Israel's rejection of Christ, (b) that the prophecies were misinterpreted as literal and were never intended to teach a literal kingdom on earth, and that they refer instead to the present experience of the church on earth (John Calvin's view), (c) that the promises of the kingdom refer to the future new heavens and new earth, not to the present situation, or (d) that the fulfillment of the promises is found in the intermediate state in heaven at the present time. There is so much variety in the refutation of premillennialism that it is quite clear that opponents of premillennialism are not agreed among themselves except on the negative conclusion that the New Testament does not confirm the premillennial view that Christ's coming will precede a one-thousand-year reign on earth.

When Christ, preceded by John the Baptist, taught the doctrine of the kingdom, the question raised was not whether the kingdom had come but whether it was coming immediately. Even John

Bright, an amillenarian, recognizes this widespread expectation of fulfillment of the prophecies of the kingdom on earth.[7] On the other hand even premillenarians like Ladd attempt to define the concept of the kingdom of God with comparatively little reference to the Old Testament teachings, giving as much attention to the Apocrypha and the Pseudepigrapha as he does to the Old Testament, and building his concept of the kingdom almost entirely on New Testament revelation.[8] Modern liberals feel free, however, to hold that the Old Testament prophets were wrong and that they were stating merely an ideal which will never be literally fulfilled. Even conservative amillenarians tend to hold that the New Testament interpretation of the Old Testament indicates that no literal kingdom and fulfillment was intended. With these varying interpretations the Gospel narratives must be searched to determine their contribution to the doctrine of the kingdom.

The Gospel of Matthew, as many recognize, is the bridge between the Old and New Testaments. Many Jews, who anticipated that the Messiah would immediately bring in the prophesied earthly kingdom, needed an explanation as to why this was not fulfilled. Matthew covers this by first proving beyond question that Christ is the expected Messiah and King. This is brought out in the genealogies and in the announcement to Joseph that Mary would have a son who would fulfill Isaiah's prophecies of a virgin-born son (Matt. 1:21–23, Isa. 7:14) and of a son who will become a world ruler (Isa. 9:6–7: Matt. 1:21). Luke took up the prophecy of Isaiah 9:7, "There will be no end to the increase of His government or of peace, on the throne of David and over his kingdom, to establish it and to uphold it with justice and righteousness from then on and forevermore. The zeal of the Lord of hosts will accomplish this." Luke stated it, "He will be great. and will be called the Son of the Most High; and the Lord God will give Him the throne of His father David; and He will reign over the house of Jacob forever; and His kingdom will have no end" (Luke 1:32–33).

Mary would have shared Israel's widespread hope for the Messiah who would reign in a political sense over them and free them from the oppression of Rome. Mary would have understood Isaiah's prophecy to refer to a literal earthly reign. If something else were intended, then Mary would have misunderstood the message and was in fact deceived by the angel. That the coming Messiah will be the spiritual Savior of those who trust Him is clear in both the Old and New Testaments. The question of whether, in addition to His work as Savior, He would also reign on earth as a king is confirmed by Luke 1:32–33, if the Scriptures are taken in the ordinary sense. Any variation would require a nonliteral interpretation of the prophecy given to Mary.

The second chapter of Matthew continues the subject of Jesus Christ as the King of the Jews (Matt. 2:2). Christ was recognized by the magi as the prophesied King, and the priests and scribes informed the magi that when the Messiah came He would fulfill the prophecy of Micah 5:2, "But as for you, Bethlehem Ephrathah, too little to be among the clans of Judah, from you One will go forth for Me to be ruler in Israel. His goings forth are from long ago, from the days of eternity." This was quoted by the scribes and chief priests to the magi (Matt. 2:5–6). Even Herod recognized it as a threat to his political kingdom and ordered the killing of male children from two years old and under in the area of Bethlehem. In Matthew 3 John the Baptist introduced the ministry of Christ by announcing, "Repent, for the kingdom of heaven is at hand" (3:2). John then quoted Isaiah 40:3 (Matt. 3:3; cf. John 1:23), which refers to clearing "the way for the LORD in the wilderness." This preparing the way for the Lord meant preparation for the coming of the kingdom. Whatever the spiritual character of the kingdom, it is clear that the Jewish people held to a political concept as well.

Though the Jews anticipated that the future messianic rule would be a political kingdom on earth, they were somewhat short in their understanding that it would also have spiritual and moral characteristics. This explains Christ's emphasis in the Sermon on the Mount (Matt. 5–7) in which He dealt with the spiritual and moral principles of the future kingdom of God. While many of the principles have present applications, some of the principles will not be fully applied until the future reign of Christ on earth.[9]

The early chapters of Matthew are designed to prove that Jesus is the prophesied King. Even the temptation of Christ by the devil is related to this purpose. The devil "showed Him all the kingdoms of the world, and their glory" (4:8), in passive recognition of the fact that Christ was promised the kingdoms of the world.

Subsequent to the Sermon on the Mount, however, as Christ offered His credentials, supported by miracles and the evident power of God on Him, the Jews increasingly opposed the idea of accepting Him as their Messiah. In contrast to the centurion who came to Christ for his paralyzed servant (8:5–10), others, because of their failure to receive Him, will be cast out (vv. 10–12).

In chapter 10 Christ instructed His disciples on their preaching mission to proclaim that "the kingdom of heaven is at hand" (10:7). The disciples clearly understood this to be a reference to the earthly kingdom. Christ warned them, however, that in His present ministry He would not bring peace on the earth. He said instead, "Do not think that I came to bring peace on the earth, I did not come to bring peace, but a sword" (v. 34).

John the Baptist, when in prison, asked whether Christ was "the Expected One" (11:3), that is, the Messiah the Jews were anticipating. Christ answered (v. 10) by quoting Malachi 3:1 as a reference to John the Baptist, who, as a messenger, preceded and prepared the way for the King. At the close of Matthew 11 Christ turned from His appeal to Israel as a nation to individuals. "Come to Me, all who are weary and heavy-laden, and I will give you rest. Take My yoke upon you, and learn from Me, for I am gentle and humble in heart; and you shall find rest for your souls. For My yoke is easy, and My load is light" (vv. 28–30).

Christ then began to predict His death, comparing His experience to that of Jonah (12:38–40).

In Matthew 13 Christ, in His second major discourse, discussed what He called "the mysteries of the kingdom of heaven" (13:11). As noted previously, interpreters differ on whether the kingdom of heaven is identical to the kingdom of God or whether it has some distinctive meaning. Unquestionably, the great majority of scholars consider the word "heaven" as simply a softened reference to God by Jews who tended, out of reverence, to avoid using the highly revered name of God. To use this explanation of Matthew's use of the kingdom of heaven, however, is seemingly contradicted by a number of facts that are sometimes overlooked. Matthew on several occasions did use the term "kingdom of God" (12:28; 19:24, 21:31, 43).[10] It is also not true that Matthew avoided the term God (θεός) for he used it almost fifty times in his gospel. Why, then, did Matthew use the term "kingdom of heaven"?

Without attempting a complete study on this question, one can observe that the kingdom of heaven has some characteristics that are not true of the kingdom of God.

As used in the New Testament, "the kingdom of God" always speaks of a realm of spiritual reality (that may include holy angels), but it never includes unsaved people. In contrast, "the kingdom of heaven" seems to refer simply to individuals and to include some who are merely professing Christians. This is illustrated in Matthew 13 where the kingdom of heaven is compared to a field with both wheat and tares, with the wheat representing the saved and the tares seemingly representing a sphere of profession without reality. Likewise, the kingdom of heaven is compared to a net that includes both good and bad fish. These parables are never used in the other Gospels to refer to the kingdom of God. Accordingly, the view that the kingdom of heaven refers to the spirit of profession including true believers while the kingdom of God includes only holy angels and true believers has some support in the Gospel of Matthew. As such, the kingdom of heaven can refer either to the present form of the kingdom as it does in Matthew 13, or in eschatological form to the kingdom which will follow the Second Advent. In both cases there is a sphere of profession as contrasted to the sphere of reality composed only of those who are the elect or angels.

Subsequent to Matthew 13 many additional references to the kingdom are included. Christ gave "the keys of the kingdom of heaven" to His disciples (16:19). He predicted that they will see the coming of the kingdom (16:28). He defined who is greatest in the kingdom of heaven (18:1, 3–4). He spoke of the King judging the works of His subjects (18:23). He referred to the qualities of those who enter the kingdom (19:12, 14, 23–24). He spoke of rewards for labor in the kingdom (20:1–16). He talked of those who will share His kingdom reign (Matt. 21–23). He said tax collectors and harlots will enter the kingdom, whereas religious Jews will be left out (21:31, 43). He likened the kingdom to a wedding feast (22:1–4). He condemned the Pharisees who seek to hinder people from entering the kingdom (23:13). He predicted the preaching of the gospel of the kingdom worldwide (24:14). He likened the kingdom of heaven to the guests of a wedding (25:1–13). He predicted that the righteous will inherit the kingdom (25:34). He predicted that the disciples will drink the fruit of the vine with Him in His Father's kingdom (26:29).

In these passages the references to the kingdom are in contexts in which the kingdom is on earth, Christ is the King, failure is judged, and righteousness is rewarded. In none of these passages did Christ make any effort to correct what amillenarians feel is the misconception of the disciples that Christ was speaking of an earthly kingdom in which He would reign triumphantly as King of Kings.

The Theme of Rejection of the King in the Gospel of Matthew

The gospel of Matthew has as its purpose to explain why Christ did not bring in the predicted kingdom in His first coming. Matthew emphasized the fact that when Christ presented Himself as King, He was rejected. While this was anticipated in the sovereign program of God and led up to the predicted death and resurrection of Christ, it does not relieve those who rejected Him of the consequences of their decision.

In his treatment of this major subject of the gospel of Matthew, Pentecost points out that there are "three major movements in the gospel of Matthew: (1) the presentation and authentication of the King (1:1–11:1); (2) the opposition to the King (11:2–16:12); and (3) the final rejection of the King (16:13–28:20)."[11]

There can be no question in any fair exposition of the gospel of Matthew that Christ is presented as the rejected King. Opponents of premillennialism argue that Christ could not make a genuine offer of Himself as King and of His millennial kingdom because in the plan of God it was necessary for Him to die on the cross for the sins of the world. This is playing games, however, with the difference between the human and the divine viewpoints. All conservative interpreters of Scripture regardless of their eschatological views agree that the death of Christ on the cross was essential to God's redemptive program. It is wrong to argue that premillenarians who insist that Christ made a genuine offer of the kingdom and of Himself as King are making unnecessary the Cross of Christ in the plan of God. Obviously God's plan included the rejection of Christ by His people when He offered Himself as their King. The fact that this was certain and essential to the ultimate plan of God that Christ be the Redeemer in no way detracts from the seriousness of the decision nor the consequences that the kingdom could not be immediately fulfilled. Nor does this contingency imply any uncertainty in the ultimate program of God to bring in His kingdom. This is the whole point of the Gospel of Matthew.

The rejection of Christ is a rejection first of His Person as the Messiah-King of Israel. To quibble that there is a difference between offering Himself as the King and offering the kingdom is again an unjustified distinction. The emphasis in Matthew is on the Person of Christ. But in His Person He is presented first as the King rather than as the Savior of the world. In rejecting Christ, of course, those who rejected Him rejected both concepts. Beginning in Matthew 11 is a constant parade of evidence of the people's rejection of Christ. This, of course, began with the rejection of John the Baptist as His forerunner. It includes all the controversies with the Jewish leaders in such matters as the Sabbath, and their accusation that He performed miracles in the power of Satan. Christ was constantly opposed by unbelievers in Nazareth, by Herod, and by the religious leaders. This opposition is the background of Christ's prediction of His sufferings and death, first mentioned in Matthew 16:21. Because Israel rejected Christ as their King, He then rejected the nation Israel (23:1–36). This passage closes with His lament over Jerusalem, whose people through the years had killed God's prophets and rejected those whom God had sent to them (23:37–39). All these steps in rejection culminated, of course, in His crucifixion as the people of Israel, influenced by the religious leaders, demanded His death.

The gospel of Matthew like the other Gospels, however, demonstrates that Christ had the right to be the Messiah-King of Israel. His resurrection, the empty tomb, and His many appearances after His resurrection combine to convince one willing to consider the evidence that Christ was indeed the Messiah-King who, though He was rejected by His people at His first coming, will return to fulfill the kingdom promises given to Israel.

The Kingdom in the Gospel of Mark

The doctrine of the kingdom in the gospel of Mark is similar to that presented in Matthew except that uniformly the expression "kingdom of God" is used instead of "kingdom of heaven." Some passages in Mark refer to earthly kingdoms (3:24; 6:23; 13:8). Other references are to the kingdom of God in general, that is, any rule of God over the earth. This seems to be its meaning in such passages as Mark 9:47; 10:14–15, 23–25. It may also be the meaning in Mark 12:34 where Christ declared that the inquiring scribe was not far from the kingdom.

Other references in Mark to the kingdom may refer to the kingdom prophesied in the Old Testament and which premillenarians believe will be fulfilled in the millennial kingdom. In Mark 1:14–15 Christ stated, "The time is fulfilled, and the kingdom of God is at hand; repent and believe the gospel." Here Christ is alluding to the kingdom predicted in the Old Testament. It was then "at hand" in the sense that the King had come, though the kingdom itself had not been inaugurated. In Mark 4:11, 26, 30 Mark used parallel references to the mysteries of the kingdom of heaven expounded in Matthew 13. This refers to the spiritual form of the kingdom which exists in the present age. The details of the kingdom are referred to as "mysteries" because this form of the kingdom was not predicted in the Old Testament. Mark 4 accordingly is a parallel to Matthew 13.

Another reference to the future kingdom is found in Mark 9:1. In the Transfiguration the disciples were given a prophetic foreview of the glorious reign of Christ on earth. The same meaning is more specific in Mark 11:10 where the kingdom is referred to as "the coming kingdom of our father David." This reference alludes to the prediction (in 2 Sam. 7:16 and Ps. 89:36–37) that David's throne would continue forever. Mark 14:25 and 15:43 also probably refer to the coming kingdom in which Christ said He will drink new wine.

The present spiritual form of the kingdom is probably in view in Mark 9:47, which refers to entering the kingdom of God. This is also true of Mark 10:14–15, 23–25, which speak of entering or receiving the kingdom of God now (cf. 12:34).

Boettner, a postmillenarian, selects passages relating to the present form of the kingdom as proof that there is no future kingdom. Premillenarians do not deny that there is a present form of the kingdom. They deny that this proves there is no future form of the kingdom as taught in other passages.[12]

Taken as a whole, no truth about the kingdom is introduced in Mark that is not also found in the gospel of Matthew, but the various usages of the word "kingdom" are found to be similar, some referring to earthly kingdoms, some to the kingdom of God in general, and others as fulfilled in the present age. In Mark, as in Matthew, some passages refer to the future predicted kingdom on earth.

The Kingdom in the Gospel of Luke

As in Matthew and Mark some references to the kingdom in the gospel of Luke have in view earthly kingdoms. This is illustrated in Luke 4:5; 11:17–18; 19:12, 15; 21:10. In these instances the term "kingdom" refers to an earthly reign of a ruler and a government under him.

Many references in Luke speak of the spiritual character of the kingdom. These references are not always clear as to whether Christ was referring to the present form of the kingdom as a spiritual rule or whether He was referring to the millennial kingdom, which also is a spiritual rule. Accordingly, in some passages there may be reference to both. In Luke 4:43 Christ referred to preaching the kingdom of God. He promised that the poor will possess the kingdom of God (6:20), and He declared that one who is in the kingdom of God is greater than John the Baptist (7:28). Luke 8:10 clearly refers to the present form of the kingdom as a spiritual rule. And in Luke 9:11, 60, 62; 10:9, 11; and 12:31–32 the present form of the kingdom is probably in view.

Although the future kingdom will also be a spiritual rule, Christ's message concerning the kingdom is referred to as "the gospel of the kingdom of God" (Luke 16:16). In Christ's answer to the Pharisees concerning when the kingdom of God would be coming, He declared, "Behold, the kingdom of God is in your midst" (17:21). While the Pharisees may have had in mind the future earthly reign of Christ, Christ pointed out that the kingdom of God was already in their midst in the form of the King Himself. Children are said to be a part of the kingdom (18:16–17). Entering the kingdom is declared to be difficult for the wealthy (18:24–25). It should be observed in all these references that the fact that there is a present form of the kingdom does not carry with it the conclusion that this is the only form of the kingdom.

Some references in Luke, as in Matthew and Mark, seem to refer specifically to the kingdom on earth which, according to the Old Testament, can be fulfilled only when the throne of David is reestablished. This is made clear early in Luke when Mary was told she would give birth to the Messiah. "And behold, you will conceive in your womb, and bear a son, and you shall name Him Jesus. He will be great, and will be called the Son of the Most High; and the Lord God will give Him the throne of His father David; and He will reign over the house of Jacob forever; and His kingdom will have no end" (Luke 1:31–33).

Amillenarians tend to ignore the obvious interpretation which Mary put on the announcement of the angel that Christ would reign over Jacob on the throne of David. They simply equate Israel with the church, which Mary certainly would have not done. They ignore the fact that the church is never called "the house of Jacob." Berkhof, a typical amillenarian, states, "Peter . . . thus virtually said of the Church that it was now in reality what Israel was once called to be. And the angel which announced to Mary the birth of Jesus used this language."[13]

It should be quite clear from the angel's words to Mary that the Jews anticipated a literal, earthly, political kingdom even though it would have spiritual characteristics and could be entered only by new birth. Many would certainly have understood it in this way. If only a present form of a spiritual kingdom was intended, Mary would have been deceived by the message of the angel.

Boettner admits that there was widespread anticipation of an earthly Davidic kingdom to be established. He states, "At the time of the first advent the Jews expected the reestablishment of the Davidic kingdom as a world power kingdom of Jewish supremacy. . . . Even the disciples shared the notion of a political kingdom and disputed among themselves concerning the chief places."[14]

Luke 8:1 and 9:2, which speak of Christ's preaching the kingdom of God, could refer to either the present or the future form of the kingdom. Most of the remaining references in Luke, however, cannot be explained by saying they refer to a present form of the kingdom. They seem definitely related to the Old Testament predictions of an earthly, political rule in which Christ will rule as the Son of David.

Accordingly, in Luke 9:27 Christ in His transfiguration referred to the future kingdom, as also recorded in the other Gospels. When Christ prayed that the Father's kingdom would come (11:2), He seems to have been referring to the predicted earthly kingdom. The reference to the kingdom in Luke 13:28–29 is a clear prophecy of an earthly kingdom in which Abraham, Isaac, and Jacob, and all the prophets will participate but from which those rejecting Christ will be cast out.

A similar reference is the blessing pronounced on those who eat bread in the kingdom of God" (14:15). The possibility of the kingdom appearing immediately (19:11) again has reference to the Jews' expectation of a literal, earthly kingdom. This is also true in 21:31. Christ referred to eating the Passover in the future kingdom of God (22:16, 18, 29–30). The future kingdom was also in view in the prayer of the thief on the cross: "Jesus, remember me when You come in Your kingdom!" (23:42). The closing reference in Luke concerns Joseph, a member of the Council, "who was waiting for the kingdom of God" (23:51).

In Luke's gospel, as in Matthew and Mark, there are several references to a spiritual rule of God, which can be conceived of in the present tense, but other references clearly picture an earthly kingdom that is not being fulfilled in the present age and that requires the personal presence of Christ on the throne of David.

Sauer points out that the future kingdom is confirmed repeatedly in the Synoptic Gospels. "Nevertheless these few references in the New Testament are quite enough to confirm the expectation of the kingdom of the Old Testament prophets. Thus the Lord Himself said, 'ye who have followed Me, in the regeneration when the Son of man shall sit on the throne of His glory, ye also shall sit upon twelve thrones, judging the twelve tribes of Israel' (Matt. 19:28)."[15]

The Kingdom in the Gospel of John

The gospel of John has relatively few references to the kingdom of God. This is because John's gospel is concerned primarily with the deity of Christ and salvation through Him. The book's prophetic sections deal with the present inter-Advent age.

In John 3:3–5 Christ's words about entering "the kingdom of God" had in mind both the present spiritual form of the kingdom and His future earthly reign. In both cases it is impossible to enter the kingdom of God without the new birth. Of importance is the fact that Christ rebuked Nicodemus for not knowing this concept, for the Old Testament clearly stated that unless a person had new life he could not enter the kingdom. As stated in Ezekiel 36:25–31, salvation in the Old Testament clearly involved a new birth, receiving a new heart, and being delivered from the power of sin. Other Old Testament references to this fact include Isaiah 44:2–4; 60:21; and Jeremiah 24:7.

The only other reference to the kingdom in the Gospel of John is in 18:36 where Christ indicated that His kingdom did not receive its power from the world which relies on physical force for its endurance. Whether referring to the present spiritual form of the kingdom or the future millennial kingdom, Christ's statement would be true in either case.

While Christ clearly offered a present form of the kingdom which believers can enter now by new birth, He also reaffirmed the hope of the Jews that there would be a future kingdom in which the Son of David will reign over the house of Israel.

The Kingdom in the Acts of the Apostles

Only seven references to the kingdom are found in Acts. In the first chapter the disciples obviously were troubled about the fact that Christ was leaving them and the predicted earthly kingdom had not been introduced (Acts 1:6). Christ gave them some teaching on the subject, but He did not answer the question whether He would restore the kingdom of David immediately (v. 7). From this it is clear that up to this time Christ had not contradicted in any way the universal hope of Israel for an earthly restoration of the kingdom of David. If this were a false expectation, it certainly would have been necessary for Christ to correct them. However, in His reply He merely told them that He could not tell them when this kingdom would come (v. 7). Meanwhile, however, they would have the power of the Holy Spirit to sustain them in their present ministry during the absence of Christ (v. 8).

Sauer points out the significance of Christ's words.

> And when, after His resurrection, the disciples asked, "Lord, dost Thou at this time restore the kingdom to Israel?" (Gr. *basileia*, kingly rule), He did not rebuke them for "fleshly conceptions," or give them a general denial of such a visible kingdom of God as they had in mind, but said only, "It is not for you to know times or seasons which the Father has reserved in His authority" (Acts 1:6–7). But precisely this prophetic expression "times or seasons" proves that the kingdom of God will be duly and actually set up.[16]

In Acts 8:12 reference is made to Philip's "preaching the good news about the kingdom of God and the name of Jesus Christ." His message probably included both the present spiritual form of the kingdom and the future reign of Christ. However, the reference to the kingdom in 14:22 seems to imply a future reign not yet realized by the present form of the kingdom. This could be a reference to the millennial kingdom. Paul's preaching in the synagogue concerning the kingdom of God (19:8) probably also included both elements as this would be the natural concern of the Jews. Paul preached "the kingdom" (20:25) and "the kingdom of God" (28:23, 31).

In these references to the kingdom of God in Acts the message of the apostles was clearly a dual message. It included the invitation to enter the spiritual kingdom (of God's rule) now by new birth and the announcement that Christ would return and reign on earth in the future. To eliminate the future aspect would be to leave the obvious question of many Jews unanswered.

The Kingdom in the Epistles

Only scattered references to the kingdom are found in the New Testament Epistles. In Romans 14:17 Paul said that the present form of the kingdom embodies "righteousness and peace and joy in the Holy Spirit." In a similar way 1 Corinthians 4:20 speaks of the present "power" of the kingdom of God.

Three other references in 1 Corinthians, however (6:9; 15:24, 50), seem to refer to a future kingdom which is not fulfilled in the present age. Qualifications for entering the kingdom are discussed and the final deliverance of the kingdom to God the Father by Christ is mentioned in 15:24. In the new heavens and the new earth all forms of the kingdom will merge in the universal rule of the Father.

Entrance into a future kingdom is also mentioned in Galatians 5:21; Ephesians 5:5; Colossians 1:13; 4:11; 1 Thessalonians 2:12; and 2 Thessalonians 1:5. The heavenly kingdom mentioned in 2 Timothy 4:18 refers to the ultimate rule of God in the new heavens and the new earth. The universal throne of Christ is mentioned in Hebrews 1:8. Hebrews 11:33 refers to earthly kingdoms, and Hebrews 12:28 seems to be a general reference to the divine kingdom regardless of its time and form. Heirs of the future kingdom are mentioned in James 2:5 and include "the poor of this world" who are "rich in faith and heirs of the kingdom which He promised to those who love Him." The eternal form of the kingdom is mentioned in 2 Peter 1:11.

In all these references it is obvious that the term "kingdom of God" is used in various senses, sometimes referring to the present form of the kingdom, sometimes to its future earthly situation in the millennium, and other times to the kingdom in its eternal form in the new heavens and the new earth. In each case the context helps determine the interpretation.

The Kingdom in the Book of Revelation

Only six verses in the Book of Revelation refer directly to the kingdom. In Revelation 1:9 John declared himself to be in the kingdom. The angel's pronouncement, "the kingdom of the world has become the kingdom of our Lord, and of His Christ; and He will reign forever and ever" (11:15), refers to the coming of Christ in His millennial kingdom which, however, will continue after the millennium. In this sense His reign will be forever. A similar prediction of the coming millennial kingdom is found in Revelation 10:12. In 16:10 the kingdom of the world government headed by the beast is mentioned, and 17:12, 17 refers to the earthly power of the kings on earth during the great tribulation.

Though the word "kingdom" does not occur in Revelation 19–22, the kingdom idea is clearly embodied in the reference to Christ in 19:16, which refers to Him as "King of Kings and Lord of Lords." His rule on earth is said to be "with a rod of iron" (19:15). The saints reigning with Christ for a thousand years are mentioned in Revelation 20:6.

Sauer provides another answer to the objections raised against the concept of the kingdom in the book of Revelation when he points out the general expectation of the Jews for a coming kingdom of one thousand years.

> . . . the doctrine of an intermediate Messianic kingdom was announced in contemporary Judaism and . . . its duration was to be exactly one thousand years. The Jewish synagogue as early as the first century distinguished between the days of Messiah and the final perfecting in 'Olam ha-ba, that is, in the world to come. The former were regarded as being limited in duration, the latter as being eternal. . . . Therefore, it cannot be justly asserted, as it often has been, that the doctrine of a millennial kingdom is nowhere found apart from the celebrated passage in Revelation 20.[17]

The future eternal reign of Christ is introduced with the concept of "a great white throne and Him who sat upon it" (20:11). Revelation 21:3 refers to the heavenly throne which will be in the holy city, the New Jerusalem, and 21:5 speaks of Christ sitting on the throne. The idea of a kingdom is obvious in all these references even though the word "kingdom" itself is not used. The continued reign of the saints with Christ is mentioned also in 22:5.

When all the New Testament references to the kingdom are examined as a whole it is seen that they fall into various categories. Some references are to earthly kingdoms, some to the concept of the general rule of God, some to a present spiritual rule of God, some to the future millennial rule of a kingdom on earth, and still others to an eternal kingdom. Confusion is introduced when one ignores the context in which the word "kingdom" is used. The fulfillment of all these anticipations of a rule of God on earth are necessary to support fully the concept of the kingdom of God in the New Testament.

Ladd refers to a "bewildering diversity of statements about the kingdom of God." He continues, "If you will take a concordance of the Bible, look up every reference in the New Testament alone where the word 'kingdom' occurs, write down a brief summary of each verse on a piece of paper, you will probably find yourself at a loss to know what to do with the complexity of teaching."[18]

Actually, it is possible to distinguish various aspects of the kingdom, as this discussion has sought to demonstrate. The doctrine of the millennium is the only cogent explanation of some references to the future kingdom.

Ladd correctly summarizes the concept of the millennium in these words.

> In the Apocalypse of the things which must shortly come to pass, Jesus revealed to John on the island of Patmos that after his glorious return, there would ensue a millennial kingdom on earth (Rev. 20:16). After his Parousia, Christ is to reign in person over human society as it is now constituted. The earth and human history will then become the realm within which God's reign will be realized to a degree beyond anything experienced before. The powers of Satan will be curtailed with special reference to the deception of the nations (Rev. 20:3). Israel as a nation is to be saved (Rom. 11) and is to become an instrument in the hands of God for the fulfillment of the divine purposes. The prophecies of God to Israel in the Old Testament which have never been fulfilled will then come to realization.[19]

Conclusion

Amillenarians frequently state that the Bible nowhere speaks of a millennial kingdom following the second coming of Christ. Such an assertion, however, does not correspond to statements in the Old and New Testaments on the kingdom.

Of course the Bible does refer to a form of the kingdom in the present age. The Bible also refers to political kingdoms that have existed on earth. Also there are references to the new heavens and the new earth in the eternal state as a form of God's continued rule. None of these concepts, however, is adequate to explain the many references in the Old and New Testaments that clearly delineate a kingdom which is subsequent to the second coming of Christ—a kingdom on earth involving a temporal rule of Christ and fulfilling the anticipations of the prophecy of a thousand-year kingdom.

Amillenarians themselves have many differing explanations on how to understand these passages that seem to refer to a future kingdom on earth. This is itself a confession that they do not have an adequate explanation. Amillenarians sometimes explain away the passages as being conditional and therefore never ones that will be fulfilled. Other times they say the supposed future millennial kingdom refers to the intermediate state or to heaven. Recently some amillenarians have revived the concept that the millennial kingdom will be fulfilled in the new heavens and the new earth.

All these explanations are in themselves inherently contradictory and disregard the normal rules of exegesis of the passages dealing with a future kingdom on earth. While the differences of opinion will continue, it should be clear that the amillennial concept explains away many significant Scriptures. This is hardly a cogent exegesis, in keeping with the revelatory character of the entire Bible.

Part 2:

Dispensationalism and the Tribulation

CHAPTER 11

The Necessity of Dispensationalism

Charles C. Ryrie

One of the evident features of the history of Christian doctrine is the fact that the church generally focused its discussions on one area of theology at a time. In the present day the area is eschatology, and discussions of eschatology are being heard in all groups. In conservative circles these discussions are raising questions in another field, namely, that of dispensationalism. This is not to say that liberals are unaware of the growing prominence being given to dispensationalism, but it is to affirm that evangelicals are having to give their attention increasingly to the dispensational question. This is shown by Bowman's pronouncement that the Scofield Bible because of its dispensational teaching "represents perhaps the most dangerous heresy currently to be found within Christian circles."[1]

Recent and current interest in eschatology is only one of the reasons for the increased interest in dispensationalism. One ventures to predict that if current discussions concerning the rapture question continue, posttribulationists will be forced to do more than just reiterate the usual arguments against pretribulationism, for they will of necessity have to reckon with the entire dispensational approach to the Scriptures. They will be forced to deal with that which they recognize, namely, that pretribulationism is "an essential element" in dispensationalism.[2]

In addition the rise of ultradispensationalism has focused increased attention on the whole question. The proponents of this view have propagated it widely and in doing so have accomplished at least two things. They have added to their own numbers, and they have done those who consider ourselves true dispensationalists the service of causing them to present more detail concerning their position in order to distinguish it from their teaching.

Too, those who embrace covenant theology have contributed and doubtless will continue to contribute to the discussion of dispensationalism. The many individuals and groups who follow the covenant theology tradition will surely not stand by if discussions of the dispensational question increase in the coming days, and by that very participation the whole matter will be brought into more prominence. Therefore because of the increasing interest in eschatology and especially in pretribulationalism, because of the aggressiveness of the ultradispensationalists, and because of the ever-present protagonists of covenant theology, one can scarcely agree with the idea that "the trend today is away from dispensationalism—away from the Scofield notes."[3]

This chapter is an attempt to state a basic approach to the concept of dispensationalism, for it is felt that if the features that make up this approach are basic enough, then the concept to which they lead will have to be deemed necessary or at least be given considered attention.

The Necessity of Biblical Distinctions

Though the statement is bold, it may be stated without fear of controversy that there is no interpreter of the Bible who does not recognize the need for certain basic distinctions in the Scriptures. Theological liberals, no matter how much they speak of the Judaistic background of Christianity, recognize that Christianity is nevertheless different from Judaism. There may be few or many features of Judaism which they say carry over into Christianity, but still the message of Jesus was something new. Therefore the material of the Old Testament is distinguished from that of the New.

Covenant theologians for all their opposition to dispensationalism also make rather important distinctions. In fairness, it must be said that their dispensational distinctions are viewed as related to the unifying and underlying covenant of grace. Nevertheless within this concept they do make some basic distinctions. After rejecting the usual dispensational scheme of biblical distinctions, Berkhof enumerates his own scheme of dispensations or administrations, reducing the number to two— the Old Testament dispensation and the New Testament dispensation. However, within the Old Testament dispensation Berkhof lists four subdivisions which, though he terms them "stages in the revelation of the covenant of grace," are distinguishable enough to be listed. In reality, then, he finds these four plus the one New Testament dispensation or five periods of differing administrations of God.[4] Thus covenant theologians find biblical distinctions a necessary part of their theology.

The word "dispensation" (οἰκονομία) is a scriptural term and is found in Luke 16:2–4; 1 Corinthians 9:17; Ephesians 1:10; 3:2, 9; Colossians 1:25; and 1 Timothy 1:4. It simply means an administration or arrangement. Dispensationalists use the word theologically as a title for the distinctive administrations of God throughout the entire Bible. For instance under Moses God administered the world in a distinctive way; therefore dispensationalists call that *administration* (not *period* necessarily) the Mosaic dispensation. To say that it is not valid to use the word this way because the Bible never uses it in connection with certain of the dispensationalists' dispensations is of no consequence. The word "atonement" is used of the work of Christ on the cross even though it is never used that way in the Bible. Certainly freedom must be granted to use a term theologically which may not be used in that way biblically as long as the theological use is not unbiblical.

Thus it is clear that all interpreters feel the need for some distinctions in the Bible. Obviously this does not prove that the dispensationalists' distinctions are the correct ones, but it demonstrates that the concept of the necessity of distinctions is basic to the proper interpretation of the Scriptures, and it shows that in a certain sense every Christian is a dispensationalist. Chafer correctly observed that "any person is a dispensationalist who trusts the blood of Christ rather than bringing an animal sacrifice" and "any person is a dispensationalist who observes the first day of the week rather than the seventh."[5] Therefore dispensationalism is based on a valid and basic approach to the Scriptures in the necessity for biblical distinctions.

The Necessity of a Philosophy of History

The Scriptures per se are not a philosophy of history but they contain one. It is true that the Bible deals with ideas, but they are ideas that are interpretations of historical events. This interpretation of the meaning of historical events is the task of theology, a task that is not without its problems. The chief problem is that both covenant and dispensational theologians claim to represent the true philosophy of history as contained in the Scriptures. The problem is further complicated by the fact that if a philosophy of history is defined as "a systematic interpretation of universal history in accordance with a principle by which historical events and successions are unified and directed toward ultimate meaning."[6] Then in a certain sense both systems of theology meet the basic requirements of the definition. However, the way in which the two systems meet these requirements shows that dispensationalism alone is the valid system. The definition focuses on three things: (a) the recognition of "historical events and successions" or a proper concept of the progress of revelation, (b) the unifying principle; (c) the ultimate goal of history. Both systems need to be examined in relation to these three features.

Concerning the goal of history, dispensationalists find it in the establishment of the millennial kingdom on earth while covenant theologians regard it as the eternal state. This is not to say that dispensationalists minimize the glory of the eternal state, but it is to insist that the display of the glory of God, who is sovereign in human history, must be seen in the present heavens and earth as well as in the new heavens and the new earth. This view of the realization of the goal of history within time is both optimistic and in accord with the requirements of the definition. The covenant view, which sees the course of history continuing the present struggle between good and evil until terminated by the beginning of eternity, obviously does not have any goal within temporal history and is therefore pessimistic. McClain points up this contrast when he writes about covenant theology.

> According to this view, both good and evil continue in their development side by side through human history. Then will come catastrophe and the crisis of divine judgment, not for the purpose of setting up of a divine kingdom in history, but after the close of history. . . . Thus history becomes the preparatory "vestibule" of eternity. . . . It is a narrow corridor, cramped and dark, a kind of "waiting room," leading nowhere *within* the historical process, but only fit to be abandoned at last for an ideal existence on another plane. Such a view of history seems unduly pessimistic, in the light of Biblical revelation.[7]

Thus in relation to a goal in a proper philosophy of history only dispensationalism with its consummating dispensation of the millennium offers a satisfactory system.

A second requirement of a philosophy of history is a proper unifying principle. In covenant theology the principle is the covenant of grace. This is the covenant the Lord supposedly made with Adam and Eve after the Fall in which He offered salvation through Jesus Christ. In short, the covenant of grace is God's plan of salvation, and therefore the unifying principle of covenant theology is soteriological. In dispensationalism the principle is theological or perhaps better eschatological, for the differing dispensations reveal the glory of God as He displays His character in the differing stewardships culminating in history with the millennial glory. If the goal of history is the earthly millennium, and if the glory of God will be manifested then in the personal presence of Christ in a way hitherto unknown, then the unifying principle of dispensationalism may be said to be eschatological (if viewed from the goal toward which history is moving) or theological (if viewed from the self-revelation of God in every dispensation). Though the dispensationalist's principle is much broader and therefore less confining, it must be admitted that this alone does not prove it is the more valid one. The third part of the definition of a philosophy of history must also be considered.

Only dispensationalism does justice to the proper concept of the progress of revelation. Covenant theology does include in its system different modes of administration of the covenant of grace and, although these modes give an appearance of an idea of progressiveness in revelation, in practice there is rigidity in covenant theology. Orr, a covenant theologian, criticizes the covenant system along this very line.

> It failed to seize the true idea of development, and by an artificial system of typology, and allegorizing interpretation, sought to read back practically the whole of the New Testament into the Old. But its most obvious defect was that, in using the idea of the covenant as an exhaustive category, and attempting to force into it the whole material of theology, it created an artificial scheme which could only repel minds desirous of simple and natural notions.[8]

Covenant theology, then, because of the rigidity of its unifying principle of the covenant of grace cannot show within its system proper progress of revelation.

Dispensationalism, on the other hand, can and does give proper place to the idea of development. Under the various administrations of God different revelation was given to man, and that revelation was increasingly progressive in the scope of its content. Though similarities are present in various dispensations, they are part of a true development and not a result of employing the unifying principle of the covenant of grace. The particular manifestations of the will of God in each dispensation are given their full yet distinctive place in the progress of the revelation of God throughout the ages. Only dispensationalism can cause historical events and successions to be seen in their own light and not to be reflected in the artificial light of an overall covenant.

Therefore a correct philosophy of history with its requirements of a proper goal, a proper unifying principle, and a proper concept of progress is best satisfied by the dispensational system.

The Necessity of Consistent Hermeneutics

Much has been written on the subject of valid hermeneutical principles. In relation to the present discussion, the question relates to literal or allegorical interpretation, for if literalism is the valid hermeneutical principle then that is an approach to the Scriptures which if consistently applied can only lead to dispensational theology.

It is not within the scope of this chapter to discuss the entire matter of allegorical and literal interpretation. It must suffice to show that only dispensationalism consistently employs the principles of literal interpretation. Covenant theologians are well known for their stand on allegorical interpretation especially as it relates to the prophetic Word, and they are equally well known for their amillennialism which is only the natural outcome of allegorizing.[9] Premillennialists who are not dispensationalists also have to depart from literal interpretation at certain points in their eschatology. For example Ladd in order to add support to his posttribulational view is forced to regard the 144,000 of Revelation 7 as referring not to literal Israel but to spiritual Israel or the church.[10] Further, he cannot abide the dispensationalists' idea of the Jewish character of Matthew's gospel,[11] but he nowhere explains, for instance, how he can interpret in any literal way Jesus' words of commission to the Twelve recorded in Matthew 10:5–10. Anyone who attempts to interpret literally this commission which *forbade* the disciples to go to the Gentiles and the commission which *commands* the same group to go to the Gentiles (28:19–20) either gives up in confusion or resorts to spiritualizing one of the passages or recognizes a dispensational distinction. If literal interpretation is the only valid hermeneutical principle and if it is consistently applied, it will cause one to be a dispensationalist. As basic as one believes literal interpretation to be, to that extent he will of necessity become a dispensationalist.

The Necessity of Proper Definition

The usually quoted definition of a dispensation is the one that appears in the notes of *The Scofield Reference Bible:* "A dispensation is a period of time during which man is tested in respect to obedience to some *specific* revelation of the will of

God."[12] The usual criticism leveled against this definition is that it is not true to the meaning of οἰκονομία since the definition says nothing about a stewardship and emphasizes the matter of a period of time. The criticism may be somewhat valid, for a dispensation is primarily a stewardship, administration, or arrangement, and not a period of time. "Age" and "dispensation" are not synonymous in meaning even though they may coincide in history. A dispensation is basically the arrangement involved, not the time involved; therefore a proper definition must emphasize this.

In addition it is obvious that dispensationalists teach that at least some features of certain dispensations overlap. Perhaps that idea would more accurately be expressed by saying that each dispensation builds on the preceding one(s). Obviously that means that similar or even the same principles obtained during former ones are sometimes included in the succeeding one. If a dispensation is an arrangement or economy, then some details of the various arrangements will be the same. Thus dispensations supersede each other in the sense of building on each other in line with the idea of progress of revelation and the philosophy of history which climaxes in an ultimate goal in time. Therefore the ideas of dispensations ending, superseding, building, progressing, and having similar and different features must also be included in the definition.

In light of the foregoing discussion, is it possible to formulate a proper definition of a dispensation? The following is suggested: "A dispensation is a distinguishable economy in the outworking of God's purpose." If one were describing a dispensation, he would include other things such as the ideas of testing, failure, and judgment, but a definition differs from a description. The definition proposed, though brief and perhaps open to the criticism of oversimplification, seems sufficiently inclusive. In this theological use of the word "economy" the emphasis is placed on the biblical meaning of the word. Economy also suggests the fact that certain features of some dispensations may be similar. Though socialistic and capitalistic economies are quite different in their basic concepts, nevertheless similar functions are performed in both systems. Likewise in the different economies of God's running of the affairs of this world certain features will be similar. However, the word "distinguishable" in the definition points out the fact that some features pertain particularly to each dispensation and mark it off as a different economy. The particular features will distinguish, though the distinguishable dispensation will not be dissimilar in all its particulars. Also the phrase "the outworking of God's purpose" in the definition indicates that the viewpoint in dispensationalism is God's. These are economies instituted and brought to their purposeful conclusion by God. The distinguishable feature is put there by God, and the purpose is His.

This definition in light of the above explanation, may be applied first to the usual dispensational scheme and second to the problem of ultradispensationalism. It is not difficult to justify most of the usual seven dispensations on the basis of this definition. If one is a premillennialist, then the distinguishable economy of God in the millennium during which Christ is visibly present is easily recognized. This present dispensation whose principal but not exclusive characteristic is grace also is easily justified by the definition. The same is apparent with the Mosaic dispensation of the Law, and the point need not be labored. The time between the beginning of creation to the giving of the Law gives rise in some minds to the question of the validity of all the dispensations which are said to belong to that period. However, before the Fall the arrangement was certainly distinguishably different from that after the Fall. Already, then, this demonstrates the existence of five dispensations: innocence, whatever name should be given to what obtained after the Fall and up to the time of Moses, the Law, the Church Age, and the millennial kingdom. The very fact that it is difficult to find a suitable name to cover the entire economy from the Fall to Moses ought to make one examine carefully the validity of trying to view that entire period as having only one dispensation operating during it. It should be apparent that up to the time of Abraham God's administration concerned all nations, whereas with Abraham he began to single out one nation, and in that singling out He made a distinctive covenant with Abraham. Therefore the distinguishable characteristic of God's dealing with Abraham in promise seems sufficient to delineate the dispensation of promise. The only question that remains is whether the dispensations of conscience and government are valid. If there was only one dispensation during this period, what should it be called? If there are two, what are the distinguishing features that justify two? The problem is complicated by the fact that the revelation of Scripture covering this long period is brief, but from what is revealed an answer must be sought. It seems to this writer that there is sufficient warrant in God's new arrangement for human government in the time of Noah to distinguish a dispensation at that time (cf. Gen. 9:6 with 4:15). If this is accepted, then there are seven dispensations, and one must admit that the more one studies in the light of a basic definition the conclusion is that there are seven dispensations. It seems to be somewhat fashionable these days to avoid this conclusion or at least to minimize the earlier dispensations, but if one has a consistently workable definition and if one applies it throughout all history, then it seems difficult not to conclude that there are seven.

But what of the ultradispensationalists who insist on dividing the present economy of grace? Is something distinguishably different being done since Paul that was not done from Pentecost to Paul? (It matters little for purposes of this discussion whether the ultradispensationalists' dispensation of grace or of the church began in Acts 9, 13, or 28. The point is that a separate dispensation is made of the so-called Jewish church and the Pauline church.) What ultradispensationalists fail to recognize is that the distinguishableness of a dispensation is related to what God is doing, not to what He revealed at the time. It is certainly true that within the scope of any dispensation there is progressive revelation, and in the present one it is obvious that not all of what God was going to do was revealed on the day of Pentecost. These are economies of God, not of man, and the limits of a dispensation are determined not by what any one person within that dispensation understood but by what may be understood now from the completed revelation of the Word. Actually today people are in a better position to understand than the writers of the New Testament themselves. Ultradispensationalists fail to recognize the difference between the progress of doctrine as it was during the time of revelation and the representation of it in the writings of Scripture.

> There would be a difference between the actual course for some important enterprise—say, of a military campaign, for instance—and the abbreviated narrative, the selected documents, and the well-considered arrangement, by which its conductor might make the plan and execution of it clear to others. In such a case the man who read would have a more perfect understanding of the mind of the actor and the author than the man who saw; he would have the whole course of things mapped out for him on the true principles of order.[13]

The distinguishable feature of this economy is the formation of the church, which is Christ's body. This is the work of God;

therefore the question that decides the beginning of this dispensation is, When did God begin to do this? not, When did individuals understand it? Only by consulting the completed revelation can one understand that God began to do this work on the day of Pentecost (Acts 1:5; 11:15–16; 1 Cor. 12:13; Col. 1:18), and therefore whether Peter and the others understood it then does not determine the beginning of the dispensation. The distinguishable feature of this dispensation is the formation of the church, and since that began at Pentecost there has been only one economy since that day. Ultradispensationalists can offer only the distinguishing feature of a Jewish church as over against a Gentile church which is the body of Christ, but such a distinction has no validity since there are Jews in today's predominantly Gentile church and since the baptism of the Spirit first occurred at Pentecost. Thus the same economy has been operative since the Day of Pentecost.

The validity of dispensational theology is based on the necessity for biblical distinctions. It alone most fully satisfies a proper philosophy of history. Only dispensationalism provides the key to consistent literalism. And properly defined, it is the only valid system of biblical interpretation.

CHAPTER 12

A New Look at Dispensationalism

Roy L. Aldrich

The current debate over dispensationalism suffers for lack of clarity and agreement in the area of basic definitions. It also suffers from an overemphasis on distinctives and a neglect of the areas of agreement. It would be naive to suppose that dispensationalists and their critics have no important theological differences. However, this study takes a new look at the dispensational debate to show that the problem of definition is not impossible, and that both sides have much more in common about essential dispensational distinctions than they have in difference. Surely this is the emphasis most needed today.

The *Oxford English Dictionary* gives the following as the theological definition of dispensation: "A religious order or system, conceived as divinely instituted, or as a state in a progressive revelation expressly adapted to the needs of a particular nation or period of time, as the *patriarchal, Mosaic* (or *Jewish*) *dispensation,* the *Christian dispensation;* also, the age or period during which such system has prevailed."[1]

Presumably this definition would be generally approved by both dispensationalists and nondispensationalists. Attention is directed to the fact that a dispensation includes the two factors of a religious order and the age during which the order is in effect.

The idea of a religious order or economy is indicated in the new Testament by the Greek word οἰκονομία. This is a compound term derived by union of the word οἶκος ("house") and νόμος ("law"). The literal meaning is thus "house rule," which is expanded to mean stewardship or economy.

The word is found nine times in the New Testament. The first three occurrences are all in the Parable of the Unjust Steward and the word has the limited and local meaning of stewardship: "Give an account of your stewardship" (Luke 16:2), "my master is taking the stewardship away from me" (v. 3), "When I am removed from the stewardship" (v. 4).

Paul used the term with a wider meaning in the following six passages. "I have a stewardship entrusted to me" (1 Cor. 9:17, ASV); "the dispensation of God's grace" (Eph. 3:2); "the stewardship from God" (Col. 1:25); "a dispensation of God which is in faith" (1 Tim. 1:4, ASV); "the administration of the mystery" (Eph. 3:9); "unto a dispensation of the fullness of the times" (Eph. 1:10, ASV).

These passages use the word "dispensation" (or "stewardship" or "administration") to describe the sacred commission or trust to preach the Gospel. However, in the last passage, Ephesians 1:10, there seems to be the additional concept of an age or epoch implied by the phrase, "the fullness of the times." Some think the reference is to the church age and some believe it describes the millennial age to come.

However, the dispensational position is not entirely dependent on the meaning of the word or its various uses in the New Testament. If no such word were found in the Bible, some term would have to be chosen to describe the concept of dispensational truth. Correct theological terms are not always biblical words.

The word αἰών ("age") is a second New Testament term that needs careful consideration in connection with the concept of a dispensation. The unfortunate translation of αἰών as "world" in the King James Version is corrected in the New American Standard Version: "and lo, I am with you always, to the close of the age" (Matt. 28:20). "so shall it be at the end of the age" (Matt. 13:40); "either in this age or in the age to come" (Matt. 12:32); "the powers of the age to come" (Heb. 6:5).

In these passages the word "age" is used to designate this Gospel economy or a new age that will follow. The use of "age" seems to be synonymous with the word "dispensation" in Ephesians 1:10—the "dispensation of the fullness of times." In Ephesians 1:10 the emphasis is on the nature of the age, but in the other passages the emphasis is on the concept of a time period.

It follows that a dispensation is a stewardship or economy that God imposes for a certain period or age. Unger writes the following:

> A dispensation is an era of time during which man is tested in respect to obedience to some definite revelation of God's will. Seven such dispensations are recognized by many premillennialists. Other premillennialists speak of only three or four. Still others prefer not to be classed as dispensationalists at all.[2]

All Bible students recognize at least two dispensations and most would acknowledge four or five. Hodge, a postmillennialist, outlines four dispensations: From Adam to Abraham, from Abraham to Moses, from Moses to Christ, and the Gospel Dispensation.[3] In regard to the last two of the four Hodge observes, "The gospel dispensation is called new in reference to the Mosaic economy, which was old, and about to vanish away."[4]

Boettner, a postmillennialist, sees only two dispensations in Bible history: "Instead of setting forth God's dealings with man under seven dispensations, the Bible sets forth two covenants—the covenant of works and the covenant of grace. It then divides the covenant of grace into two dispensations or administrations, (1) that of the Old Testament, and (2) that of the New Testament."[5] But the matter is not left quite so simple, for Boettner proceeds to divide the Old Testament covenant of grace into four stages or covenants: the revelation to Adam (Gen. 3:15), the covenant with Noah (Gen. 8:20–9:17), the covenant with Abraham (Gen. 12:1–3), and the Sinaitic Covenant (Ex. 20). Except in terminology, this is close to a dispensational approach.

Kuiper is emphatic that all biblical preaching must recognize two dispensations: "In accordance with the divine plan of history the old dispensation belongs to the irrevocable past. In the new dispensation no preacher may be satisfied to occupy the standpoint of the old. A sermon on an Old Testament text must always be a New Testament sermon."[6]

Hamilton, an amillennialist, wrote as follows.

> All Christians distinguish between at least three dispensations: (1) The dispensation of works, before the fall of man, when man was placed under a covenant according to which obedience to God's command would bring eternal life and disobedience brought eternal death to themselves and to their descendants except as God's grace brought redemption. (2) The Old Testament dispensation up to the coming of Christ, during which salvation was limited to God's chosen race and to those who were brought into the Covenant People. (3) The third dispensation is the New Testament dispensation, under which salvation is by faith in Christ for those who are mentally responsible and of God's chosen people, both Jews and Gentiles. Throughout both dispensations after the fall of man, salvation was only by grace through faith in God and His promised Redeemer. . . . The Old Testament saints and the New Testament saints are all part of the same church of God throughout the ages. Nor will there be any other basis of salvation at any time in the future, except through belief in the redemption that is in Christ Jesus. There have been several covenants, but no change in the way of salvation.[7]

Scofield gives this definition of a dispensation: "A dispensation is a period of time during which man is tested in respect to obedience to some *specific* revelation of the will of God."[8]

Pieters comments on this definition.

> Such a use of the word "dispensation" to indicate a period of time during which some specific aspect of the divine redemptive programme is prominent, is familiar to theology. We are all accustomed to the expressions: "the old dispensation," "the new dispensation," as designating the time before and after the coming of Christ, yet not merely as intervals of time but as periods during which certain distinct religious ordinances were established by divine authority. . . . On the "Dispensation of Innocency" we need waste no words. We are all agreed that there was such a period, and that the relations between God and man suffered a radical alteration by the coming in of sin.[9]

Pieters objects to more than three dispensations, but it is of interest to note that he approves of Scofield's definition of a dispensation, and he acknowledges that the concept is familiar to theology.

From what has been noted to this point, it seems that much of the debate over dispensationalism would disappear if both sides took a new look at their broad areas of agreement. The writer has no authority to speak for other dispensationalists nor for those who reject dispensationalism, but from an examination of the constructive literature of both camps it would seem that there could be agreement of several points.

A simple definition. Both sides could agree on a simple theological definition of a dispensation such as is found in most dictionaries. One definition worth noting is as follows: "The period during which a particular revelation of God's mind and will has been operative on mankind; as during the Christian dispensation; during the patriarchal dispensation."[10]

Bible history since Moses must be divided. Both sides could agree that Bible history since Moses must be divided into at least two dispensations. Some of the seven dispensations outlined by many dispensationalists may be only convenient historical divisions. After all, most of the Bible (from Exodus 20, the giving of the Law, through the Book of Revelation) contains principally the account of only two dispensations—law and grace. "The law was given by Moses, but grace and truth came by Jesus Christ" (John 1:17). Making allowance for the prophecies of a future kingdom and the brief revelation about the eternal state, it is safe to say that 90 percent of the Bible deals with only two dispensations which are not in dispute. In other words dispensationalists are actually in 90 percent agreement with nondispensationalists who see only two dispensations in the Bible.

The importance of this large area of agreement is further accentuated when it is realized that these two dispensations are the most important from a doctrinal point of view. No one thinks he belongs in the economy of the Garden of Eden with a choice between two trees, but many are confused about their exact relationship to the dispensations of law and grace. However, both dispensationalists and nondispensationalists are in agreement that, to avoid Mosaic legalism, the ages of law and grace must be distinguished.

The period from Adam to the giving of the Law must be divided into a minimum of two ages to distinguish the differences before and after the Fall. Thus all Bible history calls for at least four dispensations.

Only one way of salvation. There should be agreement that there is only one way of salvation throughout all Bible history since the Fall. The erroneous teaching of some ultradispensationalists at this point should not be attributed to dispensationalists as a whole. In Romans 4 the citing of Abraham and David as examples of justification by faith should settle any doubts about the plan of salvation in the Old Testament.

Dallas Seminary's Doctrinal Statement states, "We believe that according to the 'eternal purpose' of God (Eph. 3:11) salvation in the divine reckoning is always 'by grace, through faith,' and rests upon the basis of the shed blood of Christ."[11]

Covenant theologians speak of a covenant of grace that runs through all Bible history since the Fall. Dispensationalists object to the idea of one covenant for all the history of redemption, but would readily agree that there is but one fundamental plan of salvation for all ages. Both sides would agree that this common salvation was not fully revealed until after the death and resurrection of Christ (2 Tim. 1:9–10).

The new birth. Perhaps both sides of the dispensational debate could also agree that the new birth is characteristic of every period since the Fall, even though this doctrine is not as clearly revealed in the Old Testament as in the New. Before the inauguration of the church age the Lord said to Nicodemus, "Unless one is born again, he cannot see the kingdom of God" (John 3:3). Old Testament saints are clearly declared to be in the kingdom of God

(Luke 13:28–29) and therefore they must have experienced the new birth. The scriptural truth of the sinful nature makes the new birth a necessity for entrance into the kingdom of God.

Moral law applies in every dispensation. Both adherents and opponents of dispensationalism could agree that the eternal moral law of God applies to every dispensation. "The eternal moral law of God" does not mean the Mosaic law or the Ten Commandments but the eternal principles of righteousness as a reflection of the character of God. God's standard of holiness has always been nothing less than His own character or glory (Rom. 3:23). Moses did not originate this moral law and it did not cease at the end of the age of Mosaic Law.

When dispensationalists say the Ten Commandments are done away, they mean that believers are not under the Mosaic setting of the eternal moral law. They recognize that all the moral principles of the Mosaic age reappear for the church in a setting of grace. It is no more antinomian to say that the Mosaic Law does not apply in this age than it is for a citizen of Michigan to say he is not under the laws of Illinois. Much of the argument over law and grace is caused by a failure in definition of terms. If the eternal moral law of God is distinguished from the Mosaic laws, much of the confusion disappears. All agree that believers in this present age are still under the "righteousness of the law," that is, the moral principles contained in the Law of Moses, and all but extreme legalists also agree that believers are not under "the ministry of death, in letters engraved on stones" (2 Cor. 3:7), that is, they are not under the Mosaic economy of the moral law with its death penalties.

Saints of all ages have more in common than in difference. Both sides of the dispensational debate would doubtless agree with this generalization. "Having a common wonderful Savior surely outweighs all possible differences that will exist in the millennium or in the eternal state."

Dispensationalists believe there is a difference between Israel and the church, and that God has a literal kingdom future for Israel. Many nondispensationalists believe that Israel and the church are to be identified and that the promises to Israel find their fulfillment in the church. These are frank differences of opinion that will doubtless continue. However, the emphasis should be on the greater importance of what is held in common—the believers' "like precious faith."

In conclusion, this "new look at dispensationalism" is an attempt to show that dispensationalists have much more in common than is generally supposed. These are the suggested areas of agreement: (1) A simple definition of a "dispensation" as found in a good dictionary. (2) That Bible history since Moses must be divided into at least two dispensations, law and grace, and that these two periods cover 90 percent of Bible history. The period from Adam to Moses needs to be divided into at least two dispensations to distinguish between man's condition before and after the Fall. This gives a minimum of four dispensations for all Bible history. (3) That the Bible teaches only one way of salvation for every dispensation since the Fall. (5) That the eternal moral law of God (not the Mosaic Law) applies to all dispensations. (6) That the saints of all dispensations have far more in common than in difference.

Finally it should be agreed that the dispensational discussion should be conducted on the New Testament ethical platform. Both sides should take another look to see whether they are shooting at a real opponent or at a straw man of their own imagination. Further discussion should not only clarify differences, but also should emphasize more the great areas of agreement.

CHAPTER 13

Development of Dispensationalism by Contemporary Dispensationalists

Craig A. Blaising

D ispensationalism is undeniably a doctrinal development in the history of theology. Everyone recognizes this (in spite of sometimes tongue-in-cheek remarks such as "anybody who worships on Sunday is a dispensationalist," i.e., the whole church throughout history excluding sabbatarians such as the modern Seventh-day Adventists). John Nelson Darby had his own view of this development. As he saw it, the entire history of the church since the apostles was marked by apostasy. He saw his own theological work as a recovery of apostolic doctrine. Others have attempted to find at least some continuity with the early church fathers for dispensational distinctives, but that appeal has never really been convincing, except perhaps on the matter of belief in multiple historical dispensations.[1]

Dispensationalists are aware that their system has introduced a new theological synthesis into the history of postapostolic Christian thought. That is why they frequently counter the antidispensational tradition-polemic with *sola Scriptura*. That fact alone is clear evidence of the problem of orthodox doctrinal development. In dispensationalism there is the emergence of a new doctrinal synthesis legitimizing itself against an older synthesis (tradition) on the grounds of Scripture.[2]

Not all dispensationalists have followed Darby in relegating the whole historical church since the apostles to apostasy. In the United States for example many dispensationalists have sought to maintain some traditional continuity with the Reformation. In fact dispensationalists including Darby have had a great deal of continuity with the broad stream of orthodoxy. But when they have attempted to maintain a confessional allegiance to some more recent tradition—Reformed thought from the Westminster Confession through American Presbyterianism, for example—all the strains and pressures of the phenomena of doctrinal development are clearly sensed. In spite of this, dispensational theologians have not really grasped the problem of doctrinal development, the problem that only began to be articulated in the days of Darby by John Henry Newman and which few evangelicals have addressed directly. Actually dispensationalists because of their place in the history of doctrine should be the most concerned for proper orthodox doctrinal development and should encourage the present application of the same principles that brought into being the dispensational synthesis. Dispensationalists should be open to, sensitive to, and ready to entertain any future development of theology based on a proper theological method, giving primary consideration to the ongoing work of interpreting the Scripture. Many dispensationalists are encouraging this, and that is why development can be seen within the system.

Over the past three decades the signs of doctrinal development have clearly appeared within the dispensational system itself. But some dispensationalists still find themselves unprepared for this development and unable to contribute constructively in the proper work of theology.

The phenomena of development can be seen by examining three common concepts of dispensationalism presented by contemporary dispensational scholarship. The strength of these views lies in the perception of dispensationalism as a monolithic movement. Their weakness lies in the fact that that perception is not quite true. The three views are that dispensationalism is (a) a fixed set of confessional interpretations of Scripture, (b) a theodicy, and (c) a hermeneutical-theological system that maintains a clear essential principle. The purpose of this article is to demonstrate developments in this doctrinal area by examining these three possible concepts of dispensationalism.

Dispensationalism As a Set of Fixed, Confessional Interpretations of Scripture

This author knows of no scholarly advocate of dispensationalism who has made such a claim. However, the impression does exist. It may perhaps be due to the widespread impact of *The Scofield Reference Bible*, encouraged no doubt by the prodigious ministerial and educational activity of C. I. Scofield. With Scofield, dispensationalism entered its "scholastic" period, nurtured and supported by the educational leadership of his theological successor

Lewis Sperry Chafer.[3] It is not surprising that in many quarters dispensationalism was and even still is equated with Scofieldianism.[4]

The theological and expository output of Dallas Theological Seminary has also tended to support this confessional concept of dispensationalism, especially in the Seminary's earlier days. Its publications have sought to present a uniform, systematically integrated interpretation of the whole of Scripture. This can be seen in Chafer's *Systematic Theology*, *Bibliotheca Sacra*, and other publications as well. Differences have tended to be downplayed and traditional language maintained. This has been viewed as a strength, and in many respects it is. The concept of dispensationalism as a set of fixed interpretations of Scripture can also be seen in the frequency of inquiries regarding "the Dallas view" on any particular expositional or theological matter. Even *The Bible Knowledge Commentary* tends to support this concept in that the public sees *one* commentary by the faculty of *one* school, a commentary which claims to interpret "the Scripture *consistently* from *the* grammatical-historical approach and from *the* pretribulational, premillennial perspective."[5] Reading on, however, one finds that "the authors often present *various* views on passages where differences of opinion exist within evangelical scholarship." This does not say "differences within dispensational scholarship," but an examination of the contents shows this to be the case.[6]

Another factor that perhaps has contributed to this fixed-interpretation view of dispensationalism has been the dispensational description of its literal hermeneutic as clear, plain, or normal interpretation. This can give the idea that all the hermeneutical results presented in dispensational expositions are the clear, plain, simple, obvious interpretations of Scripture. Any other exposition is unclear, convoluted, and abnormal. Simple facts are singular; they do not allow for alternatives of equal value. Of course no dispensationalist has said that all his interpretations are obvious. But Ryrie wrote, "Normal interpretation leads to the clear distinction between words, concepts, peoples, and economies. This consistent hermeneutical principle is the basis of dispensationalism."[7] He is speaking of Israel and the church here. However, the whole Bible is made up of "words, concepts, peoples, and economies." One can see how the concept can arise of a dispensational, plain-to-see, obvious, no-alternative interpretation of the whole Bible.

Given the nature of biblical literature and a history of practicing historical-grammatical exegesis, hermeneutical developments are inevitable, including distinctions of various levels of hermeneutical certainty and the exploration and testing of multiple hermeneutical options. It is the actual practice of historical-grammatical exegesis by dispensational scholars that is proving this fixed-interpretation view of dispensationalism inadequate. For example the following well-known distinct "dispensational" interpretations illustrate this point.

THE INTERPRETATION OF THE SERMON ON THE MOUNT

The dispensational interpretation of the Sermon on the Mount as the presentation of the rules or law of the kingdom is well known. *The Scofield Reference Bible* calls it "the divine constitution for the righteous government of the earth. Whenever the kingdom of heaven is established on earth it will be according to that constitution." It also calls it "pure law" but admits that it has "a beautiful moral application to the Christian."[8] This view is repeated by Chafer with even stronger language in which he contrasts it to the Christian way of life according to his well-known dichotomy of law and grace.[9] The kingdom view can also be found in various other dispensational commentators.[10] Some, however, have stressed the qualitative more than the political aspects of this teaching.[11] Walvoord, writing in 1974, finds much greater application of the sermon to the church than did some earlier dispensationalists.[12]

Many contemporary dispensationalists deny that there is any *one* dispensational interpretation of the Sermon on the Mount.[13] One can do no better than to refer to Martin's article "Dispensational Approaches to the Sermon on the Mount" in the Pentecost *Festschrift*.[14] Martin writes, "There is a misconception that all dispensationalists hold to *the kingdom view* in the interpretation of the Sermon on the Mount. Actually, *the kingdom view* is probably a minority position among modern dispensationalists."[15] He delineates three other views besides the kingdom view, including the interim ethic approach Toussaint espoused in an earlier article of that same *Festschrift*,[16] and the believer's ethic approach to which Martin himself is attracted. This last view sees "the sermon as applicable to believers of any age (dispensation) in God's dealings with mankind."[17] The article demonstrates careful scholarly consideration of hermeneutical issues in the book of Matthew. It is primary evidence of hermeneutically based development of dispensational thought.[18]

THE INTERPRETATION OF THE KINGDOM OF HEAVEN
AND THE KINGDOM OF GOD

A distinction between the kingdom of heaven and the kingdom of God goes all the way back to Darby.[19] And Scofield's view can already be found in James Hall Brookes.[20] Of course the classic expression of the distinction between the two kingdoms is given in *The Scofield Reference Bible*.[21] Chafer also strongly maintained this distinction. "Broadly speaking, the kingdom of God . . . is the universal authority of God from everlasting to everlasting, while the term *kingdom of heaven* is fittingly applied to God's rule in the earth—it is heaven's rule on the earth—and is restricted, with respect to time . . . to limited periods and well defined situations."[22] He speaks of "vast distinctions between these two spheres of divine authority" that must be observed for proper biblical interpretation.[23] Feinberg also says, "These distinctions are vital and must be made to harmonize the Word of God."[24] Even in the 1980 revision of his book he maintains the distinction, quoting extensively from *The Scofield Reference Bible* on this point.[25]

The distinction between the kingdom of heaven and the kingdom of God was strongly attacked on exegetical grounds by Ladd in 1952.[26] Subsequent publications by dispensationalists show signs of revision. J. Dwight Pentecost writes that any distinctions between these terms exist only in their contextual usage and not in the words themselves.[27] Alva J. McClain maintained the two-kingdom distinction. But since the term "kingdom of God" can be used in different senses, sometimes even synonymously with "kingdom of heaven," McClain proposed different terminology to convey more accurately the essential distinctions: the universal kingdom and the mediatorial kingdom.[28] The revised *Scofield Reference Bible* inserted the admission that the terms are in many cases synonymous, being distinguished only "in some instances."[29] Walvoord also in recent publications clearly stresses that the terms are used interchangeably, but nevertheless he feels that some contexts do indicate a distinction, which is basically what was noted by earlier dispensationalists.[30]

Other dispensationalists have essentially abandoned any distinction between the kingdom of heaven and the kingdom of God.[31] In *The Ryrie Study Bible* the two terms have the same definition, that is, the future millennial kingdom.[32] Ryrie acknowledges that true Christians are in the kingdom today.[33] He also speaks of a present kingdom in the sense of professing

Christendom, but he makes no special use of the terms "kingdom of heaven" and "kingdom of God" in this discussion.[34]

An amazing confession was given by Mason in an article entitled "Two Kingdoms in Matthew?" After reviewing the Scofield-Chafer teaching, he wrote in 1973, "However, some forty years ago [1933!], I came to the conclusion that this distinction, which has brought enormous comfort to Scofield's enemies while baffling many of his friends, is not a valid distinction. Indeed, not only is the supposed distinction confusing; it brings with it certain unnecessary problems of interpretation."[35] He then gave seven reasons why no distinction should be seen between the two phrases, including a strong criticism of *The Scofield Reference Bible* note on Matthew 6:33. Toussaint treats the two terms as "essentially synonymous" and refers them both to the wholly future messianic or millennial kingdom.[36] Saucy also treats them synonymously but sees them both having reference to an already inaugurated messianic kingdom.[37]

Again this shows that dispensationalism is not a fixed set of confessional interpretations but that development is taking place.

THE INTERPRETATION OF ACTS 15:13–18

"Dispensationally, this is the most important passage in the New Testament." So begins the note on Acts 15:13–18 in *The Scofield Reference Bible*. Scofield presents an interpretation inherited from Brookes that relates the church and kingdom ages in succession.[38] Chafer sums up the interpretation this way:

> In defining Jehovah's new purpose in the present age, which purpose so completely set aside the essentials of Judaism for a time, the first council of the Church at Jerusalem recognized an order of events which were yet future. There was to be an outcalling of the Church from both Jews and Gentiles, which outcalling has already begun and continues to the present hour. This, in turn, was to be followed and terminated by the return of Christ; and Christ in His return would re-establish the Davidic dynasty— a restoration foreseen by Amos. . . . There is no support here or elsewhere for the Romish notion that the church is the kingdom. The elders of the early church distinguished here between the church as the present divine objective and the final return to, and completion of, the Davidic covenant.[39]

This interpretation has been quite common among dispensationalists, including Feinberg, Walvoord, Ryrie, and Pentecost.[40]

Allis attacked Scofield's interpretation of this passage, pointing out that Darby and the earlier Brethren expositors claimed to see only an analogy being expressed in Acts 15.[41] Subsequent dispensational expositions have modified or abandoned the Scofield position. Though the revised *Scofield Reference Bible* maintains the "plan of the ages" interpretation, it no longer claims that this is the most important passage for dispensationalism. And it has inserted the "analogy" interpretation surreptitiously alongside the other more famous interpretation. In the 1980 revision of his book *Millennialism*, Feinberg seems to vacillate on the passage. While leaving basically unchanged one favorable discussion of the Scofield interpretation, in another place he favors the analogy view of the earlier Brethren, saying it is "correct."[42] Toussaint, writing in *The Bible Knowledge Commentary, New Testament*, mentions the classic Scofieldian interpretation as a view "commonly held by premillenarians,"[43] but then he suggests the analogy view, which is presented by Sunukjian in *The Bible Knowledge Commentary, Old Testament* and by Elliott Johnson in the Walvoord *Festschrift*.[44] While admitting analogy, all these expositors have consistently denied any real fulfillment of Amos 9 in the early church. Some other contemporary dispensationalists, however, have argued for some measure of fulfillment in the church which does not deny a future fulfillment of Amos 9 in the millennium.[45]

Many other passages could be examined to show that dispensationalism is not a fixed set of confessional interpretations. Hermeneutical development is taking place. Obviously some hermeneutical consistency must exist in order for different expositors and theologians to maintain the name "dispensationalist." Perhaps one would include the interpretations of Romans 11:25–29 and the seventy weeks of Daniel among these. But even here, some hermeneutical refinement is not precluded.

Dispensationalism as a Theodicy

The idea that the dispensations are different tests of mankind that result in human failure and divine judgment can be traced back to Darby himself.[46] Such a view involves dispensationalism in theodicy, a vindication of God's goodness vis-à-vis evil in the world. Darby, whose writings are notoriously difficult to understand, seems to solve the theodicy in terms of the education of humanity in the perfections or attributes of God.[47] Each dispensation tests man in light of a different aspect of God's perfections. The inevitable human failure necessitates an extension of grace for those who would realize God's purpose (thus grace is in every dispensation) or judgment for those who would not. A strong doxological theme unifies the different dispensations.

Brookes also mentioned the themes of testing, failure, and judgment when he discussed the order of the dispensations. He did not expound these themes at length, but he seems to have been consciously constructing an alternative to the historical optimism of postmillennialism.[48]

These elements deeply affected Scofield's understanding of dispensationalism. This can be seen in his well-known definition of a dispensation as well as in other explanatory comments.[49] However, he said the educational purpose of the dispensations is seen in the achievement of full human comprehension of sin. Chafer agreed with this.[50]

Johnson solves the theodicy Christologically and eschatologically. Evil will be conquered by the rule of Christ. The hopes and purposes of the various dispensations, which have been frustrated by evil, will all be fulfilled in the millennium, in the dispensation of Ephesians 1:10, when all things will be consummated in Christ.[51] This emphasis can also be seen in Darby though it seems somewhat blurred in Scofield's and Chafer's writings.

A clear development of theodical dispensationalism is given by Geisler, who brings a dispensational orientation to classical theodicy.[52] From theological and anthropological considerations, Geisler argues that God "achieves the greatest good possible by allowing evil."[53] But the application of dispensationalism helps answer "the problem of why God permitted so much suffering for so long (thousands of years of human history)" and also "the problem of how men can be truly free in heaven while guaranteeing that evil will never break out again."[54] The seven dispensations provide a complete testing of mankind under all necessary conditions. With the demonstration of evil thereby complete, God is fully just to defeat it. With the conditions for sinning exhausted, the redeemed, who pledged themselves to obedience during the dispensations, have no options for evil and the omnipotence of God secures against any further outburst of it.[55]

Other dispensationalists, however, have been lessening or removing the theodicy aspect altogether from their construal of the system. Ryrie, while maintaining the governmental-responsibility aspects of the dispensations, removed the testing-failure-judgment features (those features related specifically to sin and evil) to a "secondary" status.[56] Many, including Saucy and Showers, have followed Ryrie on this point.[57] John Feinberg has stated that the idea of testing plays no important role in his view of dispensationalism.[58] Radmacher in his discussion of contemporary dispensationalism makes no mention of these features at all.[59]

From this perspective of theodicy, theological development in dispensationalism can be seen as moving in two different directions.

Dispensationalism As a Hermeneutical-Theological System That Maintains a Clear Essential Principle

Probably the clearest indication of a transition into a revisionary period for dispensationalism is Charles Ryrie's book *Dispensationalism Today*, published in 1965. While Ryrie personally endorsed many traditional features of scholastic dispensationalism, his identification of a *sine qua non* philosophically oriented dispensational scholarship in a revisionary way, for as long as one can maintain the narrowly defined essence, one can legitimately claim dispensational credentials while pursuing differences at a broad number of confessional points. The *sine qua non* is one clear way to signal continuity amid change in the process of doctrinal development. Many contemporary scholars who are contributing to dispensationalism have taken their cue from Ryrie's concept of the *sine qua non*. However, they have not all agreed with Ryrie's articulation of it, at least not completely.

Ryrie summarizes his discussion of the triadic essence of dispensationalism in this way:

> The essence of dispensationalism, then, is the distinction between Israel and the church. This grows out of the dispensationalist's consistent employment of normal or plain interpretation, and it reflects an understanding of the basic purpose of God in all His dealings with mankind as that of glorifying Himself through salvation and other purposes as well.[60]

These three aspects of the dispensational *sine qua non* must be examined in light of contemporary discussion.

THE DOXOLOGICAL PURPOSE OF GOD IN THE HISTORY OF PROGRESSIVE REVELATION

Ryrie, following Walvoord, speaks of God's glory as the unifying theme of Scripture and history. This is in contrast to salvation or redemption suggested by various covenant theologians and allows a more comprehensive inclusion of various "purposes" of God.[61] But another somewhat hidden matter in this discussion is the legitimate claim to a Reformed heritage.[62] Not all dispensationalists are or have claimed to be Reformed theologians; however, a number of them, especially those who have or have had Presbyterian affiliations (e.g., Chafer and Walvoord) have had something at stake in this claim. (The fact that Chafer and Walvoord have had a Reformed orientation in their theological writings may perhaps account for why so many think of dispensationalism as a Reformed theology.) Allis attacked dispensationalism in 1936 for dividing the unity of the Bible.[63] In his criticism he noted that this violated not only the nature of the Scriptures but also the Westminster Confession. In answering Allis, Chafer contended for both unity and diversity in Scripture, but he did not identify wherein the unity lay.[64] Regarding the Westminster Confession, Chafer argued that Scripture must take precedence over tradition. Walvoord, however, found a way to outflank covenant theologians on this confessional charge. Whereas Allis had said, "The very heart of the Bible is salvation," and other covenant theologians had also emphasized the centrality of God's redemptive work, Walvoord proposed a more comprehensive unity for the dispensational perspective taken directly from the Westminister Confession: "God . . . [works] *all things* [here are all the dispensational purposes] according to the counsel of His own immutable and most righteous will, *for His own glory*" [the overall doxological purpose].[65] Furthermore the doxological purpose is evident in the answer to the very first question of the Catechism.[66] So Walvoord writes, "This explanation fully sustains the fundamental thesis of Calvinism, that God is sovereign and all will in the end manifest His glory."[67] Many covenant theologians have been rebuffed by this one-upmanship and have complained that they never intended to deny the overall doxology in God's purpose. However, it is no longer as easy for them to charge that dispensationalists divide up the salvific unity of Scripture.

However, as some doxological unity must be agreed on by various Reformed parties, some contemporary dispensationalists have complained that consequently a doxological unity to Scripture and history cannot be the *distinctive* of dispensationalism. John Feinberg acknowledged in a recent debate with John Gerstner that a doxological unity is not a distinctive of dispensationalism and therefore cannot define its essence. Saucy also disagrees that doxology is a distinguishing principle.

One other aspect of Ryrie's treatment of the dispensational view of history seems to have been overlooked. The unity of history can also be described as eschatological.[68] That is, viewed from the goal of history all the dispensations are oriented to one goal, the millennial kingdom. Elsewhere he states that covenant theologians see history culminating in eternity whereas dispensationalists see the "entire program" culminating "not in eternity but in history, in the millennial kingdom of the Lord Christ. This millennial culmination is the climax of history and the great goal of God's program for the ages."[69] This, however, raises another question, for many theologians are taking a closer look at the nature of the eternal state. The concept of a timeless, nonhistorical eternity is giving way to the notion of a time-sequenced existence on the new earth, which is felt to be more consistent with biblical descriptions. Consequently the millennium does not properly bear the full climax of history. The goal of the dispensations is not the millennial kingdom but the eternal kingdom. The millennial kingdom is seen more as a temporary, transitional phase of God's kingdom plan, explicitly for the purpose of subjugating Christ's enemies including death and the devil. This will most likely receive further discussion by dispensationalists in the future.[70]

CONSISTENTLY LITERAL HERMENEUTICS

"Consistently literal or plain interpretation is indicative of a dispensational approach to the interpretation of the Scriptures."[71] For Ryrie, this is the second aspect of the *sine qua non*. The distinction of Israel and the church grows out of this. Literal hermeneutics does not mean literalistic.[72] Also the issue is not simply literal hermeneutics but the *consistent* practice of the same.[73] Radmacher has singled out this item as *the primary* aspect of the *sine qua non*. "It is so utterly fundamental to understand that the foundational premise of dispensationalism is not theological but hermeneutical."[74] However, he goes on to call this "the tradition of evangelical protestantism," and he quotes from nondispensationalists who point out problems with spiritual exegesis. But if this is the tradition of Protestantism, one wonders in what way it is a distinctive principle of dispensationalism? Saucy and John S. Feinberg have noted that many nondispensationalists deny that their hermeneutic is nonliteral or that it is inconsistent.[75]

One must note that some change has occurred in the debate over hermeneutics between dispensationalists and non-dispensationalists. Earlier dispensationalists were not contending over a nonissue when they charged others with what James Brookes called "the wretched habit of 'spiritualizing' the plainest testimonies of the word concerning the divine purposes with respect to the Jews."[76] Nor were they unaware that the New Testament use of the Old Testament might be appealed to by nondispensationalists. Rather they contended that the New Testament use of the Old Testament supported the dispensational view.[77]

It must be remembered that earlier dispensationalists were contending with postmillennialists and Unitarians, who disregarded historical exegesis. Boettner, often called one of the last classical postmillennialists, clearly defends "spiritual exegesis."[78]

This "nonliteral" exegesis might still be charged to amillennial evasions in Revelation 20:4–6.[79] However, over the past few decades nondispensationalists as well as dispensationalists have developed in their understanding and use of historical-grammatical exegesis and both have benefited from the study of biblical theology. Some nondispensationalists such as Ramm and Erickson have even credited dispensationalists with "contributing to an awareness of the historical development in biblical history."[80] Consequently the hermeneutical dialogue has opened onto new levels. It is even possible to see some rapprochement taking place between dispensationalists and nondispensationalists.[81] This does not mean that all differences have been resolved, but specific issues of disagreement must be identified. Today, for many scholars, to say the difference is simply between literal and spiritual exegesis is not accurate and is in fact misleading.

Contemporary dispensationalists are pointing the direction in which the discussion needs to progress. Feinberg says there are two basic issues: How does typology function? How does the New Testament use the Old Testament? These two issues are related. Regarding typology, he summarizes a dispensational position as follows: "(1) a type must have meaning in its own context; (2) the meaning of the type in its own context is essential for a type/antitype relationship (otherwise we have an example of a parable or perhaps an allegory, but not an example of typology); and (3) ignoring items 1 and 2 threatens the very integrity of the Old Testament."[82] He concludes that "the failure of nondispensational interpretation at this point, then, is that its view of typology (a misunderstanding of typology, that is), ignores or minimizes the meaning of the Old Testament event or person in its own setting, just because it takes on another meaning in a New Testament context."[83] But this understanding also implies a development in the dispensational practice of hermeneutics. Barker writes that he believes "that several passages that other dispensationalists relegate solely to the future received a literal fulfillment in the New Testament period or are receiving such a fulfillment in the continuing church age—in addition to a final, complete fulfillment in the future in the case of some of those passages." He adds, "Classic examples would be the fulfillment of Joel 2:28–32 in Acts 2:17–21 and of Amos 9:11–12 in Acts 15:16–17—without denying a final, future stage to complete the fulfillment with respect to Israel. That is to say, these are not 'either-or' propositions but 'both-and' ones."[84] Saucy says one must recognize

> that some aspects of the descriptions [made in prophetic prediction] are couched in the terminology of the time of their origin and thus allowance must be made for other forms of fulfillment corresponding to the later time. But any new theological understanding must be prescribed by the New Testament. There are types and shadows of realities which later Scriptures reveal as outmoded, but it is the position of dispensationalism that the New Testament does not *reinterpret* the meaning of the nation of Israel as much of church interpretation has done throughout its history.[85]

Turner basically agrees with these ideas, but he has drawn attention to the problem of the exegetical-theological-hermeneutical-cultural preunderstandings of dispensationalist and nondispensationalist interpreters. Differences are often a case of "conflicting preunderstandings." He also points out that the differences will not be resolved at the general level of hermeneutical rules but only in the exegesis of specific passages.[86]

Johnson essentially concurs with this as he speaks of an interpretive spiral.[87] He has also advanced a dispensational perspective of *sensus plenior* and has contributed thereby to the ongoing evangelical dialogue regarding the New Testament use of the Old Testament.[88] Bock has also helped clarify this dialogue, surveying the different positions that exist between evangelicals (dispensational and nondispensational) and has proposed an overall framework for consensus.[89]

In conclusion it can be seen that consistently literal exegesis is inadequate to describe the essential distinctive of dispensationalism. Development is taking place on how to characterize a proper hermeneutic for dispensationalists. Many do not feel, however, that the hermeneutic itself will be distinctively dispensational. Furthermore dispensational interpretations of various texts are likely to modify as this development continues.

THE DISTINCTION BETWEEN ISRAEL AND THE CHURCH

Among contemporary dispensationalists a general consensus exists that a distinction between Israel and the church is the essential distinguishing factor of dispensationalism. In spite of the fact that the other two (supporting) elements of Ryrie's triad seem less than tenable, at least in the way he stated them, this characteristic, according to many, seems to be truly representative. However, it is one thing to assert a distinction between Israel and the church; it is another to explain what the distinction is or what its implications are for dispensational theology.

The absolute distinction between Israel and the church. The ecclesiological-eschatological synthesis of Darby was his genius and the dominating conceptual center of modern dispensationalism. The most determinative portion of Scripture for him was Paul's letter to the Ephesians and particularly the description of the οἰκονομία, the dispensation, in Ephesians 1:9–10. In the future Christ will unite all things in Himself, including both heavenly and earthly spheres. The nature of the heavenly sphere is especially elaborated in Ephesians. Jesus Christ has been exalted above it already. Spiritual powers and forces of wickedness presently inhabit it, bringing misery on the earth. But the victory over them has already been won by Christ. On the earth, since the time of Christ's ascension, He has been forming a composite people (believing Jews and Gentiles with equal standing) to inhabit these heavenly regions as His body and bride. The wicked angelic hosts will be displaced, the church (those called out from the earth) will take the ruling position in the heavenlies, and the angels, who are now being educated in these things, will be subordinate to them. With Christ the church will rule the creation from the heavenlies, mediating the blessings of God on the earth (replacing thus the present flow of misery out of those places from deviate angelic hosts). When this happens, altered conditions on the earth will ensue.

This then is synthesized with the eschatological expectations of the Old Testament. Israel and the nations will have a future in an earthly kingdom-empire. The church and the church's future, however, is completely different from that of Israel and the Gentiles. The church is a heavenly people emerging on the earth now, but called out of the earthly entities of Israel and the Gentiles, having come into being since the ascension of Christ. Israel and the Gentiles are earthly people and have a future on the earth. Since history and prophecy concern the earth and earthly people, they do not concern the church. This means that the tribulation and the millennial kingdom concern earthly people only. Therefore they do not concern the church. The church's entrance into her destiny, the heavens, is not the subject of Old Testament prophecy. That entrance will take place by the rapture. The rapture is an event unrelated to earthly prophetic events, including the return of Christ to the earth before the millennium. In the future Christ will unite all things in Himself. The heavenly people will share His glory in the heavens; the earthly people will receive glory from the heavens as it shines on them and they will share in that glory on the earth.[90]

In Darby's dispensationalism the distinction between the heavenly people and the earthly people is absolutely essential. It gives meaning to all the other elements of his thought. The postponement of the kingdom, the parenthesis church, and the pretribulational rapture, for example, all fit with this distinction.

The dualism of heavenly and earthly peoples, including their heavenly and earthly destinies, is strongly affirmed by dispensationalists up to and including Lewis Sperry Chafer with only a few variations on the theme. Brookes identified this distinction as "dispensational truth" and vigorously advocated it, warning that the failure to make such a distinction would cause the church to lose sight of its nature and calling completely.[91] (Nevertheless he explicitly extended the regeneration ministry of the Spirit transdispensationally.) Kelly also strongly advocated this distinction: "The heavenly portion remains in its own unmixed character above. The believer, now gathered out from Jew or Gentile, finds his place in Christ there. The earth remains for the earthly people Israel, who will be called in their season."[92] However, Kelly noted that strictly speaking the church's inheritance is not the heavens but Christ![93] Morgan, however, began to sound a different note when he argued that the heavenly people would actually spend eternity on the new earth. The city of God, he said, will be "the earthly dwelling place of a heavenly people."[94]

Chafer stressed the absolute distinction between the heavenly and earthly peoples. He wrote, "Every covenant, promise, and provision for Israel is earthly, and they continue as a nation with the earth when it is created new. Every covenant or promise for the church is for a heavenly reality, and she continues in heavenly citizenship when the heavens are recreated."[95] It is important to note that Chafer has woven his doctrine of sanctification into this ecclesiological-eschatological dualistic synthesis. Chafer's law/grace dualism is merged with this heavenly/earthly people dualism. Thus for Chafer a distinction between Israel and the church is a soteriological doctrine (and this in spite of the fact that he has been vindicated, with some difficulty, from the charge of teaching two ways of salvation).[96]

However, a problem for Chafer's dualism is the city of God. He was forced to admit that in Revelation 21 this city is seen coming down from heaven to the earth and that Hebrews 12 places the church with Christ in that city. He had trouble with the phrase "spirits of just men made perfect." He said it "may designate saints of other dispensations or ages than the present."[97] Again he wrote, "*If* the earthly people as such are present they are indicated by the phrase, 'the spirits of just men made perfect.'"[98] In another place he admitted that Israel belongs to the class "just men made perfect," but there he had trouble landing the city on the new earth, though he admitted that it is to be considered "to some degree, as something apart from heaven."[99]

It is amazing that in the writings of Walvoord, Pentecost, Ryrie, and McClain published in the 1950s and 1960s, the heavenly/earthly dualistic language is gone.[100] A distinction between Israel and the church is vigorously asserted and all the theological structures of distinction are present except that the eternal destinies of the two peoples now share the same sphere. Consequently the heavenly/earthly descriptions are dropped. Thus is begun a slow movement away from the scholastic, classic, absolute distinction found from Darby to Chafer (with few exceptions such as G. Campbell Morgan, as noted earlier). Campbell has surveyed present differences among dispensationalists in the following way:

> Some dispensationalists make a sharp distinction between Israel as God's earthly people and the church as God's heavenly people, both continuing as such throughout eternity. Others favor a blurring of such distinction in

eternity. Charles C. Ryrie states, "The redeemed in the Body of Christ, the church of this dispensation, are the continuation of the line of redeemed from other ages, but they form a distinct group in the heavenly Zion (Heb. 12:22–24)."[101]

Relational factors between Israel and the church. Three factors that have served to relate Israel and the church in contemporary dispensational thinking are the city of God and the new earth, the New Covenant, and recognition of a present form of the kingdom.

Regarding the city of God, most dispensational scholars agree that both Israel and the church along with redeemed Gentiles will eventually share an eternal destiny in the city of God. However, some interpretive problems still remain. Does the adjective "heavenly" in "heavenly city" or "heavenly Jerusalem" as used by Paul and the writer of Hebrews refer to the city's (1) eternal position, (2) millennial position, (3) its present position before either millennial or eternal phases of the kingdom, or (4) some combination of two or three of these? The answer to this question will help determine one's response to the following: Will the church and the resurrected of Israel be a heavenly people during the millennium apart from mortal Jews and Gentiles on earth or will the resurrected and mortals be on the earth together at that time? In the eternal state will all the redeemed be a heavenly company or will they all be on the new earth? A variety of opinions have been expressed by dispensationalists on this.[102] Nevertheless most are agreed that the city of God is the common destiny of all the redeemed. It is this observation that is primarily responsible for expunging the eternal heavenly/earthly dualism. But this has created an ecclesiological problem, namely, how to describe the nature of the church vis-à-vis other groups of redeemed humanity? It is not sufficient to say simply that the church is eternally a different group than Israel nor does it help to say that the church alone is the body of Christ, unless theological content is given to that metaphor. Earlier dispensationalists seemed to offer some metaphysical and/or functional distinction that defined the nature of the church. Now that their alternative has been discarded, something needs to be put in its place.

Regarding the New Covenant, *The Scofield Reference Bible* had taken the position that both Israel and the church were related to the same New Covenant. However, Chafer recognized that this modified the sharp distinction between the two peoples, and so he taught that the New Covenant predicted for Israel in Jeremiah

31:31–34 was not the same as the New Covenant established with
the church and referred to specifically by Christ and Paul (Luke
22:20; 2 Cor. 3:6).[103] This distinction was vigorously defended
even while dispensationalists were dismantling the parallel
destinies of the two peoples.

In the words of Mason, this doctrine of two new covenants has
most certainly delighted the enemies of dispensationalism "while
baffling many of its friends."[104] It is interesting to read Ryrie's
belabored effort in *The Basis of the Premillennial Faith* to defend
this view.[105] It is doubtful that anyone could have done a better
job. However, it is really a defenseless position, and both Ryrie
and Walvoord eventually surrendered it.[106] This writer knows of
no dispensational scholar who holds it today. However, it must be
noted that according to Ryrie's argument, the surrender of this
view is an admission that the Scriptures do not "support a *sharp*
distinction between Israel and the church."[107] Ryrie rests the
dispensational position on the fact that New Covenant predictions
"have not been fulfilled in this present age. Now the question is,
does the New Testament change all this? If it does,
[dispensationalism] is weakened; if not it is further strengthened."[108]
Bringing together the exegetical work that led Walvoord and
Ryrie to abandon the view with the current work of contemporary
dispensationalists on typology and the application of Old Testament
passages to the church by the New Testament, one would have to
admit that it does change it somewhat. But many would conclude
that dispensationalism is not thereby weakened and would say
that it is instead readied for development.

Regarding a present form of the kingdom, earlier
dispensationalism did acknowledge some present divine kingdom
which it envisioned in two senses, a kingdom of heaven equivalent
to Christendom and the kingdom of God, the transdispensational
sphere of sovereignty and salvation. The messianic kingdom was
understood as the fulfillment of the Davidic Covenant in the
millennium; the present church age with its forms of kingdom was
essentially unrelated to the messianic kingdom. However, some
contemporary dispensationalists now see a connection between
the church age and the messianic kingdom that goes beyond the
older constructions of the kingdom of heaven/kingdom of God
arrangement or the theocratic kingdom view of Peters, McClain,
and Pentecost which replaced it. Noting that the New Covenant is
intimately associated with the Davidic Covenant in Old Testament

prediction, some are now saying that an inauguration of the New Covenant must involve an inauguration of the Davidic Covenant and thereby of the messianic kingdom (without denying the reality of a future millennium). Saucy writes,

> Without giving up the fulfillment of the promises for the nation of Israel when Christ returns to reign in open glory, this form of dispensationalism agrees with nondispensational premillennialism that it is preferable to interpret this age as the first phase of the fulfillment of the one promised Messianic kingdom. The present age involves the spiritual aspects of that Messianic kingdom, that is, the blessings of the New Covenant (i.e., regeneration, the indwelling Spirit, etc.). The remainder of the promises including those concerning Israel and the nations will find their fulfillment following the second advent.[109]

Present hermeneutical work in typology and the New Testament use of the Old would seem to support this understanding.

Conclusion

Dispensationalism is undergoing the process of doctrinal development in the work of contemporary dispensational scholars. Given the nature of the theological task such doctrinal development is expected and should be encouraged. Present developments are taking place on the methodological level, for example, in hermeneutical theory and practice, and this should and must continue. However, as a parting thought, certain doctrinal areas can be identified which require the attention of dispensational systematic theologians. The list is not meant to be exhaustive.

1. Ecclesiology. Dispensationalists must define the nature of the church vis-à-vis other redeemed peoples within the historical kingdom program of God. This may come in part through further study of the baptism of the Spirit seen in light of New Covenant pneumatology. Also the relationship of the church to history and thereby to society needs to be articulated.

2. Soteriology. The relationship of law and grace needs to be articulated. This will involve a reexamination of dispensational teaching on sanctification. The dispensational ministry of the Spirit with respect to the new birth and regeneration needs further examination. Is it possible that dispensationalism could offer another alternative to the Lutheran-Reformed-Wesleyan dialogue? This may lead to some new perspectives in dispensational anthropology.

3. Eschatology. The doctrine of dispensations needs to be articulated afresh. Also the change from a transcendent-present

kingdom polarity to an eschatological present-future kingdom understanding may have implications for the whole pattern or arrangement of the doctrines in a dispensational systematic theology. Finally, since biblical eschatology is Christocentric and ultimately Patrocentric, dispensationalism should clearly articulate this focus in its system.

CHAPTER 14

Is the Church in View in Matthew 24–25?

Bruce A. Ware

Robert Gundry, in his book *The Church and the Tribulation*, devotes one chapter to a discussion of the Olivet Discourse in which he argues that the church should be seen as participating in the tribulation and rapture events as described by the Lord in Matthew 24 and 25.[1] Gundry has two purposes in this chapter. First, he endeavors to show that the church is in fact in view in the events of the Olivet Discourse and that it therefore is in the tribulation described in these chapters. Second, he argues that the church (which has entered the tribulation) shall be raptured out of the world at the end of the tribulation. The concern of this chapter focuses on the first of these two purposes, namely, whether Gundry is correct in seeing the church in the tribulation period as described in the Olivet Discourse of Matthew 24–25.

Before looking at either Gundry or the biblical text, one must understand just what is (and what is not) at stake in this particular issue. First, even if Gundry is correct in asserting that the church is in view within Matthew 24–25, he still has not proved that the church will be raptured at the end of the tribulation. Certainly a posttribulational rapture *requires* that the church be in the tribulation. But to prove a *post*tribulational rapture (as opposed to a *mid*tribulational rapture) Gundry must not only show that the Olivet Discourse has the church participating in the tribulation, but that this text also shows that the church then is raptured out at the end of the tribulation (which issue he addresses in the second half of his chapter on the Olivet Discourse[2]).

Second, if Gundry is wrong and the church is not in view in the tribulation described by the Lord in His discourse on the Mount of Olives, then obviously a posttribulational rapture cannot be sustained from this text because there is no church in the tribulation of

Matthew 24–25 to be raptured. It must be acknowledged, however, that the absence of the church in Matthew 24–25 does not by itself eliminate the *possibility* of a scripturally sound posttribulational rapture, it only shows that proof for such a position cannot be derived from this passage.[3] In addition, proving the church's absence from the tribulation events of the Olivet Discourse does not necessitate the correctness of pretribulationism. To argue that the absence of the church in Matthew 24–25 proves that the church will not be in the tribulation is to argue from silence—a weak and inconclusive type of argumentation. What is needed, rather, is positive evidence that the church is in fact raptured before the tribulation, but the search for such pretribulational evidence would then go beyond the scope of this chapter.

Gundry's Position

Following the introduction to his chapter, "The Olivet Discourse," Gundry presents the fundamental issue of the first half of his chapter with the following question: "To what group of redeemed do the Jewish saints addressed by Jesus and represented by the apostles belong, Israel or the Church?"[4] Here then is the central question, namely, whether the apostles to whom Christ gave this discourse represent their nation Israel (in which case the church's presence should not be read into the discourse) or whether they represent the coming church (in which case the events described involve the church). Gundry offers five arguments in support of his position that the apostles represent tribulational church saints.

FALLACY OF HYPERDISPENSATIONALISM

Gundry first responds to hyperdispensationalism.[5] He argues that the inclusion of the Olivet Discourse within the Synoptics does not in itself make what is said irrelevant to the church. Therefore, he says, hyperdispensationalists argue wrongly for excluding the church from the events of Matthew 24–25.[6]

MATTHEW'S RELEVANCE TO THE CHURCH

Gundry addresses those who hold that Matthew alone (of the Gospels) is irrelevant to the church because of its Jewish character. He states again that Matthew's "Jewish cast" does not eliminate its having any direct relation to the church, as is evident by the church references made in Matthew 16:18 and 18:15–18.[7]

IMPORTANCE OF THE CONTEXT

Gundry argues that the context of the Olivet Discourse (both the immediate context and internal elements) supports the view that the discourse is related to the church.[8] He approaches his discussion in two stages: (a) he offers support from the immediate context that Jesus addressed the apostles as representing the church, not Israel, and (b) he argues against seeing any Jewish elements within the discourse as grounds for excluding the church.

In regard to the first stage in his discussion, Gundry asserts the following:

> The context indicates that the Jewish nation has passed into a state of divine disfavor because of their rejection of Jesus the Messiah. Since Jesus speaks from that standpoint, we might think it better logic to conclude that the discourse relates to the present dispensation characterized by Israel's setting aside.[9]

Many items are offered to show that by the time Jesus uttered His discourse on the Mount of Olives the Jewish nation had rejected Him. The Father in turn had also rejected the Jewish nation. The items mentioned include the rebuff by the Pharisees of Jesus after His triumphal entry into Jerusalem, Jesus' judgmental cleansing of the temple, Jesus' parables of judgment on the Jews who rejected Him, God's rejection of Israel as stated in Matthew 21:43, and Jesus' sorrowful "farewell" to the Jewish nation in Matthew 23:37–39.[10] Gundry concludes from this that since Israel is out of the picture (having been rejected by God), Jesus then in Matthew 24 outlined the chronology of the *present age*, relating to the church.[11]

In regard to the second stage in this discussion, Gundry attempts to show that the Jewish elements of the Olivet Discourse do not necessarily call for Jewish application if it can be shown (as he endeavors to do) that these elements are present *because* they relate not to religious Jews but only to national Jews. The Jewish elements reflect the fact that Jesus addressed Jewish Christians who *live in Israel* as opposed to His addressing Jewish, *non*church saints in the tribulation.[12] With this in mind, Gundry looks at three of the Jewish elements in the Olivet Discourse and explains their presence by arguing that Jesus was speaking of national (not religious) Jewish Christians. (1) Jesus warned of persecution from Jewish leaders. Gundry argues that such persecution can just as easily happen to Jewish Christians in the church as to nonchurch Jewish saints.[13] (2) The "gospel of the kingdom" will be preached

during the tribulation (Matt. 24:14). Gundry responds that this
gospel need not be distinguished from the church's gospel, that is,
the church can rightly be said to preach the gospel of the kingdom
today; therefore the references to the gospel of the kingdom need
not exclude the church from the tribulation.[14] (3) Jesus said to
"pray that your flight may not be . . . on a Sabbath" (24:20). This
need not be seen, says Gundry, as having been spoken to religious
Jews. Since restriction on Sabbath travel was merely of rabbinic
origin, Jesus would not be confirming these superfluous laws by
saying that their flight ought not be on the Sabbath when they are
forbidden by rabbinic teaching (not by God) to travel more than a
short distance. Rather, Gundry argues, this can be understood as
having been spoken to Christians living in Palestine who would
encounter opposition if having to travel on a Sabbath.[15]

TIME OF JERUSALEM'S DESTRUCTION

Gundry argues that the precursive (preliminary) fulfillment of
the Olivet Discourse—the destruction of Jerusalem in A.D. 70—
occurred "within the church age." This fact, he argues, negates the
contention that the final fulfillment of Matthew 24–25 must occur
when the church is removed. He states, "The falling of the
precursive fulfillment within the Church age establishes a precedent
which makes it probable that the final, tribulational fulfillment
will likewise take place while the Church is still present on the
earth."[16] In other words he sees an analogy between the church's
presence during the destruction of Jerusalem (the precursive
fulfillment) and the church's presence during the tribulation (the
final fulfillment). This analogy makes it "probable," he says, that
the church is in view in the Olivet Discourse.

APOSTLES' ASSOCIATION WITH THE CHURCH

Gundry states that since the apostles can represent both the
Jewish remnant belonging to redeemed Israel and the Jewish remnant
within the church, one can determine which group they represent in
Matthew 24–25 by seeing whether the apostles "usually represent
Israel or the Church"[17] elsewhere in Scripture. Gundry then
refers to numerous passages (Matt. 18:15–18; John 14:1–3; Acts
2:42; 1 Cor. 12:28; Eph. 2:20; 3:5–6; 4:11; and Rev. 21:12–14) to
seek to prove that the apostles stand as representatives of the church
and not of Israel in the Olivet Discourse. He concludes this section
by forcefully stating, "Hence, their [the apostles'] representative

role in the Olivet Discourse leads to the conclusion that the tribulational saints addressed through them belong to the church."[18]

These are the five arguments Gundry has advanced to support his contention that the apostles represent tribulational church saints. Each proposition will now be examined individually in an attempt to discern its strengths and/or weaknesses.

Responses to Gundry's Position

FALLACY OF HYPERDISPENSATIONALISM

In regard to Gundry's first argument, most pretribulationists would agree that hyperdispensationalists err in insisting that the Synoptics offer nothing that is directly relevant or applicable to the church. Further, Gundry is correct in concluding that "we dare not divorce the Olivet Discourse from the Church simply because of its appearance in the synoptics."[19] While Gundry is accurate here, it should be noted that this argument does not advance his position. Showing the fallacy of hyperdispensationalism does not help prove that the Olivet Discourse is dealing with the church in the tribulation. Rather, this argument only eliminates a mutually exclusive opposing position which, if true, would refute Gundry's argument.

MATTHEW'S RELEVANCE TO THE CHURCH

Gundry's second argument, too, is correct; the Jewish character of Matthew's gospel does not imply or necessitate irrelevance to the church. However, to say this is not to say that the whole Gospel is in turn directly relevant to the church. Rather, each passage must be assessed individually in its own context to determine in each case the particular group(s) addressed. While Gundry is right on this basic point, he has yet to establish the application of this point to the passage in question. Establishing that portions of Matthew *can* relate directly to the church does not automatically mean that the Olivet Discourse is one of those portions. The fact that Matthew can relate to the church makes it *possible* that the Olivet Discourse relates to the church, but it does not prove that such a position is in fact accurate.

IMPORTANCE OF THE CONTEXT

While Gundry's first and second arguments establish only the *possibility* that the apostles represent the church in the tribulation, his third argument attempts to establish the correctness of that position. However, in his analysis of the immediate context Gundry has erred not in his appraisal of Israel's rejection of Christ and God's rejection of Israel but in his conclusion. His conclusion is that *because* God had rejected Israel Jesus therefore would immediately and automatically have begun speaking of the church age to His disciples. Gundry's misunderstanding centers on his insistence that Israel's setting aside or rejection by God means that Jesus no longer says anything directly relevant to Israel as a nation. However, to make his argument valid, Gundry would have to hold that from Matthew 21:43 on God permanently cut off any direct dealings with Israel and offered no further revelation relating directly to the nation. Gundry, though, admits just the opposite, He states that God's rejection of Israel is only temporary, which necessitates a future direct relationship between God and His nation.[20] Therefore (since God's rejection of Israel is only temporary) Jesus' discourse on the Mount of Olives could well pertain to God's *future* direct dealings with Israel and need not be seen as addressed to the church.

Furthermore, the very evidence that Gundry cites to support his argument that God has rejected Israel (prior to the Olivet Discourse) actually supports the idea that the discourse is best taken as addressed to *Israel*. Gundry mentions many items (e.g., Jesus' rebuff of the Pharisees, challenges to Jesus' authority, Jesus' denunciation and rejection of Israel, Jesus' lament over Jerusalem) which, he says, show that Jesus turned from Israel to the church. However, such is not the case. The very fact that the conflict between Jesus and Israel had been constantly building in Matthew suggests that Jesus was using the discourse to focus on what further will happen to this special nation that has rejected her Messiah. In the discourse, then, Jesus did not turn His back on Israel but rather expounded God's future dealings with this rebellious nation.

Commenting on the proper understanding of Matthew 24–25, Dunham states, "The Olivet Discourse is set against the background of the twenty-third chapter of Matthew's gospel, including the rejection of the Messiah and the imposition of judicial blindness on the nation."[21] The preceding context in Matthew calls for this understanding whereas a complete break in Jesus' dealings with Israel at the end of Matthew 23 cannot be sustained.[22]

One final comment should be made in regard to this first stage of Gundry's argument. If Gundry is correct in assuming that Jesus addressed the church in the Olivet Discourse because of God's rejection of Israel, then he is forced to see the tribulation events of the Olivet Discourse as relating *only* to the church and not at all to Israel. In other words, if it is true that Jesus was addressing the *church* in His discourse rather than the now rejected nation of Israel, then what Jesus said in His discourse has *no* relationship to Israel. Gundry has in essence removed Israel altogether from the Lord's picture of the coming tribulation. This, however, contradicts posttribulationism which sees the church *with* Israel in the tribulation. Gundry (whether he wants to or not) excludes Israel from the tribulation described in the Olivet Discourse. This simply points up the serious internal problem Gundry has in this argument in addition to the previously stated scriptural problems.

The heart of Gundry's entire position is developed in the second stage of his third argument where he examines certain internal contextual elements. In evaluating this stage this writer can agree with Gundry that the "truly significant question" is whether the Jewish elements in the Olivet Discourse are there because Jesus was addressing Jewish Christians in the church who *live* in Palestine or because He was speaking to *religious* Jews who are thus not members of the church. Gundry maintains that the Jewish elements in the Olivet Discourse show that Jesus is speaking to national, Christian Jews, and that therefore the discourse relates to the church instead of Israel. However, two serious weaknesses make this conclusion untenable.

First, Gundry assumes that his argument proves something that it in fact does not. He offers three examples of the Jewish elements within the Olivet Discourse (persecution in the synagogues, the gospel of the kingdom, and the flight on the Sabbath) and attempts to show from these that the discourse relates better to the church (or to the churches within Israel) than to Jewish tribulation saints. However, even if one were to accept what Gundry says in regard to each of the three examples he sets forth, one need conclude only that it is *possible* for these elements to relate to churches in the tribulation; but it is just as possible that they relate to religious nonchurch Jews. Gundry's arguments do not prove that these Jewish elements can refer *only* to the church while excluding any possible reference to Israel. They merely show that these elements can refer either to the church or to Israel.

Each of the three elements needs to be examined individually.

Gundry speaks first of Jesus' warning of persecution from Jewish leaders in synagogues (Mark 13:9; Luke 21:12), and states that Jesus elsewhere speaks of persecution of Christians by synagogue leaders (John 16:2). Undoubtedly Jesus *could* have been addressing Christians in His warning, but He could equally have been addressing Jewish nonchurch tribulation saints and warning them of the persecution they will receive for their acceptance of the true Messiah. Second, Gundry argues that the phrase "this gospel of the kingdom" (Matt. 24:14) could appropriately describe the message of the church in the tribulation and that it cannot be regarded as "exclusively Jewish."[23] While that may be true, that phrase can just as appropriately describe the message of Jewish tribulation saints. Gundry's assertion that the "gospel of the kingdom" is "exclusively churchly" cannot be supported. Third, Gundry discusses the flight on the Sabbath (Matt. 24:20). While he very cleverly interprets this to include possible churchly relevance (as described earlier in this chapter), the same reasons he advances to show why the church would experience resistance could apply equally well to Jewish saints (or anyone, for that matter) who violated rabbinic sabbatical regulations. His answer allows for churchly relevance but does not exclude other interpretations.

Gundry fails to prove that "Jewish elements" in the Olivet Discourse must in fact be "churchly elements." He only shows that these three particular examples can apply to either the church or Israel. However, he does not offer even one example of an *exclusively* "churchly element" in the discourse. Thus what he proves again is only the possibility of his position.

The second (and major) serious weakness in Gundry's second stage in this argument is that he fails to deal with *other* Jewish elements in the discourse which must without question be Jewish and cannot be Christian. The discourse itself provides additional data not mentioned by Gundry which can be brought to bear on this issue.

The first thing to note is that Gundry does not even mention the questions asked by the disciples which prompted Christ to give the discourse. In order to interpret the discourse properly it is imperative that one understand what the disciples asked.

Dunham makes a helpful observation. "The meaning of their questions is based upon *their understanding*. One must remember they had walked and talked with the Lord for three years, that they had studied the Old Testament records, and that their understanding of Jewish apocalyptic thought was not as poor as some would like to think it was!"[24] The point here is that the disciples could not ask questions concerning things of which they were totally ignorant; they had to know enough about the problem to be able to frame an intelligent question. Further, as Dunham indicates, their knowledge (from which their questions arose) revolved around *Jewish* concerns. The disciples were Jews who recognized Jesus as the Messiah sent to Israel, and their natural concern was for their nation Israel, their questions then would center on Israel.

In addition, the apostles would obviously be concerned for their nation at the beginning of Matthew 24 because of Jesus' previous lament over Jerusalem, His sadness of heart at the nation's hardness, and His pronouncement of judgment in Matthew 24:2. Foremost in the apostles' minds would not be the church and its rapture out of the world, but rather Israel and what would happen to her because of her stubbornness. Walvoord correctly comments:

> Up to this point [Matt. 24:1] the disciples had had no instruction on this subject [rapture of the church]. They did not even clearly understand the difference between the first and second comings of Christ. Their questions indicated that they were first of all concerned about the destruction of Jerusalem which Christ had predicted in Matthew 24:2, as this obviously signaled some tremendous event.[25]

In fairness to Gundry and in the interest of honest academic pursuit, one must consider the possibility that the apostles were thinking of the church instead of Israel in forming their questions. But is this what is indicated by the text? Certainly the apostles did have some understanding of the church. In Matthew 16:18 Peter (and the apostles) first learned of a coming "church" which Christ would build, and in Matthew 18:15–20 Christ instructed them in the right approach for dealing with sin in the church. According to the scriptural record the apostles knew *only* this much concerning the church. In answer to the question of what they had in mind in forming their questions—the coming church (of which they had feeble knowledge), or their nation Israel (which had been the focus in the conflict leading up to Matt. 24)—it seems obvious that they would be feeling deep concern at this point for their beloved nation Israel.

This conclusion is confirmed by looking at the questions asked. "As Jesus was sitting on the Mount of Olives, the disciples came to him privately. 'Tell us,' they said, 'when will this happen [i.e., the destruction of the temple], and what will be the sign of your coming and of the end of the age?'" (Matt. 24:3).

> The disciples pointed to the temple and Christ predicted its destruction. Then they asked for a sign of His coming and the end of the age. Their questions are in the same frame of reference as in Acts 1:6: "Lord, wilt thou at this time restore again the Kingdom to Israel?" In the discussion which follows, there is no reference to any resurrection, nor to the Church, nor to its rapture. The questions were asked in the context of Jewish concerns and Christ answered them in terms of the Jews' future.[26]

It seems obvious that the apostles were expressing Jewish concerns in their questions. But if they were not thinking of the Jewish age (in which they were living), then to what could they possibly be referring? The *Christian* age? This is highly unlikely. The apostles' knowledge of the church was so minimal at this point in God's progressive revelation that they would not even be aware of a definite Christian age, for although they were at least knowledgeable of a coming church, they knew absolutely nothing about that coming church except that Christ would build it. Gaebelein makes the same observation, stating that "the disciples knew nothing of a Christian age. Such an age could not even begin, when they asked the question about the end of the age. They did not mean a Christian age, but their Jewish age."[27] So the apostles were asking about the termination of their present age, "during which," as Walvoord says, "from their point of view, they could still be living."[28]

By not dealing with the apostles' questions Gundry has omitted some very pertinent scriptural data concerning the context of the Olivet Discourse. The questions do not reflect the inquiry of Jesus' followers into God's activities with the church in the church age. Instead, the disciples were asking specifically about God's future direct relations with their beloved nation Israel.

With this intent of the questions in mind, it must be recognized that it is possible for Jesus to respond differently from what was indicated by the questions' intentions. Jesus could have chosen not to deal with God's future relations with Israel but rather to speak about God's future relations to the church. But did He do this? Gundry affirms that Jesus *did* speak about the church, and he shows how three particular "Jewish elements" can be seen as relating to the church. However, other "Jewish elements" in the Olivet Discourse *not* dealt with by Gundry show that Jesus was not addressing the church but was speaking about Israel and her future.

First, Jesus speaks of the "abomination of desolation which was spoken of through Daniel the prophet" (24:15). Gundry merely mentions this statement without comment.[29] Jesus' reference to this prophecy by Daniel relates *strictly* to Israel with no reference whatsoever to the church. The abomination is prophesied to the nation Israel as occurring in the 70th "week" of Daniel, and there is no reference to the church being part of this week (seven years) of judgment. This one particular "Jewish element" of the discourse then must remain exclusively Jewish and cannot refer to the church.

Second, Jesus mentioned the rise of ψευδοπροφῆται, "false prophets," who will mislead many (24:11, 24; Mark 13:22). The New Testament uses this term eight times in addition to its occurrences in the Olivet Discourse (Matt. 7:15; Luke 6:26; Acts 13:6; 2 Peter 2:1; 1 John 4:1; Rev. 16:13; 19:20; and 20:10). The references to ψευδοπροφήτης in Revelation are clearly to "*the* false prophet," who will work with the Roman beast. Of the remaining five usages, four refer clearly to false "Jewish" prophets (the only possible exception being 1 John 4:1 where the term most likely includes false Jewish prophets, but need not refer to them exclusively). By far the most common usages of the word, though, are in reference to false prophets in Judaism. For example, Acts 13:6 speaks of "a certain magician, a Jewish false prophet whose name was Bar-Jesus." Again Luke 6:26 says, "Woe to you when all men speak well of you, for in the same way their fathers [obviously Jewish] used to treat the false prophets." In His Sermon on the Mount Jesus spoke of "false prophets who come to you in sheep's clothing" (Matt. 7:15). The context here is unquestionably Jewish. Finally and most notably, 2 Peter 2:1 states, "But false prophets also arose among the people, just as there will also be false teachers among you." Here false prophets are distinguished from ψευδοδιδάσκαλοι, "false teachers." The implication is clear: False prophets were Israel's trouble; false teachers are the church's problem. Jesus' use of ψευδοπροφήτης, then, in the Olivet Discourse calls for a Jewish understanding of the term unless some contrary internal contextual evidence can be advanced to show that the word has taken on some different and rare meaning. Since there is no such evidence contextually, it is best to understand the word to refer to false prophets in Judaism. Again this "Jewish element" in the discourse remains Jewish and does not relate to the church.

One final example that can be advanced is Jesus' warning concerning ψευδόχριστοι, "false Christs," and those who claim to be ὁ χριστός , "the Christ." This reference in the Olivet Discourse of necessity must refer to Israel and simply cannot refer to the church. It is nonsensical to imagine that Jesus is warning *Christians* that they need to be aware of false Christs. A Christian is one who recognizes Jesus to be the true Christ, the real Messiah; it is this recognition followed by faith in Him that makes one a Christian. The church then is in no danger of following after a false Christ. Why? Because they know the real One. Whom then could Jesus be warning? Obviously the warning is to Israel through the apostles (who represent their nation Israel—this nation that anxiously looks for her Messiah). Jesus warned Jews in the tribulation not to be deceived by false Christs no matter what signs and wonders they perform. *Israel* is in danger of following false Christs because she has not yet recognized the true Christ. Unquestionably this is another example of an exclusively Jewish element in the context of the Olivet Discourse which proves, along with the other contextual items not discussed by Gundry, that Jesus addressed the nation Israel and its future in accord with the intent of His apostles' questions.

TIME OF JERUSALEM'S DESTRUCTION

Gundry's fourth argument concerns the destruction of Jerusalem in the church age. Gundry wrongly associates the *time* in which the fulfillment of Jesus' prophecy (Luke 21:20) occurs with the prophetic *event* itself. The occurrence of the destruction of Jerusalem during the church age does not mean that the fulfillment of that prophecy relates at all to the church. As Feinberg has commented, the destruction of the temple concerns the *Jewish* nation; it is a Jewish event, and the time (in the church age) is irrelevant to both the prophecy and its fulfillment.[30]

Further, Gundry uses an inconclusive form of argumentation here. He argues that the ultimate fulfillment of the Olivet Discourse is analogous to the precursive fulfillment. Since the precursive fulfillment happened in the church age, then by analogy the tribulational fulfillment will also occur while the church is on the earth.[31] This is extremely weak argumentation, for an analogy does not demand that every item between the two analogous events correspond in every detail. What is needed is proof that not only was the church present during the destruction of Jerusalem but that it will *in fact* be present during the tribulation. On two accounts, then, the fourth argument fails to establish Gundry's desired position.

APOSTLES' ASSOCIATION WITH THE CHURCH

Gundry falls into the trap of inconclusive argumentation in his final point when he uses an in-principle argument. In endeavoring to show which group (Israel or the church) the apostles represent, he goes to numerous New Testament passages to show that they represent the church. He is right in this, but the problem is that the bulk of the passages he presents are in the book of Acts and in the Epistles where the apostles do represent the church for they are by this time an integral *part of* the church.[32] But to show what the apostles *became* is not to prove what they were in Matthew 24. He argues that since numerous examples of the disciples representing the church can be found elsewhere in the New Testament, they must therefore represent the church in Matthew 24. This is like arguing that Abraham Lincoln represented the United States of America while he was a young, rail-splitting youth because there is much evidence from later in his life that he in fact did represent the nation as its president.

Gundry's few references to passages in the Gospels cannot show that the apostles at the time of Matthew 24 represented the church because these (Matt. 18:15–18 and John 14:1–3) speak of the *future* when the apostles will be members in Christ's church. As Walvoord states, "The question as to whom any particular passage is addressed cannot be settled by the fact that it was given to the disciples, because they represent in some sense both Israel and the Church. The issue must be settled on the subject matter. . . ."[33] Independent evidence must be sought within the immediate context of Matthew 24 to decide which group the apostles represent there. As has been shown, the immediate context compellingly calls for the apostles to represent Israel and her interests and future. Even though the apostles later came to represent the church, the immediate context of Matthew 24 supports their identification with the nation Israel.

Conclusion

In spite of Gundry's bold attempt to see the church in the tribulation of the Olivet Discourse, such a position cannot be upheld. Though some of his arguments make it possible to see the church in the tribulation, none of them shows conclusively that Jesus addressed the church through His apostles. Further, when evidence neglected by Gundry is considered, it becomes evident that the apostles represent their nation Israel. Their questions reflected an interest in Israel's future, and Jesus responded directly to their inquiries by prophesying about the coming events in their Jewish homeland.

To reiterate what was stated at the outset of this chapter, such a conclusion (that the Olivet Discourse details the coming events for Israel, not the church) does not automatically make pretribulationism the correct theory. It does, however, provide substantial support to the pretribulational position while greatly weakening the posttribulational theory. On this foundation further investigation can be done in other biblical passages to understand better God's plan for the church and its relationship to the events described in the Lord's discourse on the Mount of Olives.

CHAPTER 15

The Comforting Hope
of 1 Thessalonians 4

John F. Walvoord

Although the rapture of the church was introduced by Christ the night before His crucifixion, as recorded in John 14:1–3, the details of the rapture were not revealed in Scripture until 1 Thessalonians was written. It is not too much to say that 1 Thessalonians 4–5 is probably the most important passage dealing with the rapture in the New Testament. Additional passages are 1 Corinthians 15:51–58 and 2 Thessalonians 2:1–12; but more detail is given in 1 Thessalonians 4 than in any other passage.

Probably more pretribulationists base their conclusion for a pretribulational rapture on 1 Thessalonians 4 than on any other single passage of Scripture. By contrast, evidence indicates that posttribulationists find little of a positive character to help them in the details of this revelation. It would seem natural, if the great tribulation actually intervened before the rapture could be fulfilled, that this would have been a good place to put the whole matter into proper perspective, as Christ did in Matthew 24 in His description of the events leading up to His second coming.

The Problem of Death in Relation to the Rapture

As this central passage on the rapture is discussed, one should keep in mind that the Thessalonian Christians had had only a few weeks of doctrinal instruction before Paul, Silas, and Timothy left them. It is amazing that their instruction included such doctrines as election (1:4), the Holy Spirit (1:5–6; 4:8; 5:19), conversion (1:9), assurance of salvation (1:5), sanctification (4:3; 5:23), and teachings on the Christian life. Obviously there were great gaps in their understanding of theology in general, and more particularly of the prophetic future events.

It is most significant that in every chapter in 1 Thessalonians

199

some mention is made of the future coming of Christ. The Thessalonians are described as those who are "to wait for His Son from heaven" (1:10). They will be trophies of Paul's gospel ministry at the coming of the Lord (2:19), and their ultimate sanctification is promised when Christ comes (3:13).

Although 1 Thessalonians 4:13–18 is addressed to correct their ignorance about the rapture, it is quite clear that Paul was not introducing a new subject, but clarifying an old one. He had faithfully told them of the possibility of Christ's coming, and with this eager expectation they were exhorted to wait for the rapture. It is implied that the thought had not occurred to them that some of them would die before the rapture. Accordingly, when some of their number, after such a brief time, had passed into the presence of the Lord through death, they were unprepared for it.

As many commentators have pointed out, it is possible that the hopelessness of the pagan world may have affected their hope in resurrection. Yet the certainty of resurrection to which Paul referred in 1 Thessalonians 4:14 is so inseparable from the Gospel itself that it seems highly questionable that they had any real doubt whether their loved ones in Christ would be resurrected. Rather, their problem was how the future resurrection related to Christ's coming for the living saints. This was the problem Paul attacked and concerning which they needed further revelation.

As 1 Thessalonians 4:13–18 clearly shows, their fears were groundless. Their loved ones who had died would be resurrected, for all practical purposes, at the same time that the living would be raptured. They would therefore not have an inferior experience, and those living who were raptured would not have to wait for a period of time until their loved ones were resurrected.

Posttribulational Interpretation of 1 Thessalonians 4

Posttribulationists usually do not treat 1 Thessalonians 4–5 extensively. Gundry is an exception and devotes a whole chapter to it.[1] Ladd discusses it for only a few pages, with references scattered throughout his discussion, while devoting a third of his book to the historical argument for posttribulationism.[2]

In 1 Thessalonians 4, posttribulationists face a major difficulty. As presented here, the hope of the rapture is an imminent hope with no events such as the great tribulation regarded as intervening. Posttribulationists must find some explanation for this silence and for the major problem that the hope of the Lord's return is presented as a comfort to the Thessalonians who were sorrowing for their loved ones who had died. The hope of a rapture occurring after a literal great tribulation would be small comfort to those in this situation. Thus posttribulationists have marshaled a number of arguments in an attempt to answer both problems and others that face them in this passage.

Generally posttribulationists encounter the following problems in 1 Thessalonians 4: (a) the nature of this supposed delay of the resurrection of the dead in Christ, (b) the nature of the revelation claimed to have been received "by the word of the Lord," (c) the meaning of the revelation that saints will meet the Lord in the air, (d) the problem of emphasis on translation as opposed to resurrection, (e) the problem of silence concerning any warning of the coming great tribulation, and (f) the problem of the exhortation to comfort in view of the rapture of the church.

THE NATURE OF THE SUPPOSED DELAY

The first problem faced by all expositors is discerning the reasons for the unusual sorrow of the Thessalonians over the death of their fellow believers. Various explanations have been given as to why they feared a delay in the resurrection of the dead in Christ that would place it after the rapture of the church. Pretribulationists have a plausible explanation of that fear in that the Thessalonian believers may have assumed that the resurrection of the dead in Christ will occur at the end of the great tribulation when the tribulation martyrs will be raised (Rev. 20:4). Even Gundry mentions this. "We might think that the sorrow of the Thessalonians derived from the mistaken belief in a remaining behind of deceased believers at a pretribulational rapture with a consequent later date of resurrection, perhaps after the tribulation."[3] This would make sense if the Thessalonians had been taught pretribulationism.

In rejecting the pretribulational explanation of the Thessalonians' possible belief in the delay of the resurrection of the dead in Christ, Gundry offers instead another interpretation. He writes, "The Thessalonians further thought that departed brethren, along with the wicked dead, will not rise until after the Messianic kingdom, and thus will miss the blessedness of Christ's earthly reign. This view gives a more substantial basis for the Thessalonians' sorrow than the notion that the dead in Christ will be left out of the pretribulational rapture."[4] It is curious that

Gundry discards the pretribulational argument because it is based on an assumption, but considers as cogent and plausible the posttribulational argument also built on an assumption.

There are some real problems with Gundry's explanation. First, it is a new interpretation never before adopted by any other writer, whether pretribulational or posttribulational. Second, Gundry offers no factual support for his view. Third, pretribulationists can point to the fact that the Thessalonians had had some instruction on tribulation in general (cf. 1 Thess. 3:4), as well as the coming great tribulation specifically (2 Thess. 2:5–6). In other words they had in mind the idea of a coming great tribulation which would be a time barrier between the rapture, if viewed as imminent, and the resurrection of the dead in Christ, which might occur after the great tribulation. Fourth, there is no indication anywhere in the Thessalonian epistles that their instruction included details of the millennium.

Gundry is grasping at a straw in injecting an explanation of the problem that has no support in the Scriptures. He undoubtedly does this only because he has no more plausible view to offer. While the Thessalonians might conceivably have had some grounds for confusion concerning the time of resurrection if they were pretribulational in outlook, why would they consider a delay necessary until after the millennium which was really not their immediate concern?

While both pretribulationists and posttribulationists can only speculate concerning the reason for the Thessalonians' concern, it seems the pretribulationists at least have some scriptural support for their view, whereas Gundry has none.

THE NATURE OF THE REVELATION OF THE RAPTURE "BY THE WORD OF THE LORD"

Most scholars have little trouble with the expression "by the word of the Lord" (1 Thess. 4:15) by which Paul explained the source of his information about the rapture. Gundry seizes on this expression, however, to offer several explanations, including a rather fanciful proposal for the meaning of this term. He claims Paul may have gotten this from oral tradition of Jesus' teaching in the Olivet Discourse.[5] For this Gundry has to claim the existence of oral tradition transmitted so accurately that Paul would have before him these precise sayings of Jesus. This is extreme conjecture that has no support in any factual information possessed

by New Testament scholars and is especially contradicted by
Galatians 1:15–19, in which Paul disavowed transmission of
information from the apostles to him. As Galatians was written
about the same time or even later than 1 Thessalonians, it would
make Paul's claim that he had not received transmitted information
applicable to both epistles.

The purpose of Gundry's explanation is to avoid the idea that
the rapture is a new revelation distinct from the second coming to
the earth. One gets the impression that Gundry is unnecessarily
belaboring a point which is actually not essential to his
posttribulationism. It is much more plausible to hold, as most
other posttribulationists do, that Paul received this truth. as he did
the Gospel as a whole, by direct divine revelation. While the
doctrine of Christ's coming is a truth clearly revealed in both the
Old and New Testaments long before 1 Thessalonians was written,
the concept of a translation of living saints going to heaven
without dying was a new idea; even posttribulationists like Ladd
have no trouble accepting this. It is rather surprising that Gundry
will go to such lengths to prove a point that is actually irrelevant.

THE QUESTION OF WHY SAINTS
MEET THE LORD IN THE AIR

A crucial point in the revelation of 1 Thessalonians 4 is the
truth that the saints at the time of the rapture will meet the Lord in
the air. As this is the express statement of Scripture, both
posttribulationists and pretribulationists must accept this revelation
as valid. The question remains, however, why the saints meet the
Lord in the air, and what will happen after this event.

Pretribulationists have an easy answer because for them it is
the fulfillment of John 14:1–3 in which Christ promised to come
for His own and take them to the Father's house, which is
considered equivalent to heaven. Gundry's spiritualization of the
term "the Father's house" to avoid from the idea that the saints go
to heaven has been discussed and refuted by the present writer.[6]
Pretribulationists therefore view Christ's coming to the air above
the earth as fulfillment of His purpose to receive His bride and
take her back to heaven to the Father's house.

Posttribulationists have a twofold problem: (a) to explain why
the church will leave the earth to meet the Lord in the air, and (b)
to prove that the saints, having met the Lord in the air, will change
direction and proceed to the earth.

Gundry debates this as follows:

> Other things being equal, the word "descend" (*katabaino*) indicates a
> complete, uninterrupted descent, like that of the Spirit at Christ's baptism
> (Matt. 3:16; Mark 1:10; Luke 3:22; John 1:32, 33) and that of Christ in
> His first advent (John 3:13; 6:33, 38, 41, 42, 50, 51, 58). Where a reversal
> from downward to upward motion comes into view, a specific statement
> to that effect appears, as in Acts 10:11, 16 ("a certain object coming
> down. . . . and immediately the object was taken up into the sky"). In the
> absence of a statement indicating a halt or sudden reversal of direction,
> we naturally infer a complete descent to the earth, such as will take place
> only at the posttribulational advent.[7]

It should be noted that Gundry is attempting to solve this
problem by definition of a word, a definition quite arbitrary and
slanted in the direction of his conclusion. The text does declare
that the church will meet the Lord in the air, which at least implies
a halt for the meeting, even if it does not specify a change in
direction. Gundry here again appeals to the argument from silence,
which so often he disavows for the pretribulational view. He says,
"But surely it is strange that in this, the fullest description of the
rapture, there should be no mention of a change in direction from
earthward to heaven, or of a halt. The absence of a specific phrase
such as 'to the earth' cannot be very significant, for there is not
one NT account of the second coming which contains such a
phrase."[8] Here, on the one hand, Gundry argues from silence that
there should be mention of a change in direction if such took
place, but he discounts the silence of the passage on any indication
of its continued direction to the earth.

Actually a meeting such as this does not necessarily indicate
continued movement in the same direction. In Mark 14:13 the
disciples were to meet the man bearing a pitcher and follow him.
In Luke 17:12, which records the incident of the lepers meeting
Christ, He made no effort to accompany them back to where they
came. Although the Greek words used here are different from
those in 1 Thessalonians 4, the passage confirms the idea that to
assume a meeting in the air requires Christ to continue to earth is
reading into the passage what it does not say and does not require.

Most posttribulationists are silent on why the church rises from
the earth at all, though Gundry comments on this.[9] Why would it
not be better for the saints to remain on earth when Christ returns
and allow Him to separate them from the unsaved? This, in fact, is
what pretribulationists believe will occur at the second coming of
Christ to the earth, when the living Israelites will be separated

from other nations and gathered for judgment (Ezek. 20:34–38), and the sheep and the goats are gathered on earth to be separated (Matt. 25:31–46). Indeed, at the second coming of Christ, He will proceed directly to the earth without any interruption at all (see Rev. 19 and similar passages). His coming for the rapture, however, has a different purpose, namely, to take the church out of the earth.

From the pretribulational standpoint, therefore, it is plausible that the church should meet Him in the air. From the posttribulational standpoint, it is an unnecessary and an unlikely event. While neither posttribulationists or pretribulationists can argue with finality from the text of 1 Thessalonians 4 on this point, it becomes obvious that the posttribulationists have more of a problem than the pretribulationists on the clearly stated meeting in the air. If the purpose of Christ is to take the church out of the earth to heaven, meeting Christ in the air would be natural. If the purpose of Christ is to come to the earth, it is not really necessary for the church to rise from earth into the air. Accordingly, for the posttribulationist to say that there is implication that Christ will come all the way to the earth at the rapture is an unsupported assertion.

THE EMPHASIS ON TRANSLATION AS OPPOSED TO RESURRECTION

In the interpretation of 1 Thessalonians 4, all agree Paul was explaining that the resurrection of the saints will occur at the same time as the translation of the living. The timing of the two events is a new revelation to the Thessalonians. However, as far as Scripture as a whole is concerned, the doctrine of resurrection is a familiar truth found in both the Old and New Testaments, whereas the idea of a translation of living saints is a new revelation. Thus the main point for Christians today is that 1 Thessalonians 4 presents in clear detail the fact that Christians living in the last generation will not die, but will meet the Lord and enter into their eternal relationship to Him without experiencing death.

In these facts, posttribulationism has a specific problem. Passages relating to the second coming of Christ to the earth, such as Revelation 20:4, speak of resurrection *after* the arrival on earth at the time Christ enters His kingdom, not *during* His descent from heaven. The resurrection, however, is specified as relating to the martyred dead of those in the immediately preceding generation who had refused to worship the world ruler and consequently died for their faith. There is no indication in this text that the resurrection extends to any other class of people, such as the church as a whole.

In a similar way, Daniel 12:2 refers to a resurrection occurring after the tribulation mentioned in Daniel 12:1. This seems to refer to Old Testament saints, or at least to include them. In none of the passages in the Old or New Testaments where a resurrection is tied to the second coming of Christ to the earth is there any clear identification that the church is included. From the standpoint of pretribulational interpretation, this is no accident, but a clear revelation that all people are not raised at the same time. Revelation 20, of course, also distinguishes the resurrection mentioned in verse 4 from the resurrection of the wicked which will occur after the millennium (v. 12).

Posttribulationists usually argue that since the resurrection of Revelation 20:4–6 is said to be "the first resurrection," no resurrection can precede it, such as a rapture at the beginning of the tribulation. Arguing along this line, Ladd asks the question, "Does the Word similarly teach that the first resurrection will consist of two stages, the first of which will occur at the beginning of the Tribulation? No such teaching appears in Scripture."[10]

The problem here is the common misunderstanding of what the word "first" means. "First" does not mean the number one resurrection, but rather that the resurrection here revealed occurs before the final resurrection in the millennium, mentioned in Revelation 20:12–14. It merely means that the resurrection occurs first or *before* the later resurrection.

Indeed, everyone has to agree that the resurrection of Jesus Christ Himself is the first resurrection. Any subsequent resurrection could not be resurrection number one. Also, in Matthew 27:52–53 a token resurrection of some saints occurred in Jerusalem at the time of Christ's resurrection. The resurrection of Christ and these saints is the token of the resurrections to come. Accordingly, if there can be two separate resurrections which are already history, why should it be thought incredible that there should be more than one resurrection of the righteous still to be fulfilled, namely, the resurrection of the church (the saints of the present age) before the tribulation, and the resurrection of the Old Testament saints and the tribulation saints who die just before the time of Christ's coming to set up His kingdom? Logically, no argument can be built for posttribulationism on the word "first" because all these resurrections are "first," or before the final resurrection of the wicked at the end of the millennium.

The real embarrassment of the posttribulationists, however, is that not a single passage referring the resurrection at the time of Christ's second coming to the earth has anything at all to say about a translation of any saints, much less a specific translation for the church living on the earth. Most pretribulationists insist that there is no translation at all at the end of the tribulation; instead, the saints then living on earth enter the millennial kingdom in their natural bodies, not translated bodies. In view of the many passages that deal with both the subject of resurrection and the second coming of Christ to the earth, it is certainly a strange silence that there should be no clear passage indicating that any of the saints living on earth at that time should be translated. The alleged translation of the saints in Matthew 24:40–41 has already been demonstrated to be no rapture at all, but a taking away in judgment.

Therefore the emphasis on translation in 1 Thessalonians 4 and in other passages such as 1 Corinthians 15:51–52, which have no clear contextual relationship to Christ's second coming to the earth, leaves the posttribulationists groping for any proof that the rapture occurs at the end of the tribulation. Their frequently asserted accusation against the pretribulationists—that pretribulationism is based on inference—is a hollow charge when it follows that posttribulationism is also built on an inference. The fact that a translation is necessary to the resurrection of 1 Thessalonians 4 sets this apart as different from any other resurrection mentioned in the Bible, which includes no translation of living saints.

LACK OF WARNING OF GREAT TRIBULATION

The rapture passages are distinguished by there being no warning of an impending great tribulation. In every instance where the rapture is clearly intended there is an absence of impending events, in contrast to revelations concerning the second coming of Christ, such as Matthew 24 or Revelation 4–18. If they are at all comprehensive, they uniformly mention events that precede and serve as signs of the approaching second coming. By contrast, these signs are lacking in all the major rapture passages.

This is especially pointed out in 1 Thessalonians 4, where the truth of the rapture is presented in considerable detail. No word of caution is given contextually that believers should not look for this event until other events occur first—which is quite in contrast to the revelation concerning the second coming to the earth. Posttribulationists have no real answer to this problem, and they tend to ignore it.

THE EXHORTATION TO COMFORT

Undoubtedly the greatest problem posttribulationists face in 1 Thessalonians 4 is that the doctrine of the rapture is offered as a comfort to those who have lost loved ones in Christ through death. It is certainly a hollow argument to say that the truth presented is that of their resurrection. There seems to be no serious question that the Thessalonians believed in the doctrine of resurrection. They did have questions as to when this would occur in the prophetic scheme. This was primarily because the hope of the Lord's return for living Christians had been taught to them as an imminent hope, and they were actually waiting momentarily for His return.

If, as Gundry and Ladd agree, the great tribulation will be a time of great suffering and trial with many martyrs, and a Christian who enters this period must somehow survive the edict that all nonworshipers of the beast be put to death before he can hope to be raptured as a living saint, then the expectation of survival through such an awful period of suffering is small comfort. It would mean first that they could not possibly see their loved ones for years to come. It would mean that in the path ahead lay extreme suffering and privation and probable martyrdom. How, under these circumstances, could they derive any comfort from such a sequence of events? It would be far better from their point of view if the tribulation were to be indefinitely postponed and they were to live out normal lives and die and await resurrection at the rapture. That prospect would certainly be preferable to the possibility of survival through the great tribulation.

Though not totally ignoring this point, posttribulationists have still to explain how the Thessalonians could derive any comfort whatever out of a posttribulational rapture, and how this would add at all to their faith and expectation at the time that they had lost loved ones through death. Those who, like J. Barton Payne, deny a literal, seven-year tribulation and therefore have a concept of genuine imminency of the Lord's return can with some justification offer comfort to Christians whose loved ones have died. But others, like Ladd and Gundry, who agree to a literal seven-year tribulation offer a most unconvincing solution by simply saying that the ultimate hope of resurrection is all that is in view. If the only way a Christian can experience the rapture is to survive the tribulation, it is no longer either a comforting hope or a blessed hope. Instead there should be grim preparation for what is probable martyrdom in the most awful time of human suffering and persecution of which Scripture speaks.

Gundry posits several arguments to seek to solve this difficulty in posttribulationism. In general, he first tries to soften the rigors of the tribulation by making it a time of satanic wrath instead of divine wrath. This has been previously discussed.[11] Actually, if his view of the tribulation is right, it works against what he is trying to prove, because Satan's wrath is specifically against Christian believers and Israel. If Gundry is right, it emphasizes the rigors of the tribulation, instead of softening them. Any reasonably literal interpretation of the book of Revelation, such as Ladd and Gundry attempt, should make clear that probably the majority of believers who are in the great tribulation will perish. The percentage of Jews who perish in the land is said to be two-thirds (Zech. 13:8). The world's population as a whole will probably be reduced to less than half (Rev. 6:8; 9:15). Such a prospect is hardly harmonious with a message of comfort. Only an imminent translation could provide real comfort.

Even posttribulationists like Ladd recognize that the translation of the living saints is the most important truth. Ladd writes,

> God had never before revealed to men what would be the particular lot of the living saints at the end of the age. The doctrine of the resurrection had long been taught (cf. Dn. 12:2), but the fact that the living are to put on the resurrection bodies at the moment of the Lord's return without passing through death and join the resurrected dead in the presence of Christ is revealed for the first time through the Apostle Paul.[12]

Generally, posttribulationists tend to ignore the problem of how a posttribulational rapture could be a comfort. They dogmatically deny that comfort is affected by the prospect of the great tribulation. Gundry, for instance, attempts to dispose of the problem in two paragraphs.[13] Such a feeble attempt to erase the problem is an obvious confession that he has no realistic solution to offer. The prospect of the rapture after the tribulation is small comfort to those facing martyrdom. It is not too much to say that this is a most difficult problem to posttribulationists; as a group they tend to evade it rather than face up to it.

If a delay in the resurrection of the dead in Christ were a concern to the Thessalonian believers, how much more would have been their concern if they faced the prospect of dying as martyrs and joining these dead in Christ? Further, if martyrdom were a probability, they should have rejoiced that the dead in Christ had escaped the rigors of the tribulation. According to Revelation 14:3, the voice from heaven declares those who die as "blessed" because they will escape persecution in the great tribulation. As Hiebert expresses it, "But if they had been taught that the church must go through the great tribulation the logical reaction for them would have been to rejoice that these loved ones had escaped that great period of suffering which they felt was about to occur."[14]

Posttribulationists by and large do not solve their problems in 1 Thessalonians 4. The expectation of the Lord's return is uniformly pictured as an imminent event. Their prospect for imminent rapture was such that they feared a delay in resurrection for the dead in Christ. Posttribulationists have no adequate explanation for Paul's omission of any warning that the great tribulation was ahead and necessarily preceded the rapture; under the circumstances, such an omission would have been most misleading and contrasts sharply with the clear presentation of events leading up to the, second coming of Christ recorded in Matthew 24.

Summary of Posttribulational Interpretation of 1 Thessalonians 4

As a whole, the posttribulationists' interpretation of 1 Thessalonians 4 does little to advance their argument. They have no reasonable explanation how a posttribulational rapture offers comfort to sorrowing Thessalonians. They have no satisfactory answer why Paul was silent on the impending great tribulation. There is no good explanation why the rapture is portrayed as an impending event. There is no reasonable connection between this passage and the Olivet Discourse. The rapture of living saints was a new revelation not connected with tile second coming of Christ in previous revelations, as ever) posttribulationists like Ladd concede.

Obviously posttribulationism is at its weakest point in 1 Thessalonians 4, where the doctrine of the rapture has its most detailed revelation.

CHAPTER 16

The Rapture and the Day of the Lord in 1 Thessalonians 5

John F. Walvoord

The relationship of 1 Thessalonians 5 to the rapture has been debated by both pretribulationists and post-tribulationists with an amazing variety of opinions. The problem centers in the definition of "the day of the Lord" and its relationship to the rapture. Because there are differences of interpretation among both pretribulationists and posttribulationists, generalizations are inadvisable. The center of the problem is, first, the question of what "the day of the Lord" means. A second question is why the day of the Lord is introduced immediately after discussion of the rapture. A third issue is the meaning of specific statements relating to the time of the rapture.

The Meaning of the Day of the Lord

References to the day of the Lord abound in the Old Testament and occur occasionally in the New. Virtually everyone agrees that the judgments related to the second coming are in some sense a part of the day of the Lord. Definitions of the word "day" vary from a specific event, such as a 24-hour day, to an extended period of time stretching all the way from the rapture to the end of the thousand-year reign of Christ. Generally speaking, pretribulationists have identified the day of the Lord as the millennial kingdom, including the judgments that introduce the kingdom. This view was popularized by the 1917 edition of *The Scofield Reference Bible*.[1] In this interpretation, for all practical purposes, the day of the Lord begins at the end of or after the great tribulation.

Pretribulationists who see the day of the Lord beginning at the end of the tribulation have difficulty harmonizing this with the pretribulational rapture. Posttribulationists point out that 1 Thessalonians 5, referring to the day of the Lord, immediately follows chapter 4, which reveals the rapture. As chapter 5 is dealing with the beginning of the day of the Lord, the implication is that the rapture and the beginning of the day of the Lord occur at the same time. Capitalizing on the confusion among pretribulationists in defining the day of the Lord, Reese spends a chapter of his classic work on posttribulationism, making the most of this argument.[2]

Reese holds that the use of the expression "the day" indicates that endtime events all occur in rapid succession, including the translation of the church and the various judgments of the saints and the wicked. He identifies the day of the Lord in 1 Thessalonians 5 with other references to "the day" as found in 1 Corinthians 3:13 and Romans 13:11–12. He likewise so identifies the expressions "in that day" (2 Thess. 1:10; 2 Tim. 1:18; 4:8); "the day of Christ" (Phil. 1:6, 10; 2:16); "the day of the Lord Jesus Christ" (1 Cor. 1:7–8; 2 Cor. 1:14); and "the day of the Lord" (1 Cor. 5:4–5; 2 Thess. 2:1–3). According to Reese, all refer to the same time and the same event.

Reese and other posttribulationists, as their argument unfolds, lump together all references to "the day," ignoring the context, arguing in a circle, assuming that posttribulationism is true. As is frequently the case with difficult points of exegesis, it is of utmost importance that the context of each passage be considered before terms can be equated with similar wording elsewhere. Reese pays little attention to the variety of contextual backgrounds.

The central problem, however, is that this kind of explanation assumes that "the day" is a simple and uncomplicated reference to a point in time, whereas in fact the total view of Scripture indicates something quite different.

The subject of the day of the Lord is so extensive that a complete exposition would require a major work and would involve many references in both the Old and New Testaments. Nevertheless the matter can be simplified if truth relating to the day of the Lord is placed into three categories: (1) any period of time in the past or future when God deals directly in judgment on human sin; (2) a day of the Lord in the sense of certain specific future events constituting a judgment of God; (3) the broadest possible sense of the term, indicating a time in which God deals directly with the human situation, both in judgment and in blessing, hence broad enough to include not only the judgments preceding the millennium but also the blessings of the millennium itself.

In approaching the difficult problem of 1 Thessalonians 5, the broadest definition of the day of the Lord is indicated. This contrasts, for instance, with the use of the same term in 2 Thessalonians 2, where the narrower definition of the second category is illustrated. As this classification is not recognized by most posttribulationists and some pretribulationists, careful attention should be paid to every indication in 1 Thessalonians 5 as to the nature of the day of the Lord.

As many references to the day of the Lord make clear, the period involved is not a twenty-four-hour day, but rather an extended period of time—although the symbolism of a twenty-four-hour day is in view. Significantly the article "the" is not found in 1 Thessalonians 5, and therefore the phrase could be translated "a day of the Lord."

References to the day of the Lord, not actually a literal day, have in mind the symbolism of a day beginning at midnight and extending through twenty-four hours to the next midnight.

In this symbolism, the following points can be noted: (1) the day of the Lord indicates that the preceding day has ended as a time period, and a new time period has begun; (2) an ordinary day is usually a period of time which, at its beginning, is without major events—that is, people normally sleep from midnight until daybreak; (3) with the coming of the daylight, or after the time period is somewhat advanced, major events begin as the program for the day unfolds—as in a sense the day "comes to life" with daylight rather than at midnight; (4) as the morning hours of the day unfold, the major activities of the day take place, climaxing in the events of the evening hours; (5) as a twenty-four-hour day ends at midnight, a new day follows with a new series of events.

If the symbolism of a twenty-four-hour day is followed, the various facts revealed in Scriptures relating to the day of the Lord begin to take on meaning and relationship. In its broadest dimension, the day of the Lord follows the present day of grace in which God is fulfilling both His work of salvation by grace and His rule of life by grace; God is not attempting to deal directly in any major way with human sin. Hence the rapture could well be the end of the day of grace and the beginning of the day of the Lord. The day of grace, all agree, is followed by a period in which God does deal directly with human sin in a series of judgments continuing into the millennial kingdom, which will be also a period in which God deals directly with human sin. All agree also that after the millennium, the eternal state begins, which is another "day" that some believe is designated as "the day of God" (2 Peter 3:12), the eternal day.

Before determining the significance of 1 Thessalonians 5 in relation to eschatology as a whole, it is necessary to establish firmly exactly what the day of the Lord is, as it is variously described in the Bible. It is strange that so many expositions of 1 Thessalonians 5 do not establish a definition of the day of the Lord and do not take into consideration the specific facts furnished in the Old Testament as well as in the New.

The Old Testament Doctrine of the Day of the Lord

A study of numerous Old Testament references to the day of the Lord and "the day," as it is sometimes called, should make clear to anyone who respects the details of prophecy that the designation denotes an extensive time of divine judgment on the world. Among the texts are Isaiah 2:12–21; 13:9–16; 34:1–8; Joel 1:15–2:11, 28–32; 3:9–12; Amos 5:18–20; Obadiah 15–17; Zephaniah 1:7–18.

Examination of these references indicates, for example, that Isaiah 2 predicts that divine judgment will fall on the wicked. The passage could be applied to the Old Testament captivity, now past, or it could be applied to a future time in connection with the second coming of Christ. The main characteristic of the day of the Lord brought out in this passage is judgment on people who have been living in rebellion against God. It is clear that the judgment will extend for more than a single twenty-four-hour day, for it will be an extended period of divine judgment. It is a day of the Lord.

The dramatic picture of Isaiah 13:9–16, followed immediately by predictions concerning the destruction of Babylon by the Medes and the Persians, again gives graphic detail to the characteristics of the day of the Lord. It is described as "a destruction from the Almighty" (13:6). According to verse 9, "the day of the Lord cometh, cruel both with wrath and fierce anger, to lay the land desolate: and he shall destroy the sinners thereof out of it." Next Isaiah said the stars and sun will be darkened, a prophecy that will be fulfilled literally in the great tribulation. In Isaiah 13:11, he states, "And I will punish the world for their evil, and the wicked for their iniquity; and I will cause the arrogancy of the proud to cease, and will lay low the haughtiness of the terrible."

Beginning with verse 17, Isaiah wrote of the Medes destroying Babylon. In one sense this has already been fulfilled. In another sense this will not have a complete fulfillment until the time of the great tribulation. It is this mingled picture of judgment, regardless of when it occurs, that characterizes the day of the Lord. Any period of extensive divine judgment in the Old Testament is therefore "a day of the Lord." All of them will be eclipsed, however, with the final judgment that culminates in the great tribulation and the battle of the great day of God Almighty at the second coming of Christ.

The other references cited contain similar material. Isaiah 34:1–8 seems to indicate that judgments will fall on the world in the events leading up to the second coming of Christ.

Probably the most graphic picture is found in the Book of Joel, most of which is dedicated to describing the day of the Lord. Included is the famous prophecy of the outpouring of the Spirit, quoted in Acts 2:17–21, which occurred on the Day of Pentecost but will have its complete fulfillment in the days prior to the second coming of Christ. The judgments of God poured out on the earth, as well as disturbances in heaven, are graphically described by Joel. There will be great signs in the heavens (Joel 2:30–31), described in more detail in the book of Revelation: "And I will shew wonders in the heavens and in the earth, blood, and fire, and pillars of smoke. The sun shall be turned into darkness, and the moon into blood, before the great and terrible day of the LORD come." What is meant here is not that the day of the Lord will begin after these wonders in heaven, but that it will come to its climax when the judgment is actually executed.

The Book of Zephaniah adds another aspect to the day of the Lord. After revealing in some detail the judgments to occur at that time, the prophet described the blessings that will follow (1:7–18). In Zephaniah 3:14–17 the prophet wrote, "Sing, O daughter of Zion; shout, O Israel; be glad and rejoice with all the heart, O daughter of Jerusalem. The LORD hath taken away thy judgments, he bath cast out thine enemy: the king of Israel, even the LORD, is in the midst of thee: thou shalt not see evil any more. In that day it shall be said to Jerusalem, Fear thou not: and to Zion, Let not thine hands be slack. The LORD thy God in the midst of thee is mighty; he will save, he will rejoice over thee with joy; he will rest in his love, he will joy over thee with singing."

The significant truth revealed here is that the day of the Lord which first inflicts terrible judgments ends with an extended period of blessing on Israel, which will be fulfilled in the millennial kingdom. Based on Old Testament revelation, the day of the Lord is a time of judgment, culminating in the second coming of Christ, and followed by a time of special divine blessing to be fulfilled in the millennial kingdom.

Posttribulational Interpretation of the Day of the Lord

Generally posttribulationists like Reese and Gundry begin the day of the Lord at the end of the great tribulation. Gundry, who devotes a whole chapter to this, defines the day of the Lord in these words:

> The "day of the Lord," with its corollary the "day of Christ," figures prominently in discussion of the rapture. In these phrases the term "day" does not refer to twenty-four hours, but to a longer period of time, a period which includes the millennium and the final judgment. With reference to the time of the rapture, the crux of the argument lies in the *terminus a quo*, the beginning point, of the day of the Lord, not in its millennial extensions.[3]

In his discussion he attempts to refute the idea that the day of the Lord begins earlier than the end of the tribulation. His discussion is somewhat difficult to follow, but in general he tries to refute all the contentions that the day of the Lord begins before the end of the great tribulation.

All agree that the climax of the day of the Lord, as far as judgment on the nations is concerned, will come at Armageddon and will be furthered by the destruction of the armies at the second coming in Revelation 19. Many believe it is brought to its climax in the judgment of the nations after the second coming, as recorded in Matthew 25:31–46. The question remains whether this is all that is involved in the judgments.

Even a casual reading of the book of Revelation discloses that the divine judgments of God do not begin at the end of the tribulation, but certainly include the entire period of the tribulation itself. While Gundry attempts to rearrange the book of Revelation so that the major judgments fall at its close, it is quite clear, for instance, that the fourth seal described in Revelation 6:7–8— where one-fourth of the earth's population is destroyed is not at the end, but in the earlier phase of the great tribulation. Certainly the destruction of one-fourth of the population would qualify as a day of the Lord for the earth.

The sixth seal describes in vivid detail the very things the Old Testament attributes to the day of the Lord. It states, "And I beheld when he opened the sixth seal, and, lo, there was a great earthquake; and the sun became black as sackcloth of hair, and the moon became as blood; And the stars of the heaven fell unto the earth, even as a fig tree casteth her untimely figs, when she is shaken of a mighty wind, And the heaven departed as a scroll when it is rolled together; and every mountain and island were moved out of their places" (Rev. 6:12–14). This can be compared to Joel 2:30–31, as well as Joel 2:10–11. Unless the seals are twisted out of chronological sequence, this is not the end of the great tribulation; rather the great tribulation is in progress.

Gundry attempts to make all the catastrophic judgments of the seals, trumpets, and bowls as if they were in some way simultaneous. The very order of events described in the seven trumpets, however, as well as in the seven vials, indicates that there is chronological sequence and that all these judgments cannot be thrown together. The implication is clear that the great judgments of the day of the Lord extend over the entire great tribulation, even though all agree that they climax at its end, as God imposes final judgment on the nations.

Gundry's motive in placing the day of the Lord at the extreme end of the tribulation is to get the church raptured before major events of the day of the Lord take place. In effect, he is trying to achieve a pre-day-of-the-Lord rapture, with the great judgments at Armageddon occurring immediately afterward. If Gundry is wrong in limiting the day of the Lord to the extreme end of the great tribulation, however, his view of posttribulation rapture means that the church will go through most of the terrible judgments, even if they were raptured just before the climax. Gundry's posttribulationism is built on a faulty concept of the day of the Lord not supported by the Scriptures that define what occurs in that period.

Why Is the Day of the Lord Introduced in 1 Thessalonians 5?

In the debate between pretribulationism and posttribulationism, the question arises why the day of the Lord is introduced immediately after discussion of the rapture of the church. The fact that the rapture is mentioned first in chapter 4 before the day of the Lord is presented in chapter 5 is significant. The important subject was the rapture, including the resurrection of the dead in Christ and the translation of living believers. The rapture is not introduced as a phase of the day of the Lord and seems to be distinguished from it.

First Thessalonians 5 begins with the Greek particle δέ, which is normally used to introduce a new subject. It is found, for instance, when the rapture was introduced in 1 Thessalonians 4:13. Accordingly, it is clear that 1 Thessalonians 5 is not talking specifically about the rapture, but about another truth. The introduction of this material at this point, however, implies that it has some relationship to the preceding context. Accordingly, while it is not talking specifically about the rapture, it is dealing with the general subject of eschatology, of which the rapture is a part. To some extent, then, Paul was continuing his discussion by dealing with the broad program of endtime events as defined by the term "the day of the Lord."

For this reason Hiebert introduces his exegesis of 1 Thessalonians 5 with these words: "This paragraph is an appropriate companion piece to the preceding. It is the second half of the distinctively eschatological block of material in the epistle. The former offered needed instruction concerning the dead in Christ; this gives a word of needed exhortation to the living."[4]

The subject of chapter 5 is introduced with the statement, "But of the times and seasons, brethren, ye have no need that I write unto you." In contrast to instruction on the rapture, by which Paul was correcting their ignorance, he stated here that he need not instruct them concerning "the times" (χρόνοι) and "the seasons" (καίροι). Though these terms are sometimes used interchangeably and both relate to time, the first seems to indicate duration, and the second the character or nature of the times. The New International Version uses the words "times and dates."

In a word, Paul was saying that eschatological events involve a series of periods and events, of which the rapture is one, as he had already told the Thessalonians, and that specifically these events relate to the day of the Lord as a time period with special characteristics. In verse 2 he declared, "For yourselves know perfectly that the day of the Lord so cometh as a thief in the night." Much has been said about this figure of speech, and Paul expressed that they already knew what he meant by it. Obviously he was saying that they knew that the day of the Lord was certainly coming but, like the coming of a thief in the night, there was no way to date it.

In Paul's discussion that follows, a sharp contrast is drawn between the day of the Lord as it relates to the unsaved and as it relates to Christians. This is brought out in the use of the first and

second persons—"we," "us," and "you" (vv. 1–2, 4–6, 8–11)—
and the third person "they" and "others" (vv. 3, 6–7). In verse 3
the day of the Lord is pictured as coming on the unbelievers like
travail on a woman with child, so that they cannot escape, just as a
woman cannot escape birth pangs. Paul further stated that their
destruction will come at a time when they are saying "peace and
safety." Gundry does not explain why they will be saying "peace
and safety" toward the end of the great tribulation, as it does not
fit into his view. Payne has no problem with this and regards it as
a sense of false security that exists today in spite of atomic bombs
and the danger of a holocaust.[5]

The idea that the expression "saying peace and safety" refers to
the longing for peace and safety on the part of those who are in the
great tribulation is not an acceptable explanation and is rejected
by both posttribulationists and pretribulationists. The fact is that
Gundry is faced with the problem of trying to fit this into his
scheme with the day of the Lord beginning toward the end of the
great tribulation. First Thessalonians 5 states that people will be
saying "peace and safety" before the great tribulation begins. This
is in harmony with pretribulationism, but quite out of harmony
with posttribulationism.

Paul stated that the day of the Lord will not overtake the
Thessalonians as a thief. Why does an event coming as a thief
come unexpectedly on the world, but with proper expectation for
believers? Paul explained this in verses 4 and 5: "But you, brothers,
are not in darkness so that this day should surprise you like a thief.
You are all sons of the light and sons of the day. We do not belong
to the night or to the darkness" (NIV). Here is a crucial point in
Paul's explanation: the thief is going to come in the night, but the
believers are declared not to belong to the night or the darkness.
The implication is quite clear that believers are in a different time
reference, namely, that they belong to the day that precedes the
darkness.

On this basis Paul gave an exhortation. If the Thessalonians are
of the day, they are not to be asleep or drugged; rather they are to
be sober or self-controlled, "putting on faith and love as a
breastplate, and the hope of salvation as a helmet" (v. 8, NIV). Paul
concluded in verse 9, "For God did not appoint us to suffer wrath,
but to receive salvation through our Lord Jesus Christ" (NIV).

In the exegesis of this verse, pretribulationists and
posttribulationists part company. Posttribulationists insist that the

church is not appointed to wrath, and with this all pretribulationists agree. What the passage is talking about, however, is not wrath in the abstract, but a *time* of wrath. The judgments poured out in the tribulation do not single out unsaved people only, for war, pestilence, famine, earthquakes, and stars failing from heaven afflict the entire population except for the 144,000 of Revelation 7 singled out by God for special protection.

Here, however, the believer in Christ is assured that his appointment is not to this time of wrath. In attempting to explain this, the pretibulationist has the obvious advantage: if the church is raptured before this time of trouble, then all that is said in this passage becomes very clear; that is, the period of wrath will not overtake the church as a thief, because the church will not be there. If Gundry's use of the argument from silence is valid, it would seem here that Paul's silence on the matter of whether the church must endure this period is again another indication that the church will not even enter the period.

When the total picture of this passage is taken into consideration, the reason for Paul's introducing it becomes clearer. Though the events of the day of the Lord do not begin immediately after the rapture, the time period as such—following the symbolism of a day beginning at midnight—could easily be understood to begin with the rapture itself. The opening hours of the day of the Lord do not contain great events. Gradually the major events of the day of the Lord unfold, climaxing in the terrible judgments with which the great tribulation is brought to conclusion.

Taken as a whole, the pretribulational point of view gives sense and meaning to 1 Thessalonians 5 and explains why this is introduced after the rapture. In effect, Paul was saying that the time of the rapture cannot be determined any more than the time of the beginning of the day of the Lord, but this is of no concern to believers because our appointment is not the wrath of the day of the Lord, but rather the salvation which is ours in Christ.

Confirmation is given to this approach to 1 Thessalonians 5 in a study of 2 Thessalonians 2, where the day of the Lord is again introduced, this time in a context in which the Thessalonians misunderstood and needed correction.

A further word needs to be said concerning the relationship of the day of the Lord to "the day of Christ." Gundry argues at length that the various forms of the six occurrences of this phrase (1 Cor. 1:8; 5:5; 2 Cor. 1:14; Phil. 1:6, 10; 2:16) do not justify any distinction from the basic term "the day of the Lord." This is an exegetical problem that does not really affect the question of pretribulationism and posttribulationism. The contexts of these passages are taken by many to refer to the rapture as a specific event in contrast to the day of the Lord as an extended period of time. If the context of each passage, along with all the references to "the day," is taken into consideration, there is really no problem. Even if Gundry is right in holding that these passages refer to the day of the Lord, they can be understood to refer to the beginning of the extended period of time which follows. It is again begging the question to assume this teaches posttribulationism, as Gundry does.

Gundry summarizes his viewpoint in a way that misrepresents the pretribulational position. He states:

> In the NT sixteen expressions appear in which the term "day" is used eschatologically. Twenty times "day" appears without a qualifying phrase. In view of the wide variety of expressions and the numerous instances where "day" occurs without special qualification, it seems a very dubious procedure to select five out of the sixteen expressions, lump together four of the five as equivalent to one another, and distinguish the four from the one remaining. There is no solid basis, then, for distinguishing between the day of Christ and the day of the Lord.[6]

The reference in 1 Corinthians 5:5 has a textual problem, and some texts read "the day of the Lord." Pretribulationists are justified in distinguishing the remaining five texts from the day of the Lord because the expression "the day of the Lord" is not expressly used. Pretribulationists do not claim that this proves the pretribulation rapture; what they point to is that if the pretribulational rapture is established on other grounds, these references seem to refer specifically to the rapture rather than to the time of judgment on the world. This is based on what each passage states. It is therefore manifestly unfair to accuse pretribulationists of arbitrarily lumping things together that have no distinguishing characteristics. On the contrary, the posttribulationist is lumping together a number of different phrases that are not quite the same without any regard for the context or their precise wording.

Reese proceeds much on the same basis as Gundry when he declares that all references to "the day" refer to the day of the Lord.[7] He does this without any supporting evidence. Yet the word "day" occurs more than two hundred times in the New

Testament alone and is an eschatological term only when the context so indicates. The only way all these eschatological terms can be made to refer specifically to the day of the Lord is to assume that posttribulationism is true and to argue from this premise. Pretribulationists rightfully object to this illogical procedure.

Taken as a whole, 1 Thessalonians 5—while not in itself a conclusive argument for pretribulationism—is more easily harmonized with the pretribulational interpretation than the posttribulational interpretation. The passage is quite strange as an explanation of the time of the rapture if, in fact, the Thessalonians were taught posttribulationism and already knew that they would have to go through the day of the Lord. The beginning of the day of the Lord under those circumstances would have no relationship to the rapture and would be no comfort to them in their sorrow. On the other hand, if the rapture occurs before the endtime tribulation and the day of the Lord begins at the time of the pretribulation rapture, then the discussion is cogent because the indeterminant character of the beginning of the day of the Lord is the same as the indeterminant time of the rapture itself,

Nowhere in 1 Thessalonians 4 or 5 is the rapture specifically placed after the great tribulation and as occurring at the time of the climax of the judgments which are brought on the world at the time of the day of the Lord. On the contrary, the Thessalonians were assured that their appointment was not to a day of wrath but a day of salvation, a concept easily harmonized with the pretribulational interpretation.

CHAPTER 17

Pretribulationism As the Alternative to Posttribulationism

John F. Walvoord

hough it is not the purpose of this chapter to present pretribulationism as such, as this has been done in the author's *The Rapture Question*,[1] a summary of pretribulationism is in order.

Clarity of Pretribulational Premises

Because posttribulationists are largely in confusion in their basic presuppositions, they are open to the charge of contradiction and illogical reasoning. By contrast, pretribulationists bring into focus the major issues that relate to eschatology.

THE PRINCIPLE OF LITERAL INTERPRETATION OF PROPHECY

Among posttribulationists there is a wide divergence on the issue of the basic principles of biblical interpretation, especially as related to prophecy. Even conservative interpreters like Payne spiritualize prophecies when they seem to contradict posttribulationism.[2] Gundry, who attempts a literal interpretation of prophecy, spiritualizes when a literal interpretation would contradict posttribulationism.[3] Lack of consistency among posttribulationists in principles of interpretation have undoubtedly contributed to their lack of agreement among themselves and confusion on important points in posttribulationism. Pretribulationists do not need to spiritualize prophecy in order to support the pretribulational rapture and are more consistent in their application of the principle of literal interpretation of prophecy.

THE CHURCH CONTRASTED WITH ISRAEL

Although Gundry is a major exception, most posttribulationists fail to distinguish the scriptural program for the church, the body of Christ, and the program of God for Israel. The confusion of

Israel and the church is one of the major reasons for confusion in prophecy as a whole, as illustrated in both amillennialism and posttribulationism. Gundry attempts to distinguish Israel and the church, but in order to support his posttribulationism he has to invent some novel explanations. Only in pretribulationism is the distinct program for the church clearly defined.

A LITERAL FUTURE TRIBULATION

Posttribulationists are at odds among themselves as to the nature of the tribulation, some holding that it is a literal future period, and others that it is already past. Pretribulationism holds with clarity to a future great tribulation and to a literal fulfillment of the events and situations that will characterize this period. One of the principal causes for confusion among posttribulationists is their lack of consistency on the subject of the future tribulation.

Arguments for Pretribulationism

As presented in the author's *The Rapture Question*, at least fifty arguments may be given for pretribulationism.[4] Some of the more important arguments are stated here.

CONTRASTS BETWEEN THE RAPTURE
AND THE SECOND COMING

Probably the most important reason for pretribulationism is the evident contrast between the details revealed concerning the rapture and the description given of the second coming of Christ to establish His kingdom. These contrasts describe these two events as different in purpose, character, and result.[5]

An analogy can be drawn between the contrasts in the Old Testament between the first and second comings of Christ, and the contrasts in the New Testament between the rapture and the second coming of Christ to the earth. In the Old Testament, the first and second comings of Christ were mingled, but can now be distinguished because of the major contrasts of the sufferings of Christ relating to His first coming and the glory of Christ relating to His second coming.

It is doubtful whether anyone comprehended the difference between the first and second comings of Christ until the prophecies of the first coming were fulfilled. In interpreting the distinctions between the rapture and the second coming of Christ, interpreters do not have the benefit of fulfilled prophecy as a basis of interpretation, but the same approach that enables one to distinguish the first coming from the second coming of Christ helps distinguish the rapture from the second coming to the earth.

Only the pretribulational interpretation can account for these sharp contrasts and the literal interpretation of the various factors relating to these two future events. Inevitably posttribulationists are forced to spiritualize to some extent in order to explain away the evident contrasts.

SILENCE OF SCRIPTURE ON A POSTTRIBULATIONAL RAPTURE

Posttribulationists tend to make much of the fact that the Scriptures, in presenting the rapture, do not provide an ordered sequence of events which states in so many words that the rapture is first and the tribulation follows. Many eschatological problems, of course, would be resolved if the Scriptures specifically stated, for instance, that Christ's coming is premillennial or if the Old Testament clearly outlined the first coming of Christ to be followed by the present church age and then the second coming of Christ. The form of divine revelation given in Scripture does not always provide such an itemization.

While the argument from silence is never conclusive, most posttribulationists are not willing to admit that the silence in Scripture concerning a posttribulational rapture is much more significant than the silence in Scripture concerning the tribulation following the rapture. While no passage attempts to relate the rapture to a sequence of events, the second coming of Christ is revealed in a detailed way.

In Matthew 24, as well as in Revelation 4–19, specific revelation of events leading up to the second coming and a description of the second coming of Christ itself is provided. In view of this itemization, it is therefore most significant that the rapture is never mentioned at all when many other events are itemized. Accordingly, the rhetorical question of posttribulationists as to where the Bible teaches a pretribulation rapture actually boomerangs on the posttribulationist because he is unable to come up with any statement of a posttribulational rapture, even though the events preceding and following the second coming are given in great detail.

In the argument from silence, posttribulationists also attempt to evade the fact that the church, the body of Christ, is never mentioned in a tribulation passage. Many posttribulationists spiritualize the tribulation and make the church equivalent to the saints of all ages. The complete silence of the Scriptures on the subject of the church as such in the great tribulation has considerable weight. On the whole, the argument from silence is more damaging to the posttribulational view than it is to the pretribulational interpretation.

IMMINENCE OF THE RAPTURE

As presented in all major passages on the rapture, the coming of Christ for His church is uniformly presented as an imminent event. This is in sharp contrast to the presentation of the doctrine of the second coming, which is consistently presented as following a sequence of events—including the return of Israel to the land, the rise of the dictator in the Middle East (sometimes referred to as the Antichrist), and the forty-two months of the great tribulation detailed in the book of Revelation. The second coming of Christ to the earth in no proper sense can be called an imminent event, even though posttribulationists strain to redefine the English word "imminent" as meaning something other than an event that is immediately pending. Only by complete spiritualization of the major events leading up to the second coming of Christ can this problem be avoided by posttribulationism, and in this spiritualization a major principle of proper interpretation of eschatology is sacrificed.

The claim of many contemporary posttribulationists that they represent the historic position of the church is true only if they spiritualize the tribulation. Futurists like Ladd and Gundry offer a position that is quite different from the early church fathers and, as a matter of fact, it is more recent than pretribulationism as is commonly taught today. The fact that the rapture is presented as an imminent event is a major argument for distinguishing the rapture from the second coming of Christ to the earth.

THE DOCTRINE OF A LITERAL TRIBULATION

Pretribulationists regard the great tribulation as a future event and rightly place the rapture as occurring before this time of unprecedented trouble. By contrast, there is confusion among the posttribulationists on this point and an amazing lack of uniformity in applying the principles of interpretation. Posttribulationists are caught in the twin problem of either carrying the church through the great tribulation with resulting martyrdom for probably the majority of the church, or spiritualizing the period and thereby introducing the principles of interpretation that lead not only to posttribulationism, but also to amillennialism and a denial of any reasonable order of events for the endtime.

The difficulty of harmonizing the rapture as the blessed hope with the prospect of martyrdom and the problem of maintaining premillennialism while holding to posttribulationism has continued to plague some of the major interpreters of the posttribulational view. By contrast, the pretribulation view offers a clear and simple explanation. The blessed hope is the rapture of the church before the great tribulation. The second coming of Christ to the earth follows the tribulation. Pretribulationists accordingly are not forced to spiritualize or to evade the plain teaching of Scripture on the subject of the rapture or of the great tribulation.

AN ORDERED CHRONOLOGY OF EVENTS

The pretribulational interpretation allows the interpreter of both the Old and New Testaments to establish an order for endtime events that makes sense. While many details may not be revealed, the major events of the endtime as commonly held by pretribulationists can be established. By contrast, it would be difficult to find two posttribulationists who agree on any system of events relating to the endtime. The reason for confusion among the posttribulationists is a lack of uniformity in principles of interpretation that results in disagreements as to the extent of spiritualization required. While large prophecy conferences are held by pretribulationists with evident agreement of the speakers on major events of the endtime, no such conference has ever been held by posttribulationists for the simple reason that they do not have any major agreement among themselves. Accordingly prophecy conferences are almost the exclusive domain of the pretribulational interpretation.

Because of the confusion among posttribulationists as to how endtime events should be ordered, it is natural that there should be confusion on the interpretation of prophecy as a whole—and this is exactly what the contemporary theological scene reveals. While pretribulationism is a single system of interpretation on major events, posttribulationism is divided among many schools of interpretation, with great variation, even on major events. Pretribulationism continues to be the key to establishing a system of eschatological interpretation.

EXHORTATIONS RELATING TO THE RAPTURE
HARMONIZED WITH PRETRIBULATIONISM

An important basis for pretribulationism is found in the nature of the exhortations given in connection with the revelation of the rapture. In John 14, the disciples were exhorted, "Let not your heart be troubled" (v. 1). If it were evident that they would have to go through the great tribulation first, they had every reason to be troubled. As a matter of fact, most of the disciples had already died as martyrs when the apostle John recorded the words of John 14. It is evident that he was repeating these great promises because of their application to the church as a whole in keeping with the general revelation of the Upper Room Discourse in John 13–17.

In a similar way, the exhortation of 1 Thessalonians 4:18 extending comfort to the Thessalonians in the deaths of their loved ones, in harmony with the possibility of the return of Christ for them at any time, would be devoid of any real meaning if they had to go through the great tribulation first. While many generations of Christians have died before the rapture, it is evident that the exhortation given to the Thessalonians applies to each succeeding generation which continues to have the bright hope of an imminent return of the Lord for His own.

The exhortations of the major passage on the rapture in 1 Corinthians 15:51–58 are similar in their implications. Not a word of warning is given concerning a coming tribulation, but the readers are exhorted to live in the light of the imminent return of Christ. This hope is defined by Paul in Titus 2:13 as "that blessed hope, and the glorious appearing of the great God and our Savior, Jesus Christ." The hope of a rapture after enduring the great tribulation is hardly a happy expectation, and this passage is difficult for posttribulationists to explain. The hope is not that of resurrection after death and martyrdom, but rather the coming and revelation of Christ in His glory to them while they are still living on the earth. The exhortations relating to the rapture constitute a major problem to posttribulationism.

THE RAPTURE IN RELATION TO PREMILLENNIALISM

Posttribulationists who are premillennial are caught in the vise of a dilemma. If they spiritualize the great tribulation to avoid the problems of harmonization with a posttribulational rapture as J. Barton Payne does, they are adopting principles of interpretation that lead logically to amillennialism, which spiritualizes not only the tribulation but also the millennium itself. If, as premillenarians, they take the great tribulation literally, then they have the problem of harmonizing the imminence of the rapture and exhortations relating to it with a posttribulational rapture. The dilemma facing posttribulationism accounts for the general confusion that exists among them on endtime events.

Logically, posttribulationism leads to amillennialism and pretribulationism leads to premillennialism. Any compromise between these two points of view leads to confusion in principles of interpretation as well as in the interpretation itself. The obvious difficulty in moving from a posttribulational rapture into a millennium with saints on earth who have not been raptured forces interpreters like Gundry to postulate a second chance for salvation after the rapture, a doctrine nowhere taught in Scripture and expressly denied in the book of Revelation (14:9–11).

The evident trend among scholars who have forsaken pretribulationism for posttribulationism is that in many cases they also abandon premillennialism. For those who wish to think consistently and logically from principles of interpretation, the options continue to be (a) a pretribulational rapture followed by a premillennial return of Christ to the earth, or (b) abandoning both for a posttribulational rapture and a spiritualized millennium. It becomes evident that pretribulationism is more than a dispute between those who place the rapture before and after the tribulation. It is actually the key to an eschatological system. It plays a determinative role in establishing principles of interpretation which, if carried through consistently, lead to the pretribulational and premillennial interpretation.

Advantages of Pretribulationism

By way of summary, three major considerations point to the advantages of the pretribulational point of view.

PRETRIBULATIONISM AS A LOGICAL SYSTEM

While writers in all schools of biblical interpretation can be found who are guilty of illogical reasoning, careful observers of posttribulationism will find that so often their conclusions are based on illogical reasoning. In some cases their arguments hang on dogmatic assumptions which they do not prove. In other cases they draw conclusions from Scripture passages under consideration which the passages actually do not teach. The fact that an interpreter is a great scholar does not necessarily make him a logician; unfortunately, ability to do research and skill in linguistics do not necessarily lead to formation of logical conclusions. The writer believes that a major problem in posttribulationism is logical inconsistency. By contrast, pretribulationism moves logically from its premises and principles of interpretation to its conclusion.

EXEGETICAL ADVANTAGES OF PRETRIBULATIONISM

In contrast with posttribulational treatment of major passages on the rapture which differs widely in interpretation, pretribulationists follow a consistent pattern of literal or normal interpretation. This allows the interpreter to explain the passage in its normal meaning—which in many cases is its literal meaning—without resorting to flagrant spiritualization in order to avoid the pointed contrasts between the rapture and the second coming of Christ to the earth.

It is rather significant that, without any attempt to establish uniformity in eschatology, the Bible institute movement of America is predominantly premillennial and pretribulational. This has come from taking Scripture in its plain, ordinary meaning and explaining it in this sense. By contrast, educational institutions that have approached the Bible creedally tend to make Scriptures conform to their previously accepted creed with the result that most of them are liberal or, if conservative, tend to be amillennial.

Pretribulationism has continued to appeal to thousands of lay interpreters because it makes sense out of the passages that deal with the rapture of the church. While the majority of biblical scholars may disagree with pretribulational interpretation, it is also significant that they disagree radically among themselves as well.

PRACTICAL ADVANTAGES

In all the major rapture passages, the truth of the coming of the Lord is connected with practical exhortation. While it is undoubtedly true that eternal values remain in other interpretations, only the pretribulationists can consistently hold to a moment-by-moment expectation of the Lord's return along with the literal interpretation of the promises that are to be fulfilled following the Lord's coming. For the pretribulationist, the coming of the Lord is an imminent hope. For the great majority of others, there is only the somewhat blurred expectation of how the coming of the Lord really fits in to the pattern of future events. It is for this reason that pretribulationists hold tenaciously to their point of view, defend it earnestly, and believe the doctrine of the imminent return of Christ an important aspect of their future hope.

CHAPTER 18

The Rapture in Revelation 3:10

Jeffrey L. Townsend

E qually sincere and devout students of the prophetic Scriptures hold differing views on the time of the rapture of the church in relation to the tribulation. This is due in large measure to the fact that no verse of Scripture specifically states that relationship. But Revelation 3:10 comes close: "Because you have kept the word of My perseverance, I also will keep you from the hour of testing, that hour which is about to come upon the whole world, to test those who dwell upon the earth." Consequently, as Gundry has stated, "Probably the most debated verse in the whole discussion about the time of the Church's rapture is Revelation 3:10."[1]

In Revelation 3:10 the church at Philadelphia is promised protection from the hour of testing. The great pretribulational/ posttribulational debate over this verse concerns the nature of the protection promised. Pretribulationists maintain that the church is here promised preservation *outside* the hour of testing by means of the rapture (external preservation). Posttribulationists, on the other hand, argue that the church is preserved *in* the hour of testing (internal preservation). The solution to the problem of the nature of the protection promised the church is bound up in the phrase, σε τηρήσω ἐκ τῆς ὥρας τοῦ πειρασμοῦ   ("I will keep you from the hour of testing").

The Meaning of "Keep From"

Although τηρέω is often translated "keep," a better rendering in Revelation 3:10 would be "reserve" or "protect" since great trials are in view in the hour of testing.[2] Whatever the promise involves, its great fruit will be the genuine preservation and protection of the church during the hour of testing.

This presents an immediate problem for posttribulationism since it holds that the church will be preserved on earth during the hour of testing. Yet verses such as Revelation 6:9–10; 7:9, 13, 14;

13:15; 14:13; 16:6; 18:24; and 20:4 present a time of unprecedented persecution and martyrdom for the saints of the tribulation period. Gundry identifies these saints as members of the church.[3] One wonders with Sproule, "If multitudes of Christians are going to die under the fierce persecution of Antichrist, Satan, and the wicked, then *in what way* has God preserved them through the tribulation?"[4] Moreover, it must be questioned whether this kind of "preservation" would be of any comfort and encouragement to the persecuted Philadelphians. In effect the posttribulational scheme denies the meaning of preservation in τηρέω.[5]

The preposition ἐκ is the focal point of the debate over whether Revelation 3:10 promises internal or external preservation from the hour of testing. The standard lexicons and grammars are in agreement on the basic meaning of the preposition. According to Robertson, "The word means 'out of,' 'from within,' not like ἀπό or παρά."[6]

Applying this meaning to Revelation 3:10, posttribulationists interpret the verse in two ways. Reese states both views: "The use of *ek* in Rev. 3:10 distinctly implies that the Overseer would be in the hour of tribulation; the promise refers, either to removal from out of the midst of it, or preservation through it."[7] Posttribulationists who hold the latter view tend not to see any reference to the rapture of the church in Revelation 3:10 but only to preservation of the church during the hour of testing.[8] This is an untenable position because the idea of preservation in and through the hour of testing would normally have been expressed by ἐν or διά.[9]

This leaves Reese's first view which, in modified form, is the view of Gundry. In a rather lengthy study of ἐκ Gundry makes the following assertions:

> Essentially ἐκ, a preposition of motion concerning thought or physical direction, means *out from within*. Ἐκ does not denote a stationary position outside its object, as some have mistakenly supposed in thinking that the ἐκ of Revelation 3:10 refers to a position *already* taken outside the earthly sphere of tribulation. . . . If ἐκ ever occurs without the thought of emergence, it does so very exceptionally.[10]

These statements pose a real problem for pretribulationism for it appears that τηρέω ἐκ must look at "protection issuing in emission," a concept in line with posttribulationism.[11]

However, sufficient evidence exists throughout the history of the meaning and usage of ἐκ to indicate that this preposition may also denote *a position outside its object with no thought of prior existence within the object or of emergence from the object.*

Ἐκ IN CLASSICAL LITERATURE

Liddell and Scott list several examples of ἐκ, chiefly in the early writers, with the heading, "of Position, *outside of, beyond.*"[12] For example, in the following quotation from Murray's translation of *The Iliad*, the italicized portion is the translator's rendering of ἐκ βελέων : "Thereafter will we hold ourselves aloof from the fight, *beyond the range of missiles*, lest haply any take wound on wound. . . ."[13] In this and other references listed by Liddell and Scott[14] the meaning of ἐκ is clearly *not* motion "out from within." Gundry notes this evidence, but relegates it to early classical writers and certain lingering frozen forms of expression.[15] However, these writers have the effect of establishing that from the earliest times ἐκ can denote outside position (as well as motion "out from within").

Ἐκ IN THE SEPTUAGINT

Proverbs 21:23 exemplifies the fact that the idiom of outside position expressed by ἐκ continued into the era of the Septuagint: "The one who guards his mouth and tongue *keeps* (διατηρεῖ) his soul *from* (ἐκ) trouble."[16] This verse is significant not only because it provides an example of ἐκ meaning outside position, but also because it does so by using διατηρέω with the preposition. Though there are no examples of τηρέω with ἐκ in the Septuagint, διατηρέω with ἐκ has a very similar meaning. The preposition διά in composition with τηρέω simply intensifies the idea of keeping (hence, "to keep continually or carefully"[17]). Thus the Septuagint contains a very comparable idiom to that found in Revelation 3:10, and the meaning in the Septuagint is not "keep by bringing out from within," but rather "keep outside of." The ideas of prior existence in the object and emission from it are missing.[18]

Proverbs 21:23 is not an isolated case. Ἐκ with the idea of outside position is also found in expressions employing synonyms of τηρέω (cf. ἐξαιρέω with ἐκ in Josh. 2:13; ῥύομαι with ἐκ in Ps. 33:19 [Septuagint, 32:19]; 56:13 [Septuagint, 55:13]; Prov. 23:14).[19] Abbott notes that "Ps. 59:1–2 σῶσον ἐκ , ἐξελοῦ ἐκ , ῥῦσαι ἐκ, may mean, not 'Bring me safe *out* after I have fallen *in*,' but 'Save me [*by keeping me*] out (of the hands of my enemies who surround me).'"[20] In summary, the Septuagint offers examples of expressions which are not frozen forms and where ἐκ has the idea of outside position.

Ἐκ IN JOSEPHUS

The works of Josephus also provide examples of ἐκ used to express outside position rather than motion out from within. In perhaps the clearest example, the italicized portion is Thackeray's translation of ῥύομαι with ἐκ: "He *delivered* them *from* those dire consequences which would have ensued from their sedition but for Moses' watchful care."[21] The idea here is preservation rather than removal since the judgment of God was prevented by Moses' intercession.

Ἐκ IN THE NEW TESTAMENT

Examples of ἐκ carrying the idea of outside position have thus been found in each period of the development of the Greek language. Acts 15:29 establishes the fact that this meaning of ἐκ is also found in the New Testament. In Acts 15:28–29 the brethren in Jerusalem concluded their letter to the Gentiles in Antioch with instructions to abstain from certain practices that would be especially offensive to Jewish brethren. Their concluding remark is found at the end of verse 29: "*Keeping* yourselves *free from* (ἐξ ... διατηροῦντες) such things, you will do well." The expression employs διατηρέω in the form of a circumstantial participle with ἐκ. Like the expression with διατηρέω and ἐκ in Proverbs 21:23, the idea is outside position, not motion out from within.[22] The thrust of verses 28 and 29 is a request for future abstention (cf. ἀπέκεσθαι, v. 29a) from certain practices (outside position), not an accusation of current vices from which the brethren in Antioch must desist (motion out from within). As noted previously, διατηρέω differs from τηρέω only in the strength of the idea of keeping (hence "keeping ... free" rather than simply "keeping"). Consequently Acts 15:29 provides another construction which is very similar to τηρέω ἐκ in Revelation 3:10, and again the meaning is not keeping out from within, but keeping outside the object of the preposition.

In addition to Acts 15:29 at least four other verses in the New Testament contain verbal constructions with ἐκ in which ἐκ seems to indicate a position outside its object.[23] Each of these verses needs to be examined in some detail.

John 12:27. The use of ἐκ in John 12:27 is important because this verse, written by John, can shed light on his usage of the same preposition in the Book of Revelation.[24] Whether or not Jesus' words, "Father, save Me from this hour," express a question or a petition is relatively unimportant to the present discussion. The question at hand is whether Jesus was speaking about preservation from the coming hour of His death (ἐκ meaning outside position) or deliverance out of an hour which had already come to pass (ἐκ meaning motion out from within). The verb σώζω is capable of either idea.[25] Robertson is certain that Jesus had already entered the hour.[26] However, John 7:30 and 8:20 along with the immediate context of 12:23–24 seem to use "the hour" in reference to Jesus' betrayal and death which would be followed by His glorious resurrection. Evidently the request of the Greeks in 12:21 vividly brought to mind the hour of the Lord's impending death, but the actual occurrence of the hour was yet future. This is the conclusion of Smith who has written a helpful appendix on the significance of John 12:27 in relation to the rapture question in Revelation 3:10.

> That Jesus' suffering at this time was proleptic and anticipatory and that the "hour" spoken of was in reality still in the future is evident in that He Himself declares a few days later, "With desire I have desired to eat this Passover with you before I suffer" (Luke 22:15), and later still, just previous to His arrest, "Behold, the hour is at hand [Greek: *near*], and the Son of man is betrayed into the hands of sinners" (Matthew 26:45). The phrase "is at hand" always denotes proximity and never total arrival.[27]

It appears that Jesus was referring to preservation rather than deliverance with regard to the hour of His death. Thus John 12:27 is an example (which is parallel in many respects with Rev. 3:10) in the Johannine literature where the meaning of ἐκ is position outside the object of the preposition.

Hebrews 5:7. A second example of ἐκ indicating outside position is found in Hebrews 5:7, in which the Lord is said to have prayed "to the One [who was] able to *save* Him *from death*" (σώζειν . . . ἐκ θανάτον). The description of His prayers as being made "with loud crying and tears" and the reference to the Father as "able to save Him from death" indicates that the Gethsemane prayer is in view (Matt. 26:39; cf. Mark 14:36; Luke 22:42). This connection is significant for the present discussion since, as Hewitt points out, "If the prayer which Christ offered *with strong crying and tears* was a prayer to be saved 'out of ' death, it cannot easily be reconciled with another request made in the Garden—'Father, if thou be willing, remove this cup from me' (Luke 22:42)."[28] In order to reconcile Hebrews 5:7 with the Gospel accounts which stress preservation from death and not resurrection out of death, ἐκ must have the idea of position outside its object rather than emergence from the object.[29]

James 5:20. This passage presents yet another use of σῴζω with ἐκ where the meaning of the preposition is outside position. James writes, "He who turns a sinner from the error of his way *will save* his soul *from death*" (σώσει . . . ἐκ θανάτον). This sinner is defined in 5:19 as a brother who has strayed from the truth he once held (either doctrinal or moral) and who needs to be turned back (ἐπιστρέφω) to his former direction of life. The most natural way of understanding the context is to see this sinner as a true believer who has embraced erroneous doctrine or practice. The death in 5:20 then must be physical death. Wessel comments, "Since the NT teaches the security of the believer in Christ, it is best to take the reference to death as physical death. The early church believed and taught that persistence in sin could cause premature physical death (cf. 1 Cor. 11:30)."[30] This interpretation is supported by the context of 5:15–16 where sin is linked with the loss of physical health. If physical death is in view in James 5:20, then ἐκ cannot mean out from within. Instead it must mean position outside its object.

This study of ἐκ throughout its linguistic history and especially its usage in the New Testament has shown that the preposition may sometimes indicate outside position (whereas other times it means removal out from within). In relation to the interpretation of τηρέω ἐκ in Revelation 3:10, this finding establishes the pre-tribulational position as a bona fide grammatical possibility. To understand τηρέω ἐκ as indicating preservation in an outside position is well within the bounds of the linguistic history and usage of ἐκ.[31]

John 17:15. In order to determine the most probable meaning of τηρέω ἐκ in Revelation 3:10, its usage in John 17:15 must be considered. This is the only other occurrence of τηρέω with ἐκ in either biblical or classical Greek.[32] It is significant that both verses are Johannine and in both cases Jesus spoke the words. Hence much can be learned from John 17:15 about the meaning of τηρέω ἐκ in Revelation 3:10.

John 17:15 begins with a negative petition using αἴρω and ἐκ. Jesus uses these words to express His prayer that the disciples not be physically removed from the earth. Removal would be one way of preserving them spiritually in His absence, but it would violate their commission as witnesses (cf. John 15:27). It is significant that in the case of αἴρω with ἐκ the idea of motion in the verb naturally lends itself to the idea of taking ἐκ in the sense of motion out from within (cf. οἱ ἐρχόμενοι ἐκ , Rev. 7:14). This points up the necessity of considering the verb and the preposition together and not simply isolating the components of the expression. The context is also an important determining factor in deciding the exact force of the phrase. The disciples were in the world (John 17:11), so ἐκ must mean "out from within" in 17:15a.

In 17:15b the Lord contrasted (using ἀλλά) His first petition with a petition using τηρέω and ἐκ for preservation from the evil one.[33] Gundry asks, "How then can τηρέω ἐκ [in Rev. 3:10] refer to the rapture or to the results of the rapture, when in its only other occurrence the phrase opposes an expression [αἴρω ἐκ] which would perfectly describe the rapture?"[34] The answer lies in the combined effect of the verb and the preposition in the context—factors that Gundry tends to overlook.

Regarding the context, the disciples were in the world physically. This combined with the idea of motion in αἴρω demands that αἴρω ἐκ in John 17:15a be understood as removal out from within. However, John 17:15b *describes an entirely different situation.* The disciples were not in the evil one spiritually when Jesus prayed. This combined with the fact that τηρέω demands not the idea of motion but rather the idea of preservation indicates that τηρέω ἐκ in verse 15b be understood as preservation in an outside position.[35] This is in line with the pretribulational understanding of Revelation 3:10—just as the disciples were not in the evil one, so the Philadelphians were not in the hour of testing and the promise is that Jesus Christ will keep them outside that hour.

Gundry interprets John 17:15b as a prayer for the preservation of the disciples *in* the moral sphere of Satan, since they are to be left in the world (v. 15a).[36] However, both the immediate context and John's other writings argue against this interpretation. In the context of 17:11–16, the idea of keeping is related to salvation and the possession of eternal life, not preservation from the moral assaults of Satan. The issue is the keeping of salvation (i.e., the perseverance of the saints) not progression in sanctification (which is taken up in v. 17).

First John 5:18–19 is also against Gundry's premise. In 1 John

5:18 the evil one does not touch (ἅπτω) the one who has been born of God because the One who was born of God (Jesus Christ) keeps (τηρέω; cf. John 17:11) him. In 1 John 5:19 the apostle wrote, "We know that we are of God, and the whole world lies in the power of the evil one." Gundry's interpretation of John 17:15b as preservation *in* the moral sphere of Satan does not square with the Johannine emphasis on the separation of believers from the spiritual realm of the evil one.

Thus the idea in John 17:15b is not the moral sphere of the evil one (i.e., the world system), as Gundry and most posttribulationists suppose, but the spiritual realm of the evil one (i.e., spiritual death). The disciples were not in Satan's realm spiritually and Christ prays, using τηρέω ἐκ, that the Father would keep them so. Hence τηρέω ἐκ in John 17:15 is an expression for preservation in an outside position. Applied to Revelation 3:10, this evidence indicates that the pretribulational position is not only possible, but is also probable.

Revelation 3:10 may then be paraphrased, "Because you have held fast the word which tells of My perseverance, I also will preserve you in a position outside the hour of testing. . . ." This paraphrase points up an important nuance of meaning that must be recognized. Τηρέω ἐκ in Revelation 3:10 does not describe the rapture as such. Instead it describes the position and status of the church during the hour of testing. It describes the results of the rapture, not the rapture itself. Revelation 3:10 does not state directly how the church will be preserved outside the hour of testing. However, the remainder of the verse indicates that the proper logical deduction is preservation by means of a pretribulational rapture of the church.

The Meaning of "the Hour of Testing"

THE MEANING OF "THE HOUR"

The object of the preposition ἐκ in Revelation 3:10 is "the hour of testing" (τῆς ὥρας τοῦ πειρασμοῦ) . The preservation promised the Philadelphians is in relation to *a specific period of time*. This is indicated by the inclusion of τῆς as an article of previous reference. Jesus was speaking of *the* well-known hour of testing, a reference to the expected time of trouble, the tribulation period, before the return of Messiah (Deut. 4:26–31; Isa. 13:6–13; 17:4–11; Jer. 30:4–11; Ezek. 20:33–38; Dan. 9:27; 12:1; Zech. 14:1–4; Matt. 24:9–31).[37] This period is graphically portrayed in Revelation

6–18 (cf. "the great tribulation," 7:14; and "the hour of His judgment," 14:7).[38]

In relation to the rapture question, it is significant that the Philadelphian church is here promised preservation outside the *time period* of the tribulation. The combination ἐκ τῆς ὥρας thwarts the posttribulational view of the church being kept from trials while on earth during the hour of testing. As Thiessen notes, the promise "holds out exemption from the period of trial, not only from the trial during that period."[39] Ryrie comments, "It is impossible to conceive of being in the location where something is happening and being exempt from the time of the happening."[40]

Gundry attempts to "undercut stress on the term 'hour'"[41] in three ways. First, he claims that the hour will elapse in heaven as well as on earth. But the verse claims that this hour is coming on the οἰκουμένη (the "inhabited earth") and thus is related to the earthly time continuum. This was certainly John's perspective.

Second, Gundry claims that "the hour of testing" does not emphasize a period of time, but rather the trials during that period. Although Delling notes this possibility in his article on ὥρα, he gives Revelation 3:10 as an example of ὥρα in the general sense of "'the divinely appointed time' for the actualization [*sic*] of apocalyptic happenings."[42] Gundry's view errs in failing to square with the use of the definite article τῆς which indicates that a well-known hour (fixed in length by Dan. 9:27) is in view. A careful evaluation of the evidence seems to prove all the more that both time and event are inextricably linked.

Third, Gundry notes that in Jeremiah 30:7 (Septuagint, 37:7) Israel is given a similar promise of being saved from (σῴζω) with ἀπό in the Septuagint) the "time of Jacob's trouble" (cf. "hour of testing"). Even though ἀπό denotes separation more strongly than ἐκ, Israel is preserved within the time of trouble not outside it. Gundry concludes his argument by stating, "If a pretribulational rapture was not or will not be required for deliverance from the time of Jacob's distress, neither will a pretribulational rapture be required for preservation from the hour of testing."[43] This appears to be a strong argument until one considers the context of Jeremiah 30:7. Jeremiah 30:5–6 indicates that the nation is already in the great day of trouble when salvation comes. This is confirmed in Matthew 24 where the Jews are told to flee the persecution of the one who desecrates the temple and in Revelation 12 where the dragon persecutes the woman and her offspring. From this trouble, the nation is promised rescue in Jeremiah 30:7. Thus the promises are different and not comparable. Israel is promised rescue within the time of trouble,[44] the church is promised preservation from the hour of testing. Only the latter case demands rapture from earth to heaven.

THE SCOPE OF "THE HOUR"

The qualifying phrase, "which is about to come upon the whole inhabited earth," further describes the hour as imminent and worldwide in its impact. Τῆς μελλούσης ἔρχεσθαι goes beyond conveying future tense. It carries a note of imminency, as indicated by ἔρχομαι ταχύ which begins Revelation 3:11. Both the coming of the hour and the coming of the Lord are imminent. This connection indicates a relationship between the promise of keeping in 3:10 and the coming of the Lord in 3:11. There will be preservation outside the imminent hour of testing for the Philadelphian church when the Lord comes. This, in turn, indicates that although τηρέω ἐκ in 3:10 does not refer directly to the rapture of the church, rapture as the means of preservation is a proper deduction from the context.

"The whole inhabited earth" will be overtaken by this hour (cf. Rev. 2:10 where local persecution is in view). Since the church is to be preserved outside a period of time which encompasses the whole world, preservation by a pretribulation rapture is again seen to be a logical inference from the context. Only a rapture to heaven removes the church from the earth and its time continuum.[45]

THE PURPOSE OF "THE HOUR"

"To test those who dwell upon the earth" gives the purpose of the coming hour. In both secular and biblical Greek πειράζω has the root idea of a test that is applied in order to expose the true character of someone.[46] Usually πειράζω denotes negative intent— to test in order to break down, to demonstrate failure.[47] Hence the hour of testing will come on the whole world with the specific purpose of putting earth-dwellers to the test, which will demonstrate their utter failure before God. In other words, the tribulation period will provide condemning evidence for the judgments the Lord will carry out when He returns to the earth (cf. Matt. 25; Rev. 19:19–21; 20:4).

According to Johnson, τοὺς κατοικοῦντας ἐπί τῆς γῆς corresponds to the Hebrew idiom (יֹשְׁבֵי הָאָרֶץ) which, in Isaiah 24:1,

242 Vital Prophetic Issues

5, 6; 26:9, becomes a technical term for people on the earth during the time of Jacob's trouble.[48] The term is not all-inclusive since in each of its seven other uses in Revelation the reference is to unbelievers, and both pretribulationists and posttribulationists agree that there will be many saints in the tribulation period. The question is whether these saints are the preserved church (which is unlikely since many are martyred) or people who come to salvation during the tribulation and are martyred for their faith. In Revelation 13:8 and 17:8 an earth-dweller is further defined as one "whose name has not been written in the book of life from the foundation of the world." These are the nonelect of the tribulation period, and as a result they worship the beast (cf. Rev. 13:8, 14). On these earth-dwellers will come judgments that have the purpose of demonstrating openly their absolute and utter depravity (cf. Rev. 6:15–17; 9:20–21; 16:21). McClain notes, "In that hour the physical judgments will generally fall upon saved and unsaved alike."[49] But the special objects of testing and wrath will be the earth-dwellers.

Conclusion

In seeking a solution to the pretribulational/posttribulational debate over the nature of the preservation promised the church in Revelation 3:10, the preposition ἐκ was traced throughout its history in order to establish the fact that ἐκ may at times indicate outside position as well as at other times indicating motion out from within. This brought the pretribulational interpretation of Revelation 3:10 within the realm of possibility. In addition, John 17:15—the only other occurrence of τηρέω ἐκ in either biblical or classical Greek—was studied. Pretribulationists and posttribulationists alike note the similarity in meaning between John 17:15 and Revelation 3:10. Hence when it was determined that τηρέω ἐκ in the context of John 17:15 demanded the idea of preservation outside the evil one, this had the effect of making outside preservation the preferred (or most probable) interpretation of Revelation 3:10.

The preservation promised in Revelation 3:10 is in relation to a specific, well-known hour of trial, the future seven-year tribulation which is to precede Messiah's return and which is described in detail in Revelation 6–18. Revelation 3:10 teaches that the coming of this hour is imminent, that it is worldwide in its scope, and that the purpose of the hour is to put the ungodly earth-dwellers of the tribulation period to the test to reveal evidence of their wickedness in preparation for the Lord's judgments when He returns to the earth.

Although Revelation 3:10 describes the result of the rapture (i.e., the position and status of the church during the tribulation) and not the rapture itself, the details of the hour of testing just mentioned establish the pretribulation rapture as the most logical deduction from this verse. The promise of preservation is from a period of time which will envelope the whole world. Only a pretribulation rapture would remove the church completely from the earth and its time continuum. Thus the pretribulation rapture is found to be a proper logical deduction from the data found in Revelation 3:10.

Chapter Notes

Chapter 1

1. George N. H. Peters, *The Theocratic Kingdom* (Grand Rapids: Kregel, 1952), 1:494–95.
2. Ira D. Landis, *The Faith of Our Fathers and Eschatology* (Lititz, PA: By the author, 1946).
3. Louis Berkhof, *Systematic Theology* (Grand Rapids: Eerdmans, 1941), p. 708.
4. W. H. Rutgers, *Premillennialism in America* (Goes, Holland: Oosterbaan and Le Cointre, 1930), p. 64.
5. Ibid., p. 57.
6. A. H. Strong, *Systematic Theology* (Philadelphia: American Baptist, 1907), p. 716.
7. Arthur H. Lewis, *The Dark Side of the Millennium* (Grand Rapids: Baker, 1980), p. 6.
8. Gilbert Bilezikian, "Are You Looking for Signs—Or for Jesus?" *Christian Life*, September 1977, p. 17.
9. Ibid.
10. Ibid.
11. Ibid.

Chapter 2

1. Ramesh P. Richard, "Elements of a Biblical Philosophy of History," *Bibliotheca Sacra* 138 (April–June 1981): 108–18.
2. Ramesh P. Richard, "Non-Christian Interpretations of History," *Bibliotheca Sacra* 138 (January–March 1981): 13–21.
3. Frank C. Roberts, "Interpretation," in *A Christian View of History?* ed. George Marsden and Frank Roberts (Grand Rapids: Eerdmans, 1975), p. 11.
4. Ibid., p. 11, n. 3. He scores Hal Lindsey's book *The Late Great Planet Earth* as a clear "manifestation of a self-assured approach to history as one could find."
5. Arthur C. Danto, *Analytical Philosophy of History* (Cambridge: University Press, 1968), p. 3.
6. John F. Walvoord, *The Millennial Kingdom* (Grand Rapids: Zondervan, 1959), p. 133.
7. Ibid.

8. Robert Rendall, *History, Prophecy and God* (London: Paternoster, 1954), p. 66.

9. The main purpose of this article is to refute not postmillennialism but amillennialism, while setting up premillennialism as a viable philosophy of history. In any case postmillennialism is discounted both exegetically and theologically, for Revelation 20 proves the interregnum between the Parousia and the *telos*. If there is a millennium, it is after the second coming. The question is whether there is a millennium. The Parousia is not the *telos*, a position which most postmillennialists and amillennialists hold.

10. See *The Westminster Confession of Faith*, 7:3.

11. Charles C. Ryrie, *Dispensationalism Today* (Chicago: Moody, 1965), p. 18.

12. Alexander Patterson, *The Greater Life and Work of Christ* (Chicago: Moody, n.d.), p. 22.

13. Hoyt Chester Woodring, "Grace under the Mosaic Covenant" (Th.D. diss., Dallas Theological Seminary, May 1956), p. 37.

14. Erich Sauer, *The Dawn of World Redemption* (Grand Rapids: Eerdmans, 1951), p. 193.

15. Grant C. Richison, "God's Weltanschauung for Creation" (Th.M. thesis, Dallas Theological Seminary, May 1965), p. 17.

16. Nicolas Berdyaev, *The Meaning of History* (Chicago: Scribners' Sons, 1936), p. 21.

17. Rendall, *History, Prophecy and God*, p. 46.

18. For an excellent discussion on this view of theodicy and evil, see Norman L. Geisler, *The Roots of Evil* (Grand Rapids: Zondervan, 1978).

19. Sauer, *The Dawn of World Redemption*, p. 50.

20. Alva J. McClain, "A Premillennial Philosophy of History," *Bibliotheca Sacra* 113 (April–June 1956): 111–16.

21. Ibid., p. 115.

22. For good descriptions of the material aspects of the messianic kingdom, see Walvoord, *The Millennial Kingdom*, pp. 316–23, and J. Dwight Pentecost, *Things to Come* (Grand Rapids: Zondervan, 1958), pp. 487–90.

23. Hoyt Chester Woodring, "The Millennial Glory of Christ" (Th.M. thesis, Dallas Theological Seminary, May 1950), p. 22.

Chapter 3

1. Bernard L. Ramm, *Protestant Biblical Interpretation* (Grand Rapids: Baker, 1970), pp. 51–59.

2. J. R. de Witt, *What Is the Reformed Faith?* (Edinburgh: Banner of Truth, 1981), p. 4. As de Witt attempts to define the Reformed faith in the final paragraph, he uses "Calvinism" as a synonym for it.

3. Ibid., p. 3.
4. Louis Berkhof, *The History of Christian Doctrines* (Edinburgh: Banner of Truth, 1969), pp. 37–42.
5. H. G. MacKay, *Countdown to Eternity* (Chicago: Emmaus Bible School, 1973), p. 34. MacKay cites James Orr's lists of specific doctrines. Of interest is the fact that Orr cites eschatology as the major issue of the 19th century. His implication is that since the 19th century saw the development of modern premillennialism, this is now the orthodox view. This argument is suspect, however, since that issue is still under debate.
6. De Witt, *What Is the Reformed Faith?* p. 17.
7. Ibid.
8. Reinhold Seeburg, *The History of Doctrines* (Grand Rapids: Baker, 1977), p. 424.
9. Hermann Witsius, *The Economy of the Covenants* (London: T. Tegg and Sons, 1837). 1:26.
10. Robert G. Clouse, "Introduction," in *The Meaning of the Millennium*, ed. Robert G. Clouse (Downers Grove, IL: InterVarsity, 1977), p. 8.
11. Louis Berkhof, *Systematic Theology* (Grand Rapids: Eerdmans, 1941), p. 708.
12. Jay Adams, *The Time Is at Hand* (Phillipsburg, NJ: Presbyterian and Reformed, 1966), p. 9. Also see Anthony J. Hoekema, *The Bible and the Future* (Grand Rapids: Zondervan, 1979), pp. 173–74.
13. Ramm, *Protestant Biblical Interpretation*, pp. 53, 126; Milton Terry, *Biblical Hermeneutics* (Grand Rapids: Zondervan, 1974), p. 173; and Henry A. Virkler, *Hermeneutics: Principles and Processes of Biblical Interpretation* (Grand Rapids: Baker, 1981), p. 73.
14. Terry, *Biblical Hermeneutics*, p. 243. See also J. Dwight Pentecost, *Things to Come* (Grand Rapids: Zondervan, 1958), p. 72.
15. Witsius, *The Economy of the Covenants*, p. 259.
16. Ibid., pp. 280–81.
17. Berkhof, *Systematic Theology*, p. 279.
18. MacKay, *Countdown to Eternity*, p. 47.
19. Jack B. Rogers and Donald K. McKim, *The Authority and Interpretation of the Bible: An Historical Approach* (San Francisco: Harper and Row, 1979), p. 104.
20. C. Van der Waal, *Hal Lindsey and Biblical Prophecy* (St. Catherines: Paideria, 1978), p. 29.
21. *Westminster Confession*, chap. 7. It should be noted that even here the Reformers observed the various "dispensations" of the covenant of grace. Compare paragraphs 5 and 6.

22. MacKay, *Countdown to Eternity*, p. 48.

23. Seeburg, *The History of Doctrine*, p. 426.

24. *Catholic Encyclopedia*, s.v. "Exegesis," by A. J. Maas, 5:696, 698.

25. John A. O'Brien, *The Faith of Millions* (Huntington, IN: Our Sunday Visitor, 1938), p. 29.

26. Cf. Virkler, *Hermeneutics*, pp. 157–210; Ramm, *Protestant Biblical Interpretation*, pp. 215–88.

27. E. D. Hirsch, *Validity in Interpretation* (New Haven, CT: Yale University Press, 1967), pp. 1–6, 209–44.

28. Augustine *On Christian Doctrine* 3.10.

29. Rogers and McKim, *The Authority and Interpretation of the Bible*, p. 107.

30. Cited in Terry, *Biblical Hermeneutics*, p. 691.

31. Ibid., p. 692.

32. John R. Knott, *The Sword of the Spirit: Puritan Responses to the Bible* (Chicago: University of Chicago, 1980), pp. 115–16.

33. Rogers and McKim, *The Authority and Interpretation of the Bible*, p. 85.

34. Berkhof, *Systematic Theology*, p. 699.

35. Van der Waal, *Hal Lindsey and Biblical Prophecy*, pp. 51, 68.

36. MacKay, *Countdown to Eternity*, p. 13.

37. Virkler, *Hermeneutics*, p. 67.

38. Terry, *Biblical Hermeneutics*, pp. 405–7.

39. Virkler, *Hermeneutics*, p. 196.

40. Leland Ryken, *The Literature of the Bible* (Grand Rapids: Zondervan, 1974), p. 340.

41. Hoekema, *The Bible and the Future*, p. 20.

42. Van der Waal, *Hal Lindsey and Biblical Prophecy*, p. 9. Note the singular use of "covenant." It is assumed that this is the covenant of redemption. If that is the case, then Van der Waal has made a hypothetical covenant developed 15 centuries after the close of the canon into the *crux interpretum* of all Scripture.

43. Ibid., p. 28. It would appear that Van der Waal is not clear on the issue of a dispensational interpretation that, as noted above, is unrelated to the issue of the covenants.

44. Ibid., p. 9.

45. Since amillennialism is essentially an adjunct of covenant theology, preceding it by several centuries historically, it may be well to note several presuppositions apparently involved in the amillennial hermeneutic. One such presupposition is traditional teaching. The Reformers' eschatology, as noted, was in line with the traditional teachings of the medieval Roman Catholic Church. Another presupposition is the spirit of optimism. Hoekema pointed out that

amillennialism is an optimistic viewpoint (Anthony J. Hoekema, "Prophecy: Reformed or Dispensational?" Lecture delivered at the Pensacola Theological Institute, McIlwaine Presbyterian Church, Pensacola, FL, August 3, 1982). Therefore a person who was optimistic would tend to be drawn to it. Granted, the pretribulational, premillennial world view has a degree of pessimism. But which is the more realistic view of a fallen world? And which is more consistent with man's depravity? A third presupposition is a theological system. In amillennialism some passages are interpreted solely on the basis of one's theological system.

Chapter 4

1. C. Norman Kraus, *Dispensationalism in America* (Richmond, VA: John Knox Press, 1958), p. 25.
2. *Epistle of Barnabas* chap. 15. Unless otherwise stated, all quotations from and references to the Fathers in this study are from Alexander Roberts and James Donaldson, eds., *The Ante-Nicene Fathers*, 10 vols. (Grand Rapids: Eerdmans, n.d.) or Philip Schaff and Henry Wace, eds., *Nicene and Post-Nicene Fathers*, 2d series, 14 vols. (Grand Rapids: Eerdmans, n.d.).
3. *Epistle of Barnabas* chap. 2.
4. Ignatius *Epistle to the Ephesians* chap. 20, cited in Johannes Quasten and Joseph C. Plumpe, eds., *Ancient Christian Writers: The Epistles of St. Clement of Rome and St. Ignatius of Antioch*, trans. James A. Kleist (New York: Newman, 1946), p. 67.
5. Clement of Rome *I Clement* chap. 8.
6. *Shepherd of Hermas Vision Fourth* chap. 3.
7. Justin Martyr *Dialogue with Trypho* chap. 92. In Irenaeus *Against Heresies* 4. 16. 1–2 and Tertullian *An Answer to the Jews* chaps. 2–6, these matters received further treatment within the context of God's dispensational dealings with mankind.
8. Justin Martyr *Dialogue with Trypho* chaps. 23, 92; cf. chap. 67, for reference to "deeds God knows to be eternal and suited to every nation."
9. Ibid., chap. 23. In *Banquet of the Ten Virgins* Methodius too set forth a clear fourfold dispensational division of human history with a fourfold giving of the law in succession to Adam, Noah, Moses, and the apostles. These "laws" he explained as the means by which sinful men may "approach . . . God as suppliants, and ask His mercy, and that they may be governed by His pity and compassion" (*Banquet* disc. 10, chap. 2). As with Justin, Methodius also cited humanity's failure as the reason for each new revelation of law. Of the failure under Noah, for example, he wrote, "Those

men, having been thus rejected from the divine care, and the human race having again given themselves up to error, again God sent forth by Moses a law to rule them and recall them to righteousness. But these, thinking fit to bid a long farewell to this law, turned to idolatry" (ibid., chap. 4; cf. chaps. 2–3). Methodius concluded that "when the first laws, which were established in the times of Adam and Noah and Moses, were unable to give salvation to man, the evangelical law alone has saved all" (ibid., chap. 3).

This "law" spoken of by Methodius was also referred to by Tertullian. It seems to signify that body of revelation necessary to enable man to approach God in righteous obedience. In speaking of the law as predating Moses, Tertullian wrote that God "gave to all nations the selfsame law, which at definite and stated times He enjoined should be observed, when He willed, and through whom He willed, and as He willed." He explained that the first law was given to Adam and Eve "that they were not to eat of the fruit of the tree planted in the midst of paradise; but that, if they did contrariwise, by death they were to die" (*An Answer to the Jews* chap. 2). Tertullian maintained that this law given to Adam and Eve—which contained in embryonic form "all the precepts of God—(existing) first in paradise," was "subsequently reformed for the patriarchs, and so again for the Jews, at definite periods." Tertullian cautioned, "And let us not annul this power which God has, which reforms the law's precepts answerably to the circumstances of the times, with a view to man's salvation" (ibid.). Evidently both Methodius and Tertullian recognized the progressive nature of God's revelation of His message to man.

10. For some of the ante-Nicene Fathers the number four had special significance. The dispensations were spoken of by Irenaeus, for example, as "four covenants" (A*gainst Heresies* 3. 11. 8; 4. 9. 3); by Victorinus of Petau as "four generations of people" (*On the Creation of the World*, no divisions); and by Methodius as "four trees" or "four laws" (*Banquet of the Ten Virgins* disc. 10, chap. 2); see Appendix A. As seen in Irenaeus, the reasons given for the fourfold division were many and diverse.

11. Justin Martyr *Dialogue with Trypho* chap. 92.

12. Ibid., chap. 43. Methodius limited the first dispensation to "those before the flood," "those who had pleased God from the first-made man in succession to Noah" (*Banquet of the Ten Virgins* disc. 7, chaps. 4–5).

13. Ibid., chap. 19.

14. Ibid.

15. Ibid., chap. 92.

16. Ibid., cf. chap. 27.

17. Ibid., chap. 92; cf. chaps. 19, 23, 27.
18. Ibid., chap. 23.
19. Ibid., chaps. 19, 27, 46, 92.
20. Ibid., chap. 28 (cf. chap. 46). Justin never spelled out what the "everlasting decrees" of God are. But he spoke of God's rejoicing in the "gifts and offerings" of the one who keeps them. Elsewhere he pointed out that though Abel and others were uncircumcised, God "had respect to the gifts of Abel," translated Enoch, "saved [Lot] from Sodom," and spared Noah and his family in the ark (chap. 19; cf. Tertullian *An Answer to the Jews* chap. 2). These seem to express the more positive aspects of the means of approach to God during this period. The keeping of the everlasting decrees seems to involve simple obedience to the commands of God in the varied circumstances of life. Chapter 45 of the *Dialogue with Trypho* seems to place this within the context of the universal law of God which exists for all men. Here Justin spoke of what is "naturally good, and pious, and righteous" and of what "is universally, naturally, and eternally good" and thus "pleasing to God." (Tertullian referred to this when he said, "Before the Law of Moses, written in stone-tables, I contend that there was a law unwritten, which was habitually understood naturally, and by the fathers was habitually kept" [*An Answer to the Jews* chap. 2].) In his discussion of the New Covenant brought in by Christ, as contrasted with the covenant under Moses, Justin said that "it would be such as to show what kind of commands and deeds God knows to be eternal and suited to every nation, and what commandments He has given, suiting them to the hardness of your people's heart" (*Dialogue with Trypho* chap. 67).
21. Justin Martyr *Dialogue with Trypho* chap. 43. Here Justin's Christological focus is evident. All justification is by faith and thus the true or spiritual circumcision of the heart must point forward to the incarnate Christ, in whom all rites "have an end." For additional information on Justin's perception of the process of salvation from age to age, see note 58.
22. Ibid., chap. 23.
23. Ibid., chaps. 43 and 67; cf. chaps. 16 and 92.
24. Ibid., chaps. 43 and 16; cf. chaps. 23 and 46.
25. Ibid., chaps. 19 and 92. For Methodius the second dispensation involved "those who lived after the deluge." He said these "needed other instruction to ward off the evil, and to be their helper, since idolatry was already creeping in" (*Banquet of the Ten Virgins* disc. 7, chaps. 4 and 6).
26. Justin Martyr *Dialogue with Trypho* chaps. 23 and 43.
27. Ibid., chaps. 41 and 92. Justin's position here is not completely

clear. He certainly believed that men of all ages are justified by faith. He believed also that circumcision of the flesh was instituted on account of Israel's foreknown sin and failure. But he seemed to imply that all rites, while being brought in because of sin and being in and of themselves unable to bring justification to the individual, when observed, were nevertheless in some sense symbols of faith and obedience to God's everlasting decrees. In chapter 92 of the *Dialogue* Justin thus spoke of "those who lived between the times of Abraham and of Moses be[ing] justified by circumcision" and in chapter 41, of circumcision of the flesh as a type of the true circumcision to come. Nevertheless, Justin observed, even the difference in the sexual anatomy of men and women suggests that righteousness itself cannot be based merely on the physical act of circumcision. For while women cannot receive the physical sign, God has given them "the ability to observe all things which are righteous and virtuous." Thus, Justin concluded, "we know that neither of them [male or female] is righteous or unrighteous merely for this cause [circumcision], but [is considered righteous] by reason of piety and righteousness" (chap. 23).

Something of an expression of this twofold nature of the rites is seen in chapter 44 of the *Dialogue*. "Some injunctions were laid on you in reference to the worship of God and practice of righteousness; but some injunctions and acts were likewise mentioned in reference to the mystery of Christ, on account of the hardness of your people's hearts." This twofold character of the rites, both as signs and as a means of approach in obedience to God, will be brought out in greater detail in the discussion of the dispensation under Moses.

28. Ibid., chaps. 16, 23, 92; cf. chap. 28.
29. Ibid., chaps. 16 and 19; cf. Tertullian *An Answer to the Jews* chap. 3.
30. Justin Martyr, *Dialogue with Trypho* chap. 16.
31. Ibid., chap. 41. For Tertullian the contrast is between the "carnal circumcision" of a disobedient people given for a "sign," and the "spiritual" circumcision of an obedient people given for "salvation" (*An Answer to the Jews* chap. 3).
32. Justin Martyr *Dialogue with Trypho* chap. 23.
33. Ibid., chap. 92. As will be shown, this is a faith which, according to Justin, must have its fulfillment in the coming Christ. Tertullian too was clear in his statement that throughout human existence, justification is only by faith. As Abraham was justified by faith, so also people today are justified by faith in Jesus Christ (*Against Marcion* 5. 3).
34. Justin Martyr *Dialogue with Trypho* chap. 47. Here the term "legal

dispensation" is used twice in the course of Justin's discussion with Trypho over the status of those who confess faith in Christ yet either choose to observe "the legal dispensation" or to deny Christ altogether and then go back to "the legal dispensation."

35. Ibid., chap. 43; cf. chaps. 23, 44, 46, 67.

36. Ibid., chaps. 43 and 92; cf. Tertullian *An Answer to the Jews* chaps. 4–5.

37. Ibid., chap. 21.

38. Ibid., chap. 22.

39. Ibid.

40. Ibid., chap. 92.

41. Ibid., chap. 19. Tertullian viewed circumcision, Sabbath observance, sacrifices, and the giving of the Law to Moses as temporary, carnal prefigures of future spiritual counterparts to be found in the new dispensation or new law under Christ (*An Answer to the Jews* chaps. 4–6).

42. Justin Martyr *Dialogue with Trypho* chap. 19.

43. Ibid., chap. 20.

44. Ibid., chap. 45. See chap. 97 for a discussion of the salvation of those who kept the Law but at the same time confessed faith in Christ.

45. In chapter 45 of the *Dialogue*, in the context of successive arrangements of God among men, Justin spoke of the two advents of Christ as the means by which Satan and his angelic followers will be destroyed and death eliminated. He also wrote of final judgment and of the benefits and prospects of immortality for the faithful. All these events are rather compressed together: Incarnation-second coming-immortality (church age + millennium + eternal state = dispensation of Christ?). For Methodius the fourth dispensation is that composed of "those after Christ" (*Banquet of the Ten Virgins* disc. 7, chap. 4). It is what Tertullian called "a nobler dispensation" during which God would "choose for Himself more faithful worshipers, upon whom He would bestow His grace, and that indeed in ampler measure" (*Apology* chap. 21).

46. Justin Martyr *Dialogue with Trypho* chap. 43; cf. chap. 23. According to Methodius, the law given in the fourth dispensation is the last. He said, "There will be hereafter no other law or doctrine but judgment and fire" (*Banquet of the Ten Virgins* disc. 10, chap. 4).

47. Justin Martyr *Dialogue with Trypho* chap. 67.

48. Ibid., chaps. 23 and 43.

49. Ibid., chap. 43.

50. Ibid., chap. 87.

51. Ibid.

52. Ibid., chap. 23. For Methodius the reason for change was the failure of God's people as evidenced by their idolatry. "Hence," said Methodius, "God gave them up to mutual slaughters, to exiles, and captivities, the law itself confessing, as it were, that it could not save them" (*Banquet of the Ten Virgins* disc. 10, chap. 4).
53. Justin Martyr *Dialogue with Trypho* chap. 24.
54. Ibid., chap. 43.
55. Ibid., chap. 67; cf. Tertullian *An Answer to the Jews* chap. 6, for the "promised new law" versus the old.
56. Justin Martyr *Dialogue with Trypho* chap. 45.
57. Ibid., chap. 43.
58. Charles C. Ryrie, *Dispensationalism Today* (Chicago: Moody Press, 1965), p. 131, cf. p. 123. In chapter 45 of the *Dialogue with Trypho* it is clear from the context that when Justin wrote, "Each one . . . shall be saved by his own righteousness," he was speaking of those of all ages who demonstrate a faithful obedience to God which results in salvation "through this Christ." For Justin the process of salvation from Adam to the second advent is Christological throughout. He told Trypho that "only those who in mind are assimilated to the faith of Abraham" may expect an inheritance in the coming kingdom. And further, "there is no other (way [of salvation]) than this—to become acquainted with this Christ, to be washed in the fountain spoken of by Isaiah for the remission of sins" (*Dialogue* chap. 44).
59. Irenaeus *Against Heresies* 3. 11. 8–9. In his discussion of "the reason of the truth why the fourth day is called the Tetras," Victorinus of Petau gives a disjointed little discourse on the quadriform nature of certain things. He cites the four elements of which the world is composed, four seasons, four living creatures before God's throne (Rev. 4:6), four Gospels, and four rivers flowing in paradise (Gen. 2:10). He then makes reference without elaboration to "four generations of people from Adam to Noah, from Noah to Abraham, from Abraham to Moses, from Moses to Christ the Lord, the Son of God" (*On the Creation of the World*).
60. Irenaeus *Against Heresies* 3. 11. 8–9. Methodius, in following the figure of the four trees in Judges 9:8–15, maintained that "also four Gospels have been given, because God has four times given the Gospel [good news] to the human race and has instructed them by four laws, the times of which are clearly known by the diversity of the fruits" (*Banquet of the Ten Virgins* disc. 10, chap. 2).
61. Irenaeus *Against Heresies* 3. 11. 8. See portions of the entire paragraph.
62. Irenaeus believed that all the dispensations culminate in Christ. "For those things which have been predicted by the Creator alike

through all the prophets has Christ fulfilled in the end, ministering to His Father's will, and completing His dispensations with regard to the human race" (*Against Heresies* 5. 26. 2).

63. Irenaeus *Against Heresies* 3. 11. 8. The source for both versions is Roberts and Donaldson, eds., *The Ante-Nicene Fathers*, 1:429 (for the Greek version see their note 3).

64. "A portion of the Greek has been preserved here, but it differs materially from the old Latin version, which seems to represent the original with greater exactness, and has therefore been followed" (Roberts and Donaldson, eds., *The Ante-Nicene Fathers*, 1:429, n. 3). This note goes on to give what "seem[s] the complete system" of Irenaeus. How the writers arrived at this is not stated, but it provides data for a fascinating comparison of Irenaeus's system with the sevenfold dispensational system taught by C. I. Scofield. (1) Paradise [Innocence]—"with the tree of life," (2) Adam [Conscience]—"with the Shechinah," (3) Noah [Government]— "with the rainbow," (4) Abraham [Promise]—"with circumcision," (5) Moses [Law]—"with the ark," (6) Messiah [Grace]—"with the sacraments," (7) Heaven [Kingdom]—"with the river of life." For Scofield's dispensations see *Rightly Dividing the Word of Truth* (Fincastle, VA: Scripture Truth, n.d.), pp. 12–16, or *The Scofield Reference Bible* (New York: Oxford University Press, 1967), p. 3.

65. Irenaeus *Against Heresies* 4. 20. 6. Irenaeus's reference to the various gifts, "adapted to the times . . . and man's salvation being accomplished," reminds one of Tertullian's statement that God "reforms the law's precepts answerably to the circumstances of the times, with a view to man's salvation" (*An Answer to the Jews* chap. 2).

66. Irenaeus *Against Heresies* 4. 20. 7. Compare Irenaeus's language here with that in Tertullian *Against Praxeas* chap. 16. With reference to the appearances of Christ (Christophanies) throughout the Old Testament, Tertullian wrote that "ever from the beginning" Christ was "laying the foundation of the course *of His dispensations,* which He meant to follow out to the very last." Elsewhere Tertullian said that "the name of Christ . . . does not arise from nature, but from dispensation [*ex dispositione*]" (*Against Marcion* 3. 15). The editor's note appended here explains that "*Ex dispositione . . .* seems to mean what is implied in the phrases, 'Christian *dispensation,*' 'Mosaic *dispensation,*' etc." (Roberts and Donaldson, eds., *The Ante-Nicene Fathers*, 6:429, n. 17, italics theirs).

67. Irenaeus *Against Heresies* 4. 16. 1.

68. Ibid., 4. 16. 1–2 (italics added). Methodius maintained that those who lived before Noah (first dispensation) "had no need of precepts and laws for their salvation, the creation of the world in six days

being still recent." He spoke of the "confidence Seth had towards God, and Abel, and Enos, and Enoch, and Methuselah, and Noah, the first lovers of righteousness" (*Banquet of the Ten Virgins* disc. 7, chap. 5).

69. See Tertullian *An Answer to the Jews* chap. 2 for essentially the same question and answer concerning the giving of the Law before Moses.

70. Irenaeus *Against Heresies* 4. 16. 2.

71. Ibid., 1. 10. 3.

72. Ibid., 3. 12. 12–13.

73. Ibid., 4. 9. 1.

74. Ibid., 3. 10. 4. For other references to the "covenant of liberty," see 3. 12. 14 and 4. 34. 3.

75. For references to the "legal dispensation," or "dispensation of the Law," see *Against Heresies* 3. 10. 2; 3. 10. 4; 3. 11. 7; 3. 12. 15; and 3. 15. 3.

76. Ibid., 4. 9. 1–2. In another place, Irenaeus stated that "one and the same Lord granted, by means of His advent, a greater gift of grace to those of a later period, than what He had granted to those under the Old Testament dispensation" (cf. Tertullian *Apology* chap. 21). Irenaeus's reason for this is that Old Testament saints rejoiced and hoped in Christ's coming only in a limited sense while those of the New Testament period could rejoice because of His actual arrival. As those who obtained liberty and partook of His gifts, they were the recipients of "a greater amount of grace, and higher degree of exultation" (*Against Heresies* 4. 11. 3).

77. Ibid., 4. 9. 3. Also see 4. 28. 2, in which Irenaeus discussed the one God/one salvation theme: "There is one, and the same God the Father, and His Word, who has been always present with the human race, by means indeed of various dispensations, and has wrought out many things, and saved from the beginning those who are saved (for these are they who love God, and follow the Word of God according to the class to which they belong)."

78. Ibid., 3. 10. 2.

79. Ibid., 4. 36. 2.

80. Irenaeus *Proof of the Apostolic Preaching* chap. 58. In a note appended to this chapter, the reader is told that the Armenian word *tnawrenut'iwn* is equivalent to the Greek οἰκονομία. See Johannes Quasten and Joseph C. Plumpe, eds., *Ancient Christian Writers: St. Irenaeus, Proof of the Apostolic Preaching*, trans. Joseph P. Smith (New York: Newman, 1946), text on p. 86, and p. 194, n. 263.

81. Irenaeus *Proof of the Apostolic Preaching* chap. 99.

82. Irenaeus *Against Heresies* 4. 15. 2.

83. Kraus, *Dispensationalism in America*, p. 23.
84. Refer to Appendix A. While the absence of this incentive for a fourfold dispensational system allows greater freedom for division along more naturally biblical lines, at least in Tertullian's case, it also results in a system with less well-defined boundaries than those found in Justin Martyr and Irenaeus. As pointed out in note 64, Irenaeus developed a "complete system" (Roberts and Donaldson, eds., *The Ante-Nicene Fathers*), a sevenfold system that closely approximates what is found in contemporary dispensationalism.
85. Victorinus's scheme, with its lack of amplification, is the exception. How these divisions may have been treated elsewhere in his nonextant works is of course past finding out, but stirs interest nonetheless.
86. See Scofield, *Rightly Dividing the Word of Truth*, pp. 12–16.
87. Ryrie, *Dispensationalism Today*, p. 59. Ryrie includes Noah along with Abel and Enoch as the "heroes of faith" in the dispensation of conscience.
88. Four times Methodius calls the millennium the "new" dispensation (*Banquet of the Ten Virgins* disc. 4, chap. 5; disc. 7, chap. 3; disc. 8, chap. 11; disc. 9, chap. 1) and the "future age" (or dispensation) once (*Fragments*, "On the History of Jonah" 2). Tertullian presented the interesting notion that time is to be reckoned as consisting of two portions, separated by the millennium: creation to millennium ("millennial interspace") and "eternal economy" (*Apology* chap. 68; cf. *On the Resurrection of the Flesh* chap. 59).
89. Arnold D. Ehlert, *A Bibliographic History of Dispensationalism* (Grand Rapids: Baker, 1966).
90. Charles L. Feinberg, *Millennialism: The Two Major Views* (Chicago: Moody Press, 1980), p. 74.

Chapter 5

1. Cf. John F. Walvoord, "The Fulfillment of the Abrahamic Covenant," *Bibliotheca Sacra* 102 (January–March 1945): 27–36.
2. Albertus Pieters, *The Seed of Abraham* (Grand Rapids: Eerdmans, 1950), p. 161.
3. Louis Berkhof, *Systematic Theology* (Grand Rapids: Eerdmans, 1941), p. 277.
4. Oswald T. Allis, *Prophecy and the Church* (Philadelphia: Presbyterian and Reformed, 1945), pp. 32–33.
5. Pieters, *The Seed of Abraham*, p. 20.
6. Ibid., p. 17.
7. Ibid., pp. 19–20.
8. Ibid., pp. 11–23.
9. Allis, *Prophecy and the Church*, pp. 31–36.

Chapter 6

1. Arthur H. Lewis, *The Dark Side of the Millennium: The Problem of Evil in Revelation 20:1–10* (Grand Rapids: Baker, 1980), p. 5.
2. Ibid.
3. Ibid., p. 12.
4. Ibid., p. 6.
5. In fact Lewis disassociates himself from amillennialism. He writes, "The point of view herein defended is not amillennial, if that label means a negation of a real millennial age. Rather, it should be called historical millennialism, since it will assert the present reality of all aspects of the 'thousand years' as described in Revelation 20:1–10" (ibid.). But classic amillennialism does not negate the millennium but equates it with the present age (hence the term *a*millennial is somewhat of a misnomer). So Lewis's view, though taking a new approach, is still basically amillennial.
6. The five are John F. Walvoord, J. Dwight Pentecost, Hal Lindsey, Lewis Sperry Chafer, and Leon Wood (ibid., pp. 9–10, 22).
7. Ibid., p. 22.
8. Ibid., p. 10 (italics added).
9. Ibid., p. 40.
10. Ibid., p. 22. Cf. similar statements on his pp. 17–18, 41, 44–45.
11. Cf. René Pache, *The Return of Jesus Christ*, trans. William Sanford LaSor (Chicago: Moody, 1955), p. 397; J. Dwight Pentecost, *Things to Come: A Study in Biblical Eschatology* (Findlay, OH: Dunham, 1958), pp. 414–15, 422; Charles Caldwell Ryrie, *Revelation*, Everyman's Bible Commentary (Chicago: Moody, 1968), p. 116; John F. Walvoord, *The Millennial Kingdom* (Findlay, OH: Dunham, 1959), pp. 291, 302.
12. Lewis, *The Dark Side of the Millennium*, p. 33 (italics added).
13. Lewis does this with Psalm 2:9 on pp. 30–31; with Psalm 110 on p. 31; and with Isaiah 11:4 on p. 33.
14. Robert Jamieson, A. R. Fausset, and David Brown, *A Commentary: Critical, Experimental, and Practical on the Old and New Testaments*, 3 vols. (reprint, Grand Rapids: Eerdmans, n.d.), vol. 2: Job-Malachi, by A. R. Fausset, p. 763.
15. Lewis, *The Dark Side of the Millennium*, p. 37.
16. Ibid.
17. Ibid.
18. Ibid. Cf. Anthony A. Hoekema, *The Bible and the Future* (Grand Rapids: Eerdmans, 1979), pp. 202–3.
19. Lewis, *The Dark Side of the Millennium*, p. 37.
20. Ibid.
21. Cf. Isaiah 2:4, "And He will judge between the nations, and will reprove many peoples." No doubt Lewis would relegate this to the

judgments prior to the kingdom, but the remainder of the verse as well as the previous verse speak of conditions during the kingdom.

Zechariah 8 is another passage Lewis must face. Zechariah 8:4 also speaks of longevity during the kingdom age. But if the kingdom is the eternal state, how can there be aging? In addition, Zechariah 8:23 is revealing. "In those days ten men from the nations of every language will grasp [for knowledge of the Lord], and they will grasp the corner of the garment of a Jew saying, 'Let us go with you, for we have heard that God is with you.'" This verse clearly presents a seeking of the Lord incompatible with the eternal state.

Also as Lewis points out (ibid., p. 23), Zechariah 14:16–17 does not say explicitly that families of the earth will refuse to go up to Jerusalem to worship the King. But this does seem to be the clear implication of the passage.

22. Lewis, *The Dark Side of the Millennium*, p. 43.

23. S. Lewis Johnson, Jr., "The First Epistle to the Corinthians," in *The Wycliffe Bible Commentary*, eds. Charles F. Pfeiffer and Everett F. Harrison (Chicago: Moody, 1962), p. 1257.

24. George E. Ladd, *Crucial Questions about the Kingdom of God* (Grand Rapids: Eerdmans, 1954), p. 178.

25. Merrill C. Tenney, "The Importance and Exegesis of Revelation 20:1–8," *Bibliotheca Sacra* 111 (April–June 1954): 146.

26. Another New Testament passage that places rebellion and judgment in the earthly messianic reign is Revelation 2:27–28 in which Psalm 2:8–9 is applied to overcomers (cf. Rev. 12:5; 19:15). Also, if Revelation 20:1–10 is taken in the premillennial sense, the purpose of Satan's binding ("that he should not deceive the nations," v. 3) indicates that during the thousand years the nations are capable of being deceived and therefore are not in a perfect state.

27. Lewis, *The Dark Side of the Millennium*, p. 43.

28. Lewis claims that John 5:28–29 teaches one general resurrection (ibid., p. 45). But it should be noted that Jesus spoke of two resurrections, "a resurrection of life" and "a resurrection of judgment." In Revelation 20:4–6 the same author of Scripture gives more details of the "coming hour" of which Jesus spoke. It is an hour that encompasses the entire resurrection program with the two resurrections mentioned separated by the thousand years.

29. Ibid., p. 49. That Lewis is not alone in taking Revelation 20:1 as reverting back to the beginning of the present age can be seen in surveying amillennial literature. Others who hold similar views include William Hendriksen (*More than Conquerors: An Interpretation of the Book of Revelation* [Grand Rapids: Baker, 1982]); Hoekema (*The Bible and the Future*); R. C. H. Lenski

(*The Interpretation of St. John's Revelation* [Minneapolis: Augsburg, 1961]); and Benjamin B. Warfield (*Biblical Doctrines* [New York: Oxford University Press, 1929]).

30. J. William Fuller, "The Premillennial-Amillennial Debate: Revelation 20:1–6" (Paper for 228 The Revelation, Dallas Theological Seminary, fall 1976), p. 3.

31. Ibid.

32. He writes, "The little horn of Daniel 7 parallels the beast of Revelation 13:1–8. Both the little horn of Daniel and the beast of Revelation are said to have a worldwide empire (Dan. 7:7, 23; Rev. 13:8). Both have victory over the saints for 'a time and times and half a time' (Dan. 7:25; Rev. 12:14). Both are destroyed by the Messiah at His second advent (Dan. 7:11, 26; Rev. 19:20). Both affirm that immediately following the destruction of the world ruler the kingdom is given to the saints (Dan. 7:22, 27; Rev. 20:4–6). Thus it is apparent that at least up to the reign of the saints Revelation 19:11–20:6 is following the same pattern as Daniel 7. Since the world ruler is yet future, the millennial reign must also be future for the saints do not reign or receive their kingdom until after his destruction. Thus on the basis of Daniel 7 it is more natural to read Revelation 20:4–6 as part of a chronological progression in its larger context (19:11–20:15) than as a recapitulation" (Jack S. Deere, "Premillennialism in Revelation 20:4–6," *Bibliotheca Sacra* 135 [January–March 1978]: 60–61).

33. Lewis, *The Dark Side of the Millennium*, p. 50. In the text this sentence is followed by a footnote reference to J. Barton Payne's comment that the thousand years stands for a kingdom of "limited extent" (*Encyclopedia of Biblical Prophecy* [New York: Harper and Row, 1973], p. 626). Which is it—"extended" as Lewis says, or "limited" as Payne claims? Control on meaning can easily be sacrificed when the interpreter moves from the literal to the figurative!

34. As McClain notes, "In each recurrence the expression [a thousand years] is connected with a distinctive idea: First, Satan is bound for a thousand years (v. 2). Second, the nations will not be deceived for a thousand years (v. 3). Third, the martyred saints reign with Christ for a thousand years (v. 4). Fourth, the rest of the dead live not again till the thousand years are finished (v. 5). Fifth, all who have part in the first resurrection will be priests of God and reign with Christ a thousand years (v. 6). Sixth, Satan will be loosed after the thousand years (v. 7)" (Alva J. McClain, *The Greatness of the Kingdom: An Inductive Study of the Kingdom of God* [Chicago: Moody, 1959], p. 492).

35. Lewis, *The Dark Side of the Millennium*, p. 50.

36. Ibid., p. 51.
37. Ibid., pp. 51–60.
38. John F. Walvoord, "Is Satan Bound?" *Bibliotheca Sacra* 100 (October–December 1943): 503.
39. Lewis, *The Dark Side of the Millennium*, p. 51.
40. Ibid., p. 53.
41. Walvoord, "Is Satan Bound?" p. 501 (italics added).
42. Lewis, *The Dark Side of the Millennium*, pp. 52–53.
43. Robert H. Mounce, *The Book of Revelation*, New International Commentary on the New Testament (Grand Rapids: Eerdmans, 1977), p. 353.
44. Walvoord, "Is Satan Bound?" p. 511.
45. Lewis quotes from Matthew 12:29 (*The Dark Side of the Millennium*, p. 52). Hendriksen is an example of an amillennialist who develops this argument (*More than Conquerors*, p. 187).
46. Hendriksen, *More than Conquerors*, p. 187.
47. Hendriksen posits the following illustration, "A dog scarcely bound with a long and heavy chain can do great damage within the circle of his imprisonment. Outside that circle, however, the animal can do no damage and can hurt no-one" (ibid., p. 190).
48. S. Lewis Johnson, Jr., class notes in 228 The Revelation, Dallas Theological Seminary, fall 1976.
49. G. C. Berkouwer, *The Return of Christ*, Studies in Dogmatics (Grand Rapids: Eerdmans, 1972), p. 305.
50. Lewis, *The Dark Side of the Millennium*, pp. 55–57.
51. Ibid., p. 58.
52. "Augustine held to the believer's regeneration as the 'first resurrection.' B.B. Warfield concludes that it meant the glorification of the believers and the intermediate state following death. For Albertus Pieters it is only a symbol of the triumph for which the martyrs gave their lives" (Lewis, *The Dark Side of the Millennium*, p. 58). To this could be added Norman Shepherd, who suggests the view that water baptism is the first resurrection ("The Resurrections of Revelation 20," *Westminster Theological Journal* 37 [fall 1974]: 34–43).
53. Lewis, The Dark Side of the Millennium, p. 58. This is also the view of Hendricksen (More than Conquerors, p. 192); Meredith Kline ("The First Resurrection," *Westminster Theological Journal* 37 [spring 1975]: 371); and Lenski (*St. John's Revelation*, p. 592).
54. Alford wrote, "If, in a passage where two resurrections are mentioned, where certain ψυχαὶ ἔξησαν at the first, and the rest of the νεκροὶ ἔξησαν only at the end of a specified period after that first—if in such a passage the first resurrection may be understood to mean spiritual rising with Christ, while the second

means literal rising from the grave; then there is an end of all significance in language, and Scripture is wiped out as a definite testimony to anything. If the first resurrection is spiritual, then so is the second . . . but if the second is literal, then so is the first" (Henry Alford, *The Greek Testament*, rev. Everett F. Harrison, 4 vols. [reprint, Chicago: Moody, 1958], 4:732).

55. Lewis, *The Dark Side of the Millennium*, pp. 58–59.

56. Ladd, *Crucial Questions about the Kingdom of God*, p. 143.

57. In discussing the final resurrection and judgment, Lewis understands Revelation 20:11–15 to teach "the physical and general resurrection of all the peoples of the earth" (*The Dark Side of the Millennium*, p. 61). To do so Lewis must take the ἔξησαν of verse 5 to mean physical resurrection.

58. Ladd cautions that "no objection can be raised on the ground that it is not possible to speak of a spiritual and of a literal reality in the same context" (*Crucial Questions about the Kingdom of God*, p. 144). But "in these several passages there is a clue which is required by the context or by the words themselves which suggests and requires the literal interpretation on the one hand, and the spiritual on the other. But in Revelation 20:4–6, there is no such contextual clue for a similar variation of interpretation. The language of the passage is quite clear and unambiguous. There is no necessity to interpret either word [ἔξησαν in 20:4–5] spiritually in order to introduce meaning to the passage. At the beginning of the millennial period, part of the dead come to life; at its conclusion, the rest of the dead come to life. There is no evident play on words here. The passage makes perfectly good sense when interpreted literally" (ibid., p. 146).

59. Johnson, class notes. Lewis claims that "the new life in Christ is frequently called a 'resurrection' (Rom. 6:11; Eph. 2:4, 5; Col. 3:1)" (*The Dark Side of the Millennium*, p. 58). But the quotation marks around the word "resurrection" should alert the reader to the fact that in none of the passages listed is the word ἀναστάσις used.

60. Lewis, *The Dark Side of the Millennium*, p. 61.

Chapter 7

1. Louis Berkhof, *Systematic Theology,* 2d ed. (Grand Rapids: Eerdmans, 1911), p. 716.

2. Lewis Sperry Chafer, *Major Bible Themes* (Chicago: Bible Institute Colportage, 1930), p. 121.

3. B. B. Warfield, *Biblical Doctrines* (New York: Oxford University Press, 1929), p. 651.

4. Ibid., pp. 645–46.

5. Ibid., p. 651.
6. Masselink, *Why a Thousand Years?* p. 202.
7. Hamilton, *The Basis of Millennial Faith,* p. 130.

Chapter 8

1. Marilyn Ferguson, *The Aquarian Conspiracy* (Los Angeles: J. P. Tarcher, 1980), p. 23.
2. Bernard Pyron, *The Great Rebellion* (Waco, TX: Rebound, 1985), p. ii. Pyron notes that he has found 50 traits to describe the New Culture, all under the umbrella of the unifying emphasis on the narcissistic self.
3. Schlossberg notes the changes in today's culture by collecting a long list of "post-" descriptives, concluding that society is "post-Puritan, post-Protestant and post-Christian" (Herbert Schlossberg, *Idols for Destruction* [Nashville: Nelson, 1983], p. 1).
4. Chilton says, "The eschatology of dominion is [not] a doctrine of protection against national judgment and desolation. To the contrary, the eschatology of dominion is a *guarantee* of judgment. It teaches that world history is judgment, a series of judgments leading up to the Final Judgment" (David Chilton, *Paradise Restored: An Eschatology of Dominion* [Tyler, TX: Reconstruction, 1985], p. 220). North distinguishes between "judgment unto *restoration* and judgment unto *destruction*" (Gary North, *Unholy Spirits: Occultism and New Age Humanism* [Fort Worth: Dominion, 1986], p. 373). For a more complete discussion of this view see Herbert Bowsher, "Will Christ Return 'At Any Moment'?" *Journal of Christian Reconstruction* 7 (winter 1981): 48–60.
5. Gary North, "Cutting Edge or Lunatic Fringe?" *Christian Reconstruction* 11 (January/February 1987): 1. North coined the term "Christian Reconstruction" when he began editing the *Journal of Christian Reconstruction* (James Jordan, "The 'Reconstructionist Movement,'" *Geneva Review*, p. 1).
6. Rodney Clapp, "Democracy as Heresy," *Christianity Today*, February 20, 1987, p. 22. See also R. J. Rushdoony, *The Institutes of Biblical Law* (Nutley, NJ: Presbyterian and Reformed, 1973), p. 782. Rushdoony says, "This writer comes from an ancient line of such hereditary Armenian priests; his father, the son of a priest, was a Presbyterian clergyman, as he is also." For another reference see R. J. Rushdoony, "The Vision of Chalcedon," *Journal of Christian Reconstruction* 9 (winter 1982–83): 128.
7. Michael D. Philbeck, "An Interview with R. J. Rushdoony," *The Counsel of Chalcedon* (October 1983): 12.
8. The Chalcedon Foundation publishes the monthly newsletter *Chalcedon Report* (P. O. Box 158, Vallecito, CA 95251) and the

Journal of Christian Reconstruction. Their publishing arm is Ross House Books. Chalcedon has an expanding staff and board of affiliates which include Samuel L. Blumenfeld (an expert on the history of public education), John Lofton (a columnist for the Washington, DC *Times*, and television commentator), Mark R. Rushdoony (R. J.'s son), Otto J. Scott, and the investment counselor R. E. McMaster, Jr. Chalcedon also has representatives in Europe and other parts of the world. The *Chalcedon News* (1986) reported, "*The Conservative Digest*, now published from Colorado, has as senior editor Otto Scott, and as contributing editors John Lofton and R. J. Rushdoony."

9. John Frame, "*The Institutes of Biblical Law*: A Review," *Westminster Theological Journal* 38 (winter 1976): 195–217.

10. "The Right: A House Divided?" *Newsweek*, February 2, 1981, p. 60.

11. Clapp, "Democracy as Heresy," p. 17. See also Gary North and David Chilton, "Apologetics and Strategy," in *Tactics of Christian Resistance*, vol. 3: *Christianity and Civilization* (Tyler, TX: Geneva Divinity School Press, 1983), pp. 124–27. Here North and Chilton said that Francis Schaeffer had been reading Rushdoony for 20 years. They compared some passages from the two, showing that Schaeffer clearly picked up statements from Rushdoony.

12. North probably chose Tyler because he considered it to be one of the best locations in the United States for survival. He believes that the United States economy will soon collapse because of the nation's unbiblical practices. Therefore the best place for "the remnant" to be is a rural setting, in an estate where one can be self-supporting, from which to rebuild the apostate civilization into the kingdom of God. He gets this model from feudalism after the collapse of Rome in the 400s. He holds that this approach rebuilt European civilization with biblical law, which the modern church has squandered, resulting in judgment and paving the way for the coming millennium.

13. For some interesting insights on this matter see "Publisher's Preface" by North in David Chilton, *The Days of Vengeance: An Exposition of the Book of Revelation* (Fort Worth: Dominion, 1987), pp. xv–xxxiii.

14. The ICE currently publishes four newsletters: *Christian Reconstruction; Dominion Strategies; Biblical Economics Today*; and *Covenant Renewal* (P. O. Box 8000, Tyler, TX 75711). North also publishes his economic newsletter *Remnant Review*, and *Clipnotes* (P. O. Box 8204, Fort Worth, TX 76124). His publishing companies include Dominion Press in Fort Worth and Reconstruction Press in Tyler.

15. Geneva Ministries is operated in the basement of Westminster Presbyterian Church, P. O. Box 131300, Tyler, TX 75713. On their desktop laser printing system they publish the monthly *Geneva Review*. Their publishing branch is called Geneva Press. *Christianity and Civilization* is an occasional journal that Geneva Ministries also produces.

16. Jordan and Chilton were students at Reformed Theological Seminary when Bahnsen was dismissed from the faculty because of advocating theonomy. Both left the school when Bahnsen did. Jordan graduated from Westminster Theological Seminary, but Chilton did not pursue further institutional training.

17. Clapp, "Democracy as Heresy," p. 18. Bahnsen received his Ph.D. degree in philosophy from Southern California University. His first love is apologetics within the Van Til tradition, and some have said he was considered by Van Til to be his best ever student. As Clapp notes, "He was also the first student at Westminster Seminary to finish both the master of divinity and master of theology degrees within three years."

18. "Chalcedon Embarks on a New Beginning," *The Counsel of Chalcedon* 5 (September 1983): 3–7.

19. *The Counsel of Chalcedon*, 3032 Hacienda Court, Marietta, GA 30066.

20. Joseph C. Morecraft III, "The Future of Evangelism," cassette recording from the 1984 Conference on "Eschatology and Dominion," in Tyler, Texas. Michael Gilstrap sounds a similar note, "It is my fear, however, that in our beehive of dominion activity, we often neglect the more personal and individual aspects of personal piety" ("Dominion from Our Knees," *Geneva Review* 36 [March 1987]: 2).

21. Gary DeMar, American Vision Press, P. O. Box 720515, Atlanta, GA 30328.

22. Joe Kickasola, "Law and Society: A Basic Course in Theonomy," cassette recordings from the Mount Olive Tape Library, P. O. Box 422, Mount Olive, MS 39119. Clapp notes that Pat Robertson is highly influenced by these views, as is Robertson's dean of the Schools of Law and Public Policy, Herbert Titus, a Harvard Law School graduate ("Democracy as Heresy," p. 21). Titus published an essay, "The Constitutional Law of Privacy: Past, Present and Future," in R. J. Rushdoony, *Law and Society*, vol. 2 of *The Institutes of Biblical Law* (Vallecito, CA: Ross House, 1982).

23. North, "Publisher's Preface," in Chilton, *The Days of Vengeance*, pp. xviii-xxxiii.

24. He credits Kline's studies on the suzerainty treaties as a breakthrough (ibid., pp. xvii-xviii). This in turn gave rise to Sutton's

five points of the covenant, which were the key to Chilton's understanding of Revelation. Also it seems that Kline has had significant influence on the thinking of James Jordan, who praises Kline's *Images of the Spirit* as a brilliant study in biblical theology in a review of that book. North says that "Kline without Jordan produces confusion about biblical symbolism" ("Chilton, Sutton, and Dominion Theology," an essay in the January 1987 ICE monthly mailing, p. 3). Kline's work seems to have had some role in Jordan's "maximalist" approach to biblical interpretation displayed in his work *Judges: God's War against Humanism* (Tyler, TX: Geneva Ministries, 1985), p. xii. See especially Sutton's "Covenant: What Is It Anyway?" *Covenant Renewal* 1 (February 1987), in which he wrote, "In the next newsletter I shall discuss in what sense I've used Kline and in what way I've rejected him. The title of the essay is 'Kline vs. Kline,'" (p. 2, n. 3).

25. Meredith G. Kline, "Comments on an Old-New Error," *Westminster Theological Journal* 41 (fall 1978): 74–80.

26. Bahnsen goes to great length to argue that the suggested novelty of theonomy is only "apparent." "Theonomic ethics does not then ask that something new be added to the Confessional understanding of God's law, but simply that we be consistent with its outlook— as were the Puritans. It is, therefore, inaccurate to speak of theonomic ethics as 'the latest approach to the law.' It is among the oldest, and therein lies its modern offense. It is unpopular to support the Puritans in a secular age" ("The Authority of God's Law," *Presbyterian Journal*, December 6, 1978, p. 9).

27. Some examples are Gary North, *Dominion Strategies* 2 (June 1986); David Chilton, *Paradise Restored*, pp. 4–7; idem, *The Days of Vengeance*, pp. 494–96; idem, "Orthodox Christianity and the Millenarian Heresy," *Geneva Review* 19 (June 1985): 3; Greg Bahnsen, "The Prima Facie Acceptability of Postmillennialism," *Journal of Christian Reconstruction* 3 (winter 1976–77): 50–52; James Jordan, "Christian Zionism and Messianic Judaism," appendix B in *The Days of Vengeance*, pp. 615–16; and R. J. Rushdoony, *God's Plan for Victory* (Tyler, TX: Thoburn, 1977), p. 13.

28. North wrote, "I see myself as a neo-Puritan" ("Preface to the Second Edition" in David Chilton, *Productive Christians in an Age of Guilt-Manipulators* [Tyler, TX: ICE, 1982], p. 14).

29. Examples are North's recent claim that Sutton's "remarkable, path-breaking discoveries" concerning the five-point nature of the biblical covenants is a key to understanding not only the books of Exodus, Deuteronomy, and Revelation, but also "Psalms, Hosea, Matthew, Hebrews 8, and several of Paul's epistles." North's

excitement continues as he further observes, "Sutton's thoroughgoing development . . . has to be regarded as the most important single theological breakthrough in the Christian Reconstruction movement since the publication of R. J. Rushdoony's *Institutes of Biblical Law*, in 1973" ("Publisher's Preface," pp. xvii-xviii). North and Chilton say concerning Van Til's philosophy, "His apologetic system marks the first total break with humanism in all its forms." And they added that Van Til "will be understood in the history of the church as equal in importance to, and probably greater than, the contribution of the scholastics or the Protestant Reformers" ("Apologetics and Strategy," p. 112).

30. Contrary to what many might think, Rushdoony often castigates Calvin's incomplete view of the law. For example in one place Calvin is cited for declaring that the Old Testament Law is no longer in full force. Rushdoony calls this "silly and trifling reasoning" (*The Institutes of Biblical Law*, p. 653).

31. North, "Chilton, Sutton, and Dominion Theology," p. 3. Clapp, however, lists three: presuppositional apologetics, theonomy (biblical law), and postmillennialism ("Democracy as Heresy," pp. 18–19). Jordan sees three ingredients under the sovereignty of God: "What [Reconstructionists] have in common is a belief in three specific manifestations of the sovereignty of God: a triumphant eschatology (postmillennialism), grounded in a presuppositional philosophy (articulated best by Van Til), and guided by Biblical law ('theonomy')" ("The 'Reconstructionist Movement,'" p. 1). These three themes also are the main issues for Rushdoony and Bahnsen. North has recently added the covenant factor as another "path-breaking discovery."

32. North, "Apologetics and Strategy," p. 107.

33. Ibid.

34. See Frame, "*The Institutes of Biblical Law*: A Review"; idem, "*Theonomy and Christian Ethics*: A Review," *Presbyterian Journal*, August 31, 1977, p. 18; Kline, "Comments on an Old-New Error"; R. Laird Harris, "*Theonomy and Christian Ethics*: A Review," *Presbyterian: Covenant Seminary Review* 5 (spring 1979): 1–15; Douglas E. Chismar and David A. Rausch, "Regarding Theonomy: An Essay of Concern," *Journal of the Evangelical Theological Society* 27 (September 1984): 315–23; Robert P. Lightner, "Theonomy and Dispensationalism," *Bibliotheca Sacra* 143 (January–March 1986): 26–36; idem, "Nondispensational Responses to Theonomy," *Bibliotheca Sacra* 143 (April–June 1986): 134–45; idem, "A Dispensational Response to Theonomy" *Bibliotheca Sacra* 143 (July–September 1986): 228–45; Mark W.

Karlberg, "Reformation Politics: The Relevance of OT Ethics in Calvinist Political Theory," *Journal of the Evangelical Theological Society* 29 (June 1986): 179–91; Aiken G. Taylor, "Theonomy Revisited," *Presbyterian Journal*, December 6, 1978, pp. 12–13, 22; idem, "Theonomy and Christian Behavior," *Presbyterian Journal*, September 13, 1978, pp. 9–10, 18–19; William B. Tucker, "Theonomic Application for a Sociology of Justification by Faith: Weakness in the Social Criticisms of Rousas John Rushdoony as Revealed in the Doctrine of Sanctification by Law" (M.A. thesis, Gordon-Conwell Theological Seminary, 1984).

35. According to a recent sampling of *Christian Today* readers, 9 percent of those who responded said they think Christ will come after the millennium (February 6, 1987, p. 9–I). This is certainly an "optimistic" turn of events.

36. Chilton revises what constitutes a postmillenarian and an amillenarian. He calls optimistic amillenarians "postmills," and pessimistic amillenarians "premills." He says, "The Millennium' is thus simply the Kingdom of Christ. . . . In this objective sense, therefore *orthodox Christianity has always been postmillennialist.* . . . orthodox Christians have always confessed that Jesus Christ will return *after* ('post') Christ's mediatorial reign has come to an end. In this sense, all 'amils' are also 'postmils'" ("Orthodox Christianity and the Millenarian Heresy," p. 3). Chilton wrote, "What I'm saying is this: *Amillennialism and Postmillennialism are the same thing.* The *only fundamental difference* is that 'postmils' believe the world will be converted, and 'amils' don't. Otherwise, I'm an amil. Meredith Kline is a postmil. Got it?" (David Chilton to Thomas D. Ice, December 17, 1986, p. 4).

37. Aiken Taylor, "Postmillennialism Revisited," *Presbyterian Journal*, September 6, 1978, p. 11.

38. North, *Unholy Spirits*, pp. 388–89.

39. Ibid., pp. 392–93. The March 17, 1987 issue of the *Austin American-Statesman* published an article entitled "Born-again Christians, 'Kingdom Theology' vs. Communists" (p. A-11). The story centered around Bishop Earl Paulk of the 10,000–member congregation at Chapel Hill Harvester Church in Decatur, Georgia. The article tells of Paulk's conversion to "kingdom theology" about six years earlier. Gary North was a keynote speaker at a recent conference at Paulk's church, and North serves as an adviser to one of the church's ministries. Paulk in his book *Held in the Heavens Until . . .* (Atlanta: Kingdom Dimension, 1985) argues that Christ cannot come back to the earth until a certain amount of dominion (maturity) is achieved by the church. This appears to be a blend of postmillennialism with the old Pentecostal error often called the "Manifest Sons of God" teaching.

40. "Chilton, Sutton, and Dominion Theology," p. 4. Rushdoony acknowledged growth of their views among the charismatics also. "So, years ago I came to the post-mil faith. NOW IT'S GROWING LIKE WILDFIRE ALL OVER THE COUNTRY. It is spreading into Baptist circles, as is theonomy. A very large section of the charismatic movement is becoming Reformed, theonomic, and postmillennial, also" ("An Interview with R. J. Rushdoony," p. 14, capital letters his).

41. Gary Scott Smith, "The Men and Religion Forward Movement of 1911–12," *Westminster Theological Journal* 49 (spring 1987): 92–93.

42. Chilton, "Orthodox Christianity and the Millenarian Heresy," p. 3.

43. Chilton writes, "The dominion outlook is equated with the liberal 'Social Gospel' movement in the early 1900's. Such an identification is utterly absurd, devoid of any foundation whatsoever. The leaders of the Social Gospel movement were evolutionary humanists and socialists, and were openly hostile toward Biblical Christianity. It is true that they *borrowed* certain terms and concepts from Christianity, in order to pervert them for their own uses. Thus they talked about the 'Kingdom of God,' but what they meant was far removed from the traditional Christian faith" (*Paradise Restored*, p. 228). Why would Shirley Jackson Case (a social gospel advocate) write a whole book defining what he called postmillennialism, against the pessimistic premillennialism of his day, if he did not view himself as an optimistic postmillennialist? (*The Millennial Hope* [Chicago: University of Chicago Press, 1918], p. 209).

44. North wrote, "I am probably the person most responsible for devising a strategy for speeding up this drift toward postmillennialism, which I think Mr. Hunt is aware of" (*Unholy Spirits*, p. 391).

45. North admits that people like Robert Tilton have some theological problems. "Mr. Hunt points out that the language used by other 'positive confession' ministers is similar to the man-deifying language of the New Age 'positive thinking' theology. There is no doubt that this accusation can be documented, and that some of these leaders need to get clear the crucial distinction between the imputed *human* perfection of Jesus Christ and the non-communicable divinity of Jesus Christ. This Creator-creature distinction is the most important doctrine separating the New Agers and orthodox Christianity" (p. 388). "Mr. Hunt implies that the poor wording of the 'positive confession' charismatics' Christology reflects their eschatology. It doesn't. It simply reflects their sloppy wording and their lack of systematic study of theology and its

implications, at least at this relatively early point in the development of the 'positive confession' movement's history" (ibid., p. 392).

46. In a break with Van Til on the issue of common grace, North argues that God increasingly restrains evil as the current kingdom age moves toward a fuller manifestation of the kingdom. One of the means is the corresponding increase in what North calls "common curse." God's increasing curse of evil is one of the means of His restraint of evil (common grace). This is his explanation as to why the millennium does not appear to be on its way in. It is because Western civilization has retreated from its Christian foundation and God is disciplining her, much as He did Israel during her times of unfaithfulness in the Old Testament. See North, "Common Grace, Eschatology, and Biblical Law," *Journal of Christian Reconstruction* 3 (winter 1976–77): 13–47 (reprinted in Chilton, *The Days of Vengeance*, pp. 623–64). Also see Gary North, "Competence, Common Grace, and Dominion," *Biblical Economics Today* 8 (June/July 1985), and Gary North, *Dominion and Common Grace: The Biblical Basis of Progress* (Fort Worth: Dominion, 1987).

47. The CRM believes that Van Til has solved one of the major roadblocks that hindered the New England Puritans from bringing in the kingdom. The Puritans have been purged of epistemological rationalism, with Van Til's biblically centered method. This is argued by Terrill Irwin Elniff, *The Guise of Every Graceless Heart: Human Autonomy in Puritan Thought and Experience* (Vallecito, CA: Ross House, 1981). However, one of Van Til's foundational ideas is that one cannot reach the kind of logical certainty that their dogmatism on certain issues projects. In fact North bemoans the fact that Van Til never became either a theonomist or a postmillennialist. North said, "Van Til was like a demolition expert; he spent his life blowing up bridges between covenant-breakers and covenant-keepers. But he offered no solutions. Thus, he gained few followers, and he offered no earthly hope. His amillennial pessimism was fully consistent with his cultural pessimism. He never trusted theonomic postmillennialism, which is why we search in vain for any public acknowledgment on his part of the existence of Rushdoony or me, or any favorable printed words for either of us. He regarded the Christian Reconstruction movement as a fringe movement, not the cutting edge" ("Cutting Edge or Lunatic Fringe?" p. 2).

48. See note 29.

49. North says, "The missing element in 1967 was biblical law. Once the details of the 'theonomist' position began to take shape, Christian Reconstructionism became a full-fledged system. . . .

Biblical law establishes the basis of a positive alternative" ("Cutting Edge or Lunatic Fringe?" p. 1).

50. See a series of essays on things like tape ministries, computers, television technology, and church newsletters in *Backward, Christian Soldiers?* (Tyler, TX: Institute for Christian Economics, 1984), pp. 171–226.

51. "Law and Society: A Basic Course in Theonomy: A Response to Rushdoony, and the Millennium," cassette recording.

52. One of the latest displays of this is North's "Publisher's Preface" in *The Days of Vengeance* in which he boasts, "Someone had better be prepared to write a better commentary on Revelation than *The Days of Vengeance*. I am confident that nobody can. From this time on, there will only be three kinds of commentaries on the Book of Revelation: Those that try to extend Chilton's. Those that try to refute Chilton's. Those that pretend there isn't Chilton's" (pp. xxxii-iii).

53. G. Aiken Taylor, "Theonomy Revisited," p. 10 (italics added).

54. J. I. Packer, "Biblical Authority, Hermeneutics, Inerrancy," in *Jerusalem and Athens*, ed. E. R. Geehan (Nutley, NJ: Presbyterian and Reformed, 1971), pp. 146–47.

55. See R. J. Rushdoony, *The One and the Many* (Tyler, TX: Thoburn, 1971) for an explanation of what it means to think in a Trinitarian way.

56. Chilton, *Paradise Restored*, p. 213.

57. Chilton, *The Days of Vengeance*, p. 38.

58. North, "Publisher's Preface," in *The Days of Vengeance*, p. xxiii. Chilton's "exegesis" of the thousand years in Revelation 20 is primarily an approach in which he calls his opponents heretics. He says, "The answer to this precise question [the millennium] cannot be determined *primarily* by the exegesis of particular texts" (*The Days of Vengeance*, p. 493). Chilton is correct that exegesis certainly will not yield a postmillennial view of the thousand years.

59. Kline, "Comments on an Old-New Error," pp. 182–83.

60. John F. Walvoord, *The Millennial Kingdom* (Grand Rapids: Zondervan, 1959), pp. 33–34.

61. "Exposition of Matthew 24," cassette tapes, Geneva Media, Tyler, Texas.

62. D. A. Carson, "Matthew," in *The Expositor's Bible Commentary*, ed. Frank E. Gaebelein (Grand Rapids: Zondervan, 1984), 8:506.

63. Chilton, *The Days of Vengeance*, p. 34. See also Jordan's three lectures on "How to Interpret Prophecy," Geneva Ministries.

64. Chilton, *The Days of Vengeance*, p. 35.

65. Ibid., pp. 32–33 (italics his).

66. Elliott E. Johnson, "Apocalyptic Genre in Literal Interpretation,"

in *Essays in Honor of J. Dwight Pentecost*, ed. Stanley D. Toussaint and Charles H. Dyer (Chicago: Moody, 1986), pp. 204–5. See the essay for specific examples.

67. The neopostmillenarians see this, however, as a reference to the period from Christ's ascension to the destruction of Jerusalem in A.D. 70, when the day/kingdom dawned.

68. Kline, "Comments on an Old-New Error," p. 178.

69. Charles A. Clough, "Dispensational Premillennialism and the Present Social Order" (A paper presented to the Department of Systematic Theology, Dallas Theological Seminary, 1966), p. 11.

70. Chilton, *The Days of Vengeance*, pp. 519–29. Bahnsen, "Satan Loosed: Rev. 20:1–10," cassette recording, Mount Olive Tape Library.

71. North, "Optimistic Corpses," *Backward, Christian Soldiers?* pp. 231–32; idem, *Unholy Spirits*, pp. 372–74. Also see R. J. Rushdoony, *Salvation and Godly Rule*, p. 10, and Chilton, *Paradise Restored*, pp. 10–12.

72. North, *Moses and Pharaoh: Dominion Religion versus Power Religion* (Tyler, TX: Institute for Christian Economics, 1985), pp. 259–60.

73. Clough, "Dispensational Premillennialism," pp. 17–18.

74. Alva J. McClain, *The Greatness of the Kingdom* (Winona Lake, IN: BMH, 1959), p. 531.

Chapter 9

1. J. Dwight Pentecost, *Things to Come* (Grand Rapids: Zondervan, 1958), pp. 427–45.

2. Rutgers states, for instance, "Again the New Testament gives plain indication that Christ will remain in heaven until the end of the world. That kingdom will not be one of earthly, material felicity and blessing, but spiritual. In Christ and His true disciples that kingdom is already established, and in harmony with the confession of the church of all ages, not to establish an earthly, Jewish kingdom, Himself visible and bodily reigning in this semi-earthly, semi-heavenly realm of material existence, but for judgment. An unprejudiced reading of the Scripture renders one universal judgment, one universal resurrection. Nowhere is there intimation of a millennial reign intervening" (William H. Rutgers, *Premillennialism in America* [Goes, Holland: Oosterbaan and Le Cointre, 1930], pp. 286–87). Hoekema states, "That the millennial reign depicted in Revelation 20:4–6 occurs before the Second Coming of Christ is evident from the fact that the final judgment, described in verses 11–15 of this chapter, is pictured as coming after the thousand-year reign . . . . it is obvious that the thousand-

year reign of Revelation 20:4–6 must occur *before* and *not after* the Second Coming of Christ" (Anthony A. Hoekema, *The Bible and the Future* [Grand Rapids: Eerdmans, 1979], p. 227).

3. Pentecost, *Things to Come*, p. 427.
4. Ibid., pp. 428, 433.
5. Ibid., pp. 435–37, 441.
6. John F. Walvoord, *The Millennial Kingdom* (Grand Rapids: Dunham, 1959), pp. 18–36.
7. Jay Adams, *The Time Is at Hand* (Phillipsburg, NJ: Presbyterian and Reformed, 1970), p. 63.
8. Ibid., p. 27.
9. Ibid.

Chapter 10

1. Oswald Allis, *Prophecy in the Church* (Philadelphia: Presbyterian and Reformed, 1945), p. 5.
2. A. H. Strong, *Systematic Theology* (Philadelphia: Judson Press, 1907), p. 1013.
3. D. H. Kromminga, *The Millennium in the Church* (Grand Rapids: Eerdmans, 1945), p. 20.
4. Earl Miller, *The Kingdom of God and the Kingdom of Heaven* (Kansas City, KS: Walterick, 1950).
5. J. Dwight Pentecost, *Things to Come* (Findlay, OH: Dunham, 1958), pp. 446–75.
6. G. N. H. Peters, *Theocratic Kingdom*, 3 vols. (Grand Rapids: Kregel, 1952), 1:183.
7. John Bright, *The Kingdom of God* (Nashville: Abingdon-Cokesbury, 1953). pp. 17–18.
8. George E. Ladd, *Crucial Questions about the Kingdom of God* (Grand Rapids: Eerdmans, 1952).
9. John F. Walvoord, *Matthew: Thy Kingdom Come* (Chicago: Moody, 1974), pp. 43–62.
10. Some include Matthew 6:33, but some ancient Greek manuscripts have only "the kingdom" and omit "of God."
11. Pentecost, *Things to Come*, p. 456.
12. Loraine Boettner, *The Millennium* (Philadelphia: Presbyterian and Reformed, 1958), pp. 285–86.
13. Louis Berkhof, *The Second Coming of Christ* (Grand Rapids: Eerdmans, 1953), p. 62.
14. Boettner, *The Millennium*, pp. 286–87.
15. Erich Sauer, *From Eternity to Eternity* (Grand Rapids: Eerdmans, 1954), p. 147.
16. Ibid., pp. 147–48.
17. Ibid., p. 148.

18. George E. Ladd, *The Gospel of the Kingdom* (Grand Rapids: Eerdmans, 1952), p. 16.
19. Ibid., pp. 94–95.

Chapter 11

1. John Wick Bowman, "The Bible and Modern Religions, Part 2: Dispensationalism," *Interpretation* 10 (April 1956): 172.
2. George E. Ladd, *The Blessed Hope* (Grand Rapids: Eerdmans, 1956), p. 37.
3. "Is Evangelical Theology Changing?" *Christian Life,* March 1956, p. 18.
4. Louis Berkhof, *Systematic Theology* (Grand Rapids: Eerdmans, 1941).
5. Lewis Sperry Chafer, *Dispensationalism* (Dallas, TX: Dallas Theological Seminary, 1936), p. 9.
6. Karl Lowith, *Meaning in History* (Chicago: University of Chicago Press, 1949), p. 11.
7. Alva J. McClain, "A Premillennial Philosophy of History," *Bibliotheca Sacra* 113 (April–June 1956): 113–14 (italics his).
8. James Orr, *The Progress of Dogma* (London: Hodder and Stoughton, 1901), p. 303.
9. However, not all covenant theologians are amillenarians.
10. Ladd, *The Blessed Hope,* p. 126.
11. Ibid., pp. 133–34.
12. C. I. Scofield, ed., *The Scofield Reference Bible,* rev. ed. (New York: Oxford University Press, 1917), p. 5 (italics added).
13. Thomas Dehany Bernard, *The Progress of Doctrine in the New Testament* (1864; reprint, Minneapolis: Klock & Klock, 1978), p. 35.

Chapter 12

1. *Oxford English Dictionary*, 13 vols. (Oxford: Clarendon, 1933), 3:481 (italics original).
2. Merrill F. Unger, *Unger's Bible Dictionary*, rev. ed. (Chicago: Moody, 1961), p. 269.
3. Charles Hodge, *Systematic Theology*, 3 vols. (New York: Scribner, 1906), 2:373–77.
4. Ibid., p. 376.
5. Loraine Boettner, *The Millennium* (Philadelphia: Presbyterian and Reformed, 1957), p. 155.
6. R. B. Kuiper, "Scriptural Preaching," in *The Infallible Word*, ed. N. B. Stonehouse and Paul Woolley (Philadelphia: Presbyterian and Reformed, 1946), p. 236.
7. Floyd E. Hamilton, *The Basis of Millennial Faith* (Grand Rapids: Eerdmans, 1942), pp. 26–27.

8. C. I. Scofield, ed., *The Scofield Reference Bible*, rev. ed. (Oxford: Oxford University Press, 1917), p. 5 (italics added).
9. Albertus Pieters, *A Candid Examination of the Scofield Bible* (Swengel, PA: Bible Truth Depot, 1938), p. 14.
10. *Funk and Wagnalls New Standard Dictionary*, 2 vols. (New York: Funk & Wagnalls, 1949).
11. *Doctrinal Statement*, Dallas Theological Seminary, Article V, "The Dispensations."

Chapter 13

1. Apparently some earlier opponents of dispensationalism (e.g., Oswald T. Allis on occasion) were unwilling to grant this. For a recent attempt to establish the dispensational *sine qua non* in the early patristic period, see Larry V. Crutchfield, "Israel and the Church in the Ante-Nicene Fathers," *Bibliotheca Sacra* 144 (July–September 1987): 254–76.
2. Craig A. Blaising, "Doctrinal Development in Orthodoxy," *Bibliotheca Sacra* 145 (April–June 1988): 133–40.
3. John Hannah, "The Early Years of Lewis Sperry Chafer," *Bibliotheca Sacra* 144 (January–March 1987): 17–18.
4. It would be helpful here to note how *The Scofield Reference Bible*, published in 1909, was presented to the public. The second paragraph under the introduction reads: "The last fifty years have witnessed an intensity and breadth of interest in Bible study unprecedented in the history of the Christian Church. Never before have so many reverent, learned, and spiritual men brought to the study of the Scriptures minds so free from merely controversial motive. A new and vast exegetical and expository literature has been created, inaccessible for bulk, cost, and time to the average reader. The winnowed and attested results of this half-century of Bible study are embodied in the notes, summaries, and definitions of this edition. Expository novelties, and merely personal views and interpretations, have been rejected" (*The Scofield Reference Bible* [Oxford: Oxford University Press, 1909]). This is an amazing statement. "The last fifty years" includes the great Bible and prophetic conference movement. The intention of *The Scofield Reference Bible* is undoubtedly to present itself as the culmination of this great evangelical expository movement. The interpretations of *The Scofield Reference Bible* are presented with a kind of ecumenical authority, for "merely personal views and interpretations have been rejected." Of course it is dispensational, but that admission comes later (par. 10) and the impression is created that dispensationalism is the consensus of the Bible conference movement. That was not the case though it did have strong

representation. Nevertheless it can be seen how the bearing and self-presentation of *The Scofield Reference Bible* could create a kind of confessionalism among its receptive readers, for to disagree with *The Scofield Reference Bible* would be to assert one's own private interpretation against what was presumed to be an agreed consensus of the greatest assemblage of calm and learned minds in the history of the church.

5. John F. Walvoord and Roy B. Zuck, eds., *The Bible Knowledge Commentary*, 2 vols. (Wheaton, IL: Victor, 1983, 1985), 1:7 and 2:5 (italics added).

6. Compare again the claims of *The Scofield Reference Bible* to have omitted personal views and interpretations (see n. 4).

7. Charles C. Ryrie, *Dispensationalism Today* (Chicago: Moody, 1965), pp. 97–98.

8. *The Scofield Reference Bible*, note on Matthew 5:2.

9. Lewis S. Chafer, *Systematic Theology*, 8 vols. (Dallas, TX: Dallas Seminary, 1948; reprint [8 vols. in 4], Grand Rapids: Kregel, 1992), 4:207–25; 5:97–114.

10. Pettingill, an editor of *The Scofield Reference Bible*, gives one of the clearest statements of the kingdom view: "The Sermon on the Mount, then, is not the way of salvation for the sinner. Neither is it the rule of life for the Christian. . . . He [Christ] has not neglected to give to His church ample directions for her guidance, but these directions are not to be found in the Sermon on the Mount. The Sermon on the Mount is pure law, and the Christian is not under law, but under grace. . . . The Sermon on the Mount is the code of laws of the kingdom of Heaven, which kingdom, though for the time being rejected and held in abeyance, will one day be set up on this earth. . . . The Anointed King in this great discourse plainly sets forth the nature of the proposed kingdom and the laws by which He will govern the earth when He re-establishes and occupies the Throne of David" (William L. Pettingill, *The Gospel of the Kingdom: Simple Studies in Matthew* [Findlay, OH: Durham, n.d.], pp. 57–58). The kingdom view can also be found in E. Schuyler English, *Studies in the Gospel according to Matthew* (New York: Revell, 1935), p. 45; A. C. Gaebelein, *The Gospel of Matthew: An Exposition*, 2 vols. (New York: Our Hope Publication Office, 1910), 1:105–11. Charles L. Feinberg sees the Sermon on the Mount as "laws for the regulation of conduct in His [Christ's] kingdom. . . . The King is still offering the covenanted kingdom to those to whom it was promised. Now He promulgates laws for the carrying on of that kingdom. There is no message of salvation in this sermon. It tells us not how to be acceptable to God, but it does reveal those

who will be pleasing to God in the kingdom." In the third edition of this work (1980), Feinberg has added a footnote: "It is wrong to hold that the Sermon on the Mount has no relevance or profit for the believer today" (*Millennialism: The Two Major Views* [Chicago: Moody, 1980], p. 145, n. 7). Alva J. McClain writes that the Sermon on the Mount "is concerned specifically with the things of the 'kingdom of heaven'!" (*The Greatness of the Kingdom* [Winona Lake, IN: BMH, 1959], p. 278).

11. See for example J. N. Darby, *The Collected Writings of J. N. Darby*, ed. William Kelly, 34 vols. (reprint, Sunbury, PA: Believer's Bookshelf, 1972) 11:144–45; and William Kelly, *Lectures on the Gospel of Matthew*, rev. ed. (Neptune, NJ: Loizeaux Bros., n.d.), pp. 103–7. Kelly sees it as a discourse on the moral character of the kingdom of heaven in contrast to the earthly expectations of the Jews. He does not, however, subordinate its application to the church.

12. John F. Walvoord, *Matthew: Thy Kingdom Come* (Chicago: Moody, 1974), pp. 43–46.

13. Robert L. Saucy writes, "Although there are many dispensationalists today who yet hesitate to see the primary interpretation of the sermon's teaching for the church, there are few who would argue for a strict kingdom interpretation" ("Dispensationalism and the Salvation of the Kingdom," *Tyndale Student Fellowship Bulletin* 7 [May-June 1984]: 6).

14. John A. Martin, "Dispensational Approaches to the Sermon on the Mount," in *Essays in Honor of J. Dwight Pentecost*, ed. Stanley D. Toussaint and Charles H. Dyer (Chicago: Moody, 1986), pp. 35–48.

15. Ibid., p. 48.

16. Stanley D. Toussaint, "The Kingdom and Matthew's Gospel," in ibid., pp. 19–34. Apparently this view is also shared by Charles C. Ryrie, *Basic Theology* (Wheaton, IL: Victor, 1986), pp. 255–56.

17. Martin, "Dispensational Approaches to the Sermon on the Mount," p. 46.

18. See also Martin's note on the well-known dispensational interpretation of "the offer of the kingdom" (ibid., p. 37, n. 6).

19. "The kingdom of God is the exercise or exhibition of the ruling power of God under any circumstances. . . . The kingdom of heaven is the kingdom of God in its heavenly character" (J. N. Darby, T*he Collected Writings of J. N. Darby*, 2:55). It is not claimed that this is original with Darby. It would be helpful to see to what extent this is shared by other expositors in his day. Such, however, is beyond the scope of this chapter. Note also in the quotation that Darby stressed the *heavenly* character of the kingdom

of heaven. Contrast this to later dispensationalists who see it as the *earthly* rule.

20. James Hall Brookes, *Maranatha* (New York: Revell, n.d.) p. 255.
21. "The phrase, kingdom of heaven . . . signifies the Messianic earth rule of Jesus Christ, the Son of David. . . . It is the rule of the heavens over the earth. . . . It is the kingdom covenanted to David's seed described in the prophets . . . ; and confined to Jesus the Christ, the Son of Mary, through the angel Gabriel. . . . The kingdom of heaven has three aspects in Matthew: (a) "at hand" from the beginning of the ministry of John the Baptist . . . to the virtual rejection of the king . . . (b) in seven "mysteries of the kingdom of heaven" to be fulfilled during the present age . . . and which have to do with the sphere of Christian profession during this age; (c) the prophetic aspect—the kingdom to be set up after the return of the king in glory" (*The Scofield Reference Bible*, n. 1 on Matt. 3:2). "The kingdom of God is to be distinguished from the kingdom of heaven in five respects: (1) the kingdom of God is universal, including all intelligences willingly subject to the will of God . . . (2) the kingdom of God is entered only by new birth . . . the kingdom of heaven, during this age, is the sphere of profession which may be real or false . . . (3) . . . the kingdom of heaven is the earthly sphere of the universal kingdom of God . . . (4) the kingdom of God 'comes not with outward show,' but is chiefly that which is inward and spiritual . . . while the kingdom of heaven is organic, and is to be manifested in glory on the earth . . . (5) the kingdom of heaven merges into the kingdom of God . . . (1 Cor. 15:24–28)" (*The Scofield Reference Bible*, n. 1 on Matt. 6:33).
22. Chafer, *Systematic Theology*, 5:316; cf. 4:26.
23. Ibid., 5:316.
24. Charles L. Feinberg, *Premillennialism or Amillennialism* (Grand Rapids: Zondervan, 1936), p. 196; and idem, *Millennialism*, p. 253.
25. Feinberg, *Millennialism*, pp. 253–54.
26. George E. Ladd, *Crucial Questions about the Kingdom of God* (Grand Rapids: Eerdmans, 1952).
27. J. Dwight Pentecost, *Things to Come* (Grand Rapids: Zondervan, 1958), p. 144.
28. McClain, *The Greatness of the Kingdom*, pp. 19–21.
29. *The Scofield Reference Bible*, rev. ed. (1980), n. 3 on Matt. 3:2; and n. 1 on Matt. 6:33.
30. Walvoord, *Matthew: Thy Kingdom Come*, p. 30; and idem, "The New Testament Doctrine of the Kingdom," *Bibliotheca Sacra* 139 (July–September 1982): 211–13.
31. Robert L. Saucy, "The Critical Issue between Dispensational and

Non-Dispensational Systems," *Criswell Theological Review* 1 (1986): 154–55.
32. *The Ryrie Study Bible*, n. on Matthew 3:2; and n. on Mark 1:15. Cf. the appendix, "A Synopsis of Bible Doctrine," The Doctrine of Future Things IV.B.
33. Ibid., n. on Colossians 1:15.
34. Ibid., Matthew 13:3; n. on 13:33; and *Basic Theology*, p. 398.
35. Clarence E. Mason, Jr., *Prophetic Problems with Alternative Solutions* (Chicago: Moody, 1973), pp. 102–3.
36. Toussaint, "The Kingdom and Matthew's Gospel," p. 23.
37. Robert L. Saucy, "Contemporary Dispensational Thought," *Tyndale Student Fellowship Bulletin* (March–April 1984): 6–7.
38. James Hall Brookes, *"Till He Come"* (Chicago: Gospel, 1891), pp. 76–77; *The Scofield Reference Bible*, n. 1 on Acts 15:13.
39. Chafer, *Systematic Theology*, 5:329; cf. 4:267–69.
40. See Feinberg, *Premillennialism or Amillennialism*, pp. 118–19; idem, *Millennialism*, pp. 154–55; Pentecost, *Things to Come*, pp. 109–11. Also see *The Ryrie Study Bible*, n. on Acts 15:15–17.
41. Oswald T. Allis, *Prophecy and the Church* (Philadelphia: Presbyterian and Reformed, 1947), pp. 149–50.
42. Feinberg, *Millennialism*, pp. 154–55, 238.
43. Stanley D. Toussaint, "Acts," pp. 394–95.
44. "But James also knew from Amos' succinct statement and from extended passages in other prophets . . . that when the promised kingdom would come, the Gentiles will share in it as Gentiles and not as quasi-Jews. Since this was God's millennial purpose, James concluded that the church should not require Gentiles to relinquish their identity and live as Jews. James was not saying the church fulfills the promises to Israel in Amos 9:11–12. He was saying that since Gentiles will be saved in the yet-to-come Millennium, they would not become Jews in the church age (see extended comments on Acts 15:15–18)" (Donald R. Sunukjian, "Amos," in *The Bible Knowledge Commentary*, 1:1451). See also Elliott E. Johnson, "Hermeneutics and Dispensationalism," in *Walvoord: A Tribute*, ed. Donald K. Campbell (Chicago: Moody, 1982), pp. 243–44.
45. Kenneth L. Barker, "False Dichotomies between the Testaments," *Journal of the Evangelical Theological Society* 25 (March 1982): 4, n. 5.
46. Larry V. Crutchfield, "The Doctrine of Ages and Dispensations as Found in the Published Works of John Nelson Darby (1800–1881)" (Ph.D. diss., Drew University, 1985), pp. 82–83.
47. Ibid.
48. Brookes, *"Till He Come,"* p. 106. "Thus do we see that in each of

the five preceding dispensations, man, tried under any and all circumstances, has proved to be a wretched failure; and each has closed amid increasing tokens of human depravity and divine wrath. Why will it not be so in the sixth dispensation?" (Brookes, *Maranatha*, p. 286).

49. "A dispensation is a period of time during which man is tested in respect of obedience to some specific revelation of the will of God" (*The Scofield Reference Bible*, p. 5). "These periods are marked off in Scripture by some change in God's method of dealing with mankind, or a portion of mankind, in respect of the two questions of sin and of man's responsibility. Each of the dispensations may be regarded as a new test of the natural man, and each ends in judgment—marking his utter failure" (C. I. Scofield, *Rightly Dividing the Word of Truth* [Grand Rapids: Zondervan, 1965], p. 19).

50. "It has been necessary to bring fallen man into divine testing. This, in part, is God's purpose in the ages, and the result of the testings is in every case an unquestionable demonstration of the utter failure and sinfulness of man. In the end, every mouth will have been stopped because every assumption of the human heart will be revealed as foolish and wicked by centuries of experience" (Lewis Sperry Chafer, *Major Bible Themes*, rev. John F. Walvoord [Grand Rapids: Zondervan, 1947], p. 127). As far as the character of God is concerned, which Darby seemed to relate differently to the dispensations, Chafer (and Ryrie also) taught it as a transdispensational constant.

51. Johnson, "Hermeneutics and Dispensationalism," pp. 239–55. See also the brief discussion in McClain, *The Greatness of the Kingdom*, pp. 529–30.

52. Norman L. Geisler, "God, Evil, and Dispensation," in *Walvoord: A Tribute*, pp. 95–112. It should be noted that Geisler does not see theodicy as the only way to construe dispensationalism, but he sees it as an important yet often neglected aspect of it.

53. Ibid., p. 103.

54. Ibid., p. 104.

55. Ibid., pp. 105–7.

56. Ryrie, *Dispensationalism Today*, pp. 38–39.

57. Saucy, "Contemporary Dispensational Thought," p. 10; and Renald Showers, "A Presentation of Dispensational Theology," *Israel My Glory* (February–March 1984): 26–29.

58. John S. Feinberg, "What Are the Distinctions of a Covenantal System as Opposed to a Dispensational?" A debate between Dr. John Feinberg and Dr. John Gerstner, Peninsula (FL) Bible Church, n.d.

59. He may mention them in other contexts; however, in this article in

which he discusses the essence of the system, he makes no mention of them ("The Current Status of Dispensationalism and Its Eschatology," in *Perspectives on Evangelical Theology: Papers from the Thirtieth Annual Meeting of the Evangelical Theological Society*, ed. Kenneth S. Kantzer and Stanley N. Gundry [Grand Rapids: Baker, 1979], pp. 163–76).

60. Charles C. Ryrie, *Dispensationalism Today*, p. 47 (see the full discussion of the *sine qua non* on pp. 43–47).

61. Ibid., pp. 46–47, 102–5. Cf. John F. Walvoord, *Millennial Kingdom* (Grand Rapids: Zondervan, 1959), p. 92.

62. One way this can be seen is that *Dispensationalism Today* sets the context for defining dispensationalism totally within Reformed parameters (primarily as a dialogue/debate with covenant theology).

63. Oswald T. Allis, "Modern Dispensationalism and the Doctrine of the Unity of Scripture," *Evangelical Quarterly* 8 (1936): 22–35.

64. Lewis Sperry Chafer, "Dispensationalism," *Bibliotheca Sacra* 93 (October–December 1936): 390–449; reprinted as *Dispensationalism* (Dallas, TX: Dallas Theological Seminary, 1936). "The real unity of the Bible is preserved only by those who observe with care the divine program for Gentiles, for Jews, and for Christians in their individual and unchanging continuity" (p. 33). "The true unity of the Scriptures is not discovered when one blindly seeks to fuse these opposing principles into one system, but rather it is found when God's plain differentiations are observed" (p. 51).

65. *Westminster Confession of Faith* 2.1 (italics added).

66. "What is the chief and highest end of man? Man's chief and highest end is to glorify God, and fully to enjoy him forever."

67. Walvoord, *Millennial Kingdom*, p. 92.

68. "In dispensationalism the principle [unifying a philosophy of history] is theological or perhaps better eschatological, for the differing dispensations reveal the glory of God as He manifests His character in the differing stewardships culminating in history with the millennial glory. . . . If the goal of history is the earthly millennium, and if the glory of God will be manifest at that time in the personal presence of Christ in a way hitherto unknown, then the unifying principle of dispensationalism may be said to be eschatological (if viewed from the goal toward which we are moving) or theological (if viewed from the self-revelation of God in every dispensation)" (Ryrie, *Dispensationalism Today*, p. 18).

69. Ibid., p. 104.

70. The "historical" nature of the eternal state is confirmed in the statements by Pentecost, *Things to Come*, p. 561, and Herman Hoyt, *The End Times* (Chicago: Moody, 1969), pp. 241–43. Some nondispensationalists emphasizing this view are George E. Ladd,

The Last Things (Grand Rapids: Eerdmans, 1978), p. 112; and Anthony A. Hoekema, *The Bible and the Future* (Grand Rapids: Eerdmans, 1979), p. 274. The eschatological unity of Scripture and history is emphasized by Elliott E. Johnson, who also sees it as a Christological unity. He writes, "That final season will combine the purposes of each preceding season and will bring them to full realization in history." Also "the stewardship of Christ's rule brings to full realization all of the purposes of God in world history" ("Hermeneutics and Dispensationalism," pp. 241–42).

71. Ryrie, *Dispensationalism Today*, p. 46.

72. "Symbols, figures of speech and types are all interpreted plainly in this method and they are in no way contrary to literal interpretation" (ibid., p. 87).

73. "Of course literal interpretation is not the exclusive property of dispensationalists. . . . The difference [between dispensationalists and nondispensationalists] lies in the fact that the dispensationalist claims to use the normal principle of interpretation consistently in all his study of the Bible" (ibid., p. 89).

74. Earl D. Radmacher, "The Current Status of Dispensationalism and Its Eschatology," in *Perspectives on Evangelical Theology*, p. 166.

75. Robert L. Saucy, "The Critical Issue between Dispensational and Non-Dispensational Systems"; and John S. Feinberg, "Salvation in the Old Testament," in *Tradition and Testament: Essays in Honor of Charles Lee Feinberg*, ed. John S. Feinberg and Paul D. Feinberg (Chicago: Moody, 1981), p. 45.

76. Brookes, *Maranatha*, p. 402.

77. "It may be asked, however, whether the New Testament does not compel this spiritual interpretation of such passages. The answer is, the New Testament cannot be in conflict with the Old Testament, and the fact is, the New Testament confirms the view here taken of the literal application of the Old Testament to the Jews and Jerusalem" (ibid., p. 439).

78. Lorraine Boettner, *The Millennium*, rev. ed. (Nutley, NJ: Presbyterian and Reformed, 1984), pp. 82–105. See also his discussion in Robert G. Clouse, *The Meaning of the Millennium* (Downers Grove, IL: InterVarsity, 1977), pp. 136–38.

79. See Ladd's response to Hoekema in Clouse, *The Meaning of the Millennium*, pp. 189–91. Also see Deere's response to Hughs ("Premillennialism in Revelation 20:4–6," *Bibliotheca Sacra* 135 (January–March 1978): 58–73. Reference is made ahead to David Turner's identification of the problem of different preunderstandings in dispensational and nondispensational exegesis. Perhaps this more accurately describes the difference of interpretation than literal versus spiritual. But note Alford's

criticism of "the spiritual interpretation now in fashion" which makes "an end of all significance in language" wiping Scripture out "as a definite testimony to anything" (Henry Alford, *The Greek Testament*, 4 vols. [reprint, Chicago: Moody, 1958], 4:732.

Another example of this kind of interpretation is identified in Brookes's contention for a literal bodily return of Christ in 1 Thessalonians 1:9–10: believers "wait for His Son from heaven, whom He raised from the dead, that is Jesus, who delivers us from the wrath to come." Brookes writes, "This [coming] cannot possibly mean that they waited for the destruction of Jerusalem, for they had, in their distant home, no interest in that event; nor can it mean that they waited for the Holy Ghost, for He had already come; nor can it mean that they waited for death, for death had not been raised from the dead, and it had not delivered them from the wrath to come; *but it means precisely what it says, that these first Christians waited for Jesus to come from heaven*" (*Maranatha*, p. 72 [italics added]).

80. See Saucy, "Contemporary Dispensationalist Thought," p. 11.
81. Radmacher, writing in 1979, said that it has been going on "over the last decade or so" ("Current Status of Dispensationalism," p. 163). The same fact has been noted by Barker ("False Dichotomies between the Testaments," p. 3), and by other scholars in public and private conversations.
82. John S. Feinberg, "Salvation in the Old Testament," p. 47.
83. Ibid., p. 46.
84. Barker, "False Dichotomies between the Testaments," p. 4, n. 5.
85. Saucy, "Contemporary Dispensationalist Thought," p. 11 (italics added).
86. David Turner, "The Continuity of Scripture and Eschatology: Key Hermeneutical Issues," *Grace Theological Journal* 6 (fall 1985): 275–87.
87. Paul's use of οἰκονομία in Ephesians provides "the direction for a theological system of progressive revelation. That system in turn influences subsequent biblical interpretation in terms of the unity of biblical revelation and of the individual identity of particular revelations" (Johnson, "Hermeneutics and Dispensationalism," pp. 240, 251).
88. Elliott E. Johnson, "Dual Authorship and the Single Intended Meaning of Scripture," *Bibliotheca Sacra* 143 (July–September 1986): 218–27.
89. Darrell L. Bock, "Evangelicals and the Use of the Old Testament in the New," part 1, *Bibliotheca Sacra* 142 (July–September 1985): 209–23; and part 2 (October–December 1985): 306–19.
90. Some of the best essays on this are in Darby's *Collected Writings*,

vols. 2 and 11. Some suggestions are "Divine Mercy in the Church and toward Israel," 2:122–64, esp. pp. 122–23, 127; "The Purpose of God," 2:266–77, esp. 266–67, 271–72; "The Hopes of the Church of God," 2:278–383, esp. 288–89, 376–78; and "Elements of Prophecy, in Connection with the Church, the Jews, and the Gentiles," 11:41–54, esp. 41–47.

91. It remains for someone to search out Darby's view of the relationship of regeneration to the dispensations. Brookes's comments in *"Till He Come,"* pp. 108–9, and *Israel and the Church* (Chicago: Bible Institute Colportage, n.d.), p. 12, are interesting in light of Chafer's tendency to restrict its beginning to this dispensation (Chafer, *Systematic Theology* 6:105–6). For the strong heavenly/earthly distinction in Brookes's writings, see *Israel and the Church*, pp. 7, 12–15; *"Till He Come,"* p. 95; and *Maranatha*, pp. 393, 401–2, 521–23.

92. William Kelly, *Lectures on the Second Coming* (London: N.p., n.d.), p. 70, see also pp. 65–69.

93. Ibid., pp. 68–69.

94. G. Campbell Morgan, *God's Methods with Man* (Chicago: Revell, 1898), pp. 136–38.

95. Chafer, *Systematic Theology*, 4:47. At other times he simply says that the heavenly destiny of the church is to be with Christ "wherever He goes" (7:130) and to share in His reign (4:33). It is interesting that in discussing the eternal state, he stops short of explicitly saying that the church will forever be in the heavenlies. He says that heaven is being populated "at the present time" and that "all believers [church age] will be brought into that place of glory at the coming of the Lord" (4:438). He does say that "heaven is also the appropriate home of Christ, of the Spirit, and of the Church of the first-born, and of the 'spirits of just men made perfect'" (4:364). It is clear that Chafer relates the classic doctrine of heaven with the new heavens of Revelation 21 (4:419).

96. "The heavenly people, by the very exalted character of their salvation being 'made' to stand in all the perfection of Christ, . . . have no burden laid upon them of establishing personal merit before God since they are perfected forever in Christ . . . but they do have the new responsibility of 'walking worthy' of their high calling. . . . No system of merit, such as was the law, could possibly be applied to a people who by riches of divine grace have attained to a perfect standing, even every spiritual blessing in Christ Jesus. . . . It is to be expected that the injunctions addressed to a perfected heavenly people will be exalted as heaven itself; and they are. . . . Similarly, as these requirements are superhuman and yet the doing of them is most essential, God has

provided that each individual thus saved shall be indwelt by the Holy Spirit to the end that he may by dependence on the Spirit and by the power of the Spirit, live a supernatural, God-honoring life—not, indeed, to be accepted, but because he is accepted. Those who would intrude the Mosaic system of merit into this heaven-high divine administration of superabounding grace either have no conception of the character of that merit which the law required, or are lacking in the comprehension of the glories of divine grace" (ibid., 4:18–19). It is interesting to note that this follows right after a statement that the Law never was nor could be a means of justification. The passage quoted is in the context in which Chafer contrasts the rule of life in the past and future dispensations.

97. Ibid., 4:419.
98. Ibid., 4:131.
99. Ibid., 5:366–67.
100. Chafer's language can be found in two places in Pentecost's book *Things to Come*, pp. 202, 212. However, it is not a major characteristic of Pentecost's understanding of the distinction between Israel and the church. Since that time he has dispensed with the heavenly/earthly people dualism altogether. However, Charles L. Feinberg has persisted in maintaining the dualism even in the 1980 revision of his book *Millennialism* (p. 232).
101. Donald K. Campbell, "The Church in God's Prophetic Program," in *Essays in Honor of J. Dwight Pentecost*, pp. 149–50.
102. See John F. Walvoord, *The Church in Prophecy* (Grand Rapids: Zondervan, 1964), pp. 154–65; Pentecost, *Things to Come*, pp. 546, 561–62, 574–77; McClain, *The Greatness of the Kingdom*, pp. 511–15; Erich Sauer, *From Eternity to Eternity* (Grand Rapids: Eerdmans, 1972), p. 193; W. Robert Cook, *The Theology of John* (Chicago: Moody, 1970), p. 237; and Campbell, "The Church in God's Prophetic Program," pp. 158–61.
103. "There remains to be recognized a heavenly covenant for the heavenly people, which is also styled like the preceding one for Israel a 'new covenant.' It is made in the blood of Christ (cf. Mark 14:24) and continues in effect throughout this age, whereas the new covenant made with Israel happens to be future in its application. To suppose that these two covenants—one for Israel and one for the Church—are the same is to assume that there is a latitude of common interest between God's purpose for Israel and His purpose for the Church. Israel's covenant, however, is new only because it replaces the Mosaic, but the Church's covenant is new because it introduces that which is God's mysterious and unrelated purpose. Israel's new covenant rests

specifically on the sovereign 'I will' of Jehovah, while the new covenant for the Church is made in Christ's blood. Everything that Israel will yet have, to supply another contrast, is the present possession of the Church—and infinitely more" (Chafer, *Systematic Theology*, 7:98–99).

104. Mason, *Prophetic Problems with Alternative Solutions*, p. 103.
105. Charles C. Ryrie, *The Basis of the Premillennial Faith* (New York: Loizeaux Brothers, 1953), pp. 106–25.
106. *The Wycliffe Bible Encyclopedia*, s.v. "Covenant, New," by Charles C. Ryrie, pp. 391–92. Also see Homer A. Kent, Jr., "The New Covenant and the Church," *Grace Theological Journal* 6 (fall 1985): 289–98; and Walvoord, "Revelation," in *The Bible Knowledge Commentary, New Testament*, pp. 560–61, 800.
107. Ryrie, *The Basis of the Premillennial Faith*, p. 107.
108. Ibid., p. 115.
109. Saucy, "Contemporary Dispensationalist Thought," p. 11.

Chapter 14

1. Robert H. Gundry, *The Church and the Tribulation* (Grand Rapids: Zondervan, 1973), pp. 129–39.
2. Ibid., pp. 134–39.
3. Gundry, however, seems to imply that his posttribulation position is based primarily on the Olivet Discourse and only secondarily "on what is believed to be confirmation of natural inferences from the discourse in subsequent N. T. teaching" (ibid., p. 129). If, in fact, Gundry's one primary New Testament source for the substantiation of posttribulationism is Matthew 24–25, then in reality Gundry's argument *for* posttribulationism can be eliminated if it can be shown that those chapters do not have the church in view in the tribulation events they describe.
4. Ibid., p. 129.
5. Little will be said here because the author and most (if not all) of those within his theological circle do not hold to hyper-dispensationalism.
6. Gundry, *The Church and the Tribulation*, pp. 129–30.
7. Ibid., pp. 130–31.
8. This is by far the most crucial of Gundry's five arguments.
9. Gundry, *The Church and the Tribulation*, p. 131. It should be noted that within this quotation, Gundry provides an important footnote stating that posttribulationists agree to the *temporariness* of God's rejection of Israel. Gundry does believe in a future for Israel in which God will again relate Himself directly to her.
10. Ibid.
11. Ibid., p. 132.

12. Ibid.
13. Ibid.
14. Ibid., pp. 132–33.
15. Ibid., p. 133.
16. Ibid.
17. Ibid.
18. Ibid., p. 134.
19. Ibid., p. 130.
20. Ibid., p. 131, n. 1.
21. Duane A. Dunham, "An Examination of Some Eschatological Problems in the Olivet Discourse" (Th.M. thesis, Western Conservative Baptist Seminary, 1964), p. 23.
22. This argument does not attempt to prove conclusively that the Olivet Discourse is beyond doubt addressed to Israel as opposed to the church; it rather shows the distinct possibility (and even likelihood) that the discourse relates to Israel rather than to the church. The next argument presented (on internal elements) is the attempt to prove that the discourse is addressed to Israel.
23. Gundry, *The Church and the Tribulation*, pp. 132–33.
24. Dunham, "An Examination of Some Eschatological Problems in the Olivet Discourse," p. 26 (italics added).
25. John F. Walvoord, *The Blessed Hope and the Tribulation* (Grand Rapids: Zondervan, 1976), p. 87.
26. Gordon R. Lewis, "Biblical Evidence for Pretribulationism," *Bibliotheca Sacra* 125 (July–September 1968): 220.
27. A. C. Gaebelein, *The Gospel of Matthew*, 2 vols. in 1 (New York: Our Hope Publishing Office, 1914), 2:169.
28. Walvoord, *The Blessed Hope and the Tribulation*, p. 87.
29. Gundry, *The Church and the Tribulation*, p. 133.
30. John S. Feinberg, class notes in T303 Eschatology, Western Conservative Baptist Seminary, spring 1978.
31. Gundry, *The Church and the Tribulation*, p. 133.
32. Feinberg, class notes.
33. Walvoord, *The Blessed Hope and the Tribulation*, p. 86.

Chapter 15

1. Robert H. Gundry, *The Church and the Tribulation* (Grand Rapids: Zondervan, 1973), pp. 100–111.
2. George E. Ladd, *The Blessed Hope* (Grand Rapids: Eerdmans, 1956), pp. 77–80.
3. Gundry, *The Church and the Tribulation*, p. 100.
4. Ibid., p. 101.
5. Ibid., p. 102.

6. John F. Walvoord, "Pretribulationism Today; Part VII: *Bibliotheca Sacra* 133 (July–September 1976).
7. Gundry, *The Church and the Tribulation*, p. 103.
8. Ibid., p. 104.
9. Ibid.
10. Ladd, *The Blessed Hope*, p. 82.
11. See John F. Walvoord, "Posttribulationism Today; Part VI: Posttribulational Denial of Imminency and Wrath," *Bibliotheca Sacra* 133 (April–June 1976): 108–18; or John F. Walvoord, *The Blessed Hope and the Tribulation* (Grand Rapids: Zondervan, 1976), chapter 6.
12. Ladd, *The Blessed Hope*, p. 80.
13. Gundry, *The Church and the Tribulation*, pp. 101–2.
14. D. Edmond Hiebert, *The Thessalonian Epistles* (Chicago: Moody, 1971), p. 205.

Chapter 16

1. C. I. Scofield, ed., *The Scofield Reference Bible*, rev. ed. (New York: Oxford University Press, 1917), p. 1272, note.
2. Alexander Reese, *The Approaching Advent of Christ* (London: Marshall, Morgan & Scott, 1937), pp. 17–83. Cf. discussion by John F. Walvoord, *The Rapture Question* (Findlay, OH: Dunham, 1957), pp. 161–72.
3. Robert H. Gundry, *The Church and the Tribulation* (Grand Rapids; Zondervan, 1973), p. 89.
4. D. Edmond Hiebert, *The Thessalonian Epistles* (Chicago: Moody, 1971), p. 207.
5. J. Barton Payne, *The Imminent Appearing of Christ* (Grand Rapids: Eerdmans, 1962), p. 108.
6. Gundry, *The Church and the Tribulation*, p. 98.
7. Reese, *The Approaching Advent of Christ*, pp. 167–83.

Chapter 17

1. John F. Walvoord, *The Rapture Question* (Findlay, OH: Dunham, 1957).
2. J. Barton Payne, *The Imminent Appearing of Christ* (Grand Rapids: Eerdmans, 1962).
3. Robert H. Gundry, *The Church and the Tribulation* (Grand Rapids: Zondervan, 1973).
4. Walvoord, *The Rapture Question*, pp. 191–99.
5. John F. Walvoord, "Unresolved Problems of Posttribulationism," *Bibliotheca Sacra* 134 (October–December 1977): 299–313.

Chapter 18

1. Robert H. Gundry, *The Church and the Tribulation* (Grand Rapids: Zondervan, 1973), p. 54.

2. Gundry claims that "where a situation of danger is in view, τηρέω means to *guard*," and that "throughout the LXX and the NT τηρέω always occurs for protection within the sphere of danger" (Gundry, *The Church and the Tribulation*, p. 58). Although "to guard" does not differ much from "to protect," Gundry's second statement is questionable. In 2 Peter 2:9 and Jude 21, for example, the idea of protection within the sphere of danger is inappropriate.

3. Ibid., p. 80.

4. John A. Sproule, "A Revised Review of *The Church and the Tribulation* by Robert H. Gundry" (Paper delivered at the Postgraduate Seminar in New Testament Theology, Grace Theological Seminary, Winona Lake, IN, May 15, 1974), p. 32 (italics his).

5. Gundry's comment that "were the Church absent from the hour of testing, keeping would not be necessary" (Gundry, *The Church and the Tribulation*, p. 58) looks at the situation from a posttribulational viewpoint within the tribulation where keeping seems necessary. There is also the viewpoint of the Philadelphians prior to the hour of testing. To them, protection from that hour definitely necessitated some form of keeping. In relation to a worldwide judgment, it would seem that keeping in heaven would be a necessity.

6. A. T. Robertson, *A Grammar of the Greek New Testament in the Light of Historical Research*, 4th ed. (New York: George H. Doran Co., 1923). p. 596.

7. Alexander Reese, *The Approaching Advent of Christ: An Examination of the Teaching of J. N. Darby and His Followers* (London: Marshall, Morgan, & Scott, 1937), p. 205.

8. As Ladd puts it, "This verse neither asserts that the Rapture is to occur before the Tribulation, nor does its interpretation require us to think that such a removal is intended" (George E. Ladd, *The Blessed Hope* [Grand Rapids: Eerdmans, 1956], p. 86).

9. Cf. E. Schuyler English, *Re-Thinking the Rapture: An Examination of What the Scriptures Teach as to the Time of the Translation of the Church in Relation to the Tribulation* (Travelers Rest, SC: Southern Bible, 1954), p. 89.

10. Gundry, *The Church and the Tribulation*, pp. 55–56.

11. Ibid., p. 59.

12. Henry George Liddell and Robert Scott, *An Intermediate Greek-English Lexicon* (Oxford: Clarendon Press, 1968), pp. 498–99.

13. Homer *The Iliad* 2.14.130 (italics added).

14. Cf. ἐκ καπνοῦ, "out of the smoke" (Homer *The Odyssey* 2.19.7); ἐκ μέσου κατῆσατο, "stood aside" (Herodotus 2.3.83).
15. Gundry, *The Church and the Tribulation*, p. 55.
16. Old Testament citations are based on the Masoretic text. Variations in the Septuagint are indicated in parentheses.
17. Joseph Henry Thayer, *A Greek-English Lexicon of the New Testament* (Grand Rapids: Zondervan, 1962), p. 142. Cf. *Theological Dictionary of the New Testament*, s.v. "τηρέω," by Harald Riesenfeld, 8:151.
18. Preservation in an outside position is also found in Psalm 12:8 (Septuagint, 11:7) using διατηρέω with ἀπό. Thus ἐκ in the Septuagint is capable of the idea of separation normally found in ἀπό.
19. Also compare ἐκκλίνω with ἐκ in Proverbs 1:5 and ἀνέχω with ἐκ in Amos 4:7
20. Edwin A. Abbott, *From Letter to Spirit: An Attempt to Reach through Varying Voices the Abiding Word*, Diatessarica, part 6 (London: Adam & Charles Black, 1903), p. 311. In the Septuagint the reference is Psalm 58:1–2.
21. Josephus *Jewish Antiquities* 4.2.1 (italics added). Cf. ῥύομαι ἐκ in *Jewish Antiquities* 12.10.5; 13.6.3.
22. In a similar context of keeping from idols, 1 John 5:21 employs τηρέω with ἀπό, indicating that, as in the Septuagint, ἐκ and ἀπό are difficult to distinguish as to meaning in the New Testament. Both may mean "separation from." (Compare John 17:15 with James 1:27; Mark 1:10 with Matt. 3:16; and 1 Thess. 1:10 with Rom. 5:9.)
23. In addition to the verbal constructions with ἐκ, the nonverbal expression ἐλεύθερος . . . ἐκ πάντων ("free from all") in 1 Corinthians 9:19 seems to use ἐκ in a way that indicates a position outside its object.
24. Smith notes a further correlation with Revelation 3:10. "It is significant that Jesus is the speaker and John the writer just as is the case in the Revelation [3:10] text, and that in each case mention is made of a coming hour of suffering. In all probability, therefore, the meaning of the phrase *from the hour* is similar in both instances" (J. B. Smith, *A Revelation of Jesus Christ: A Commentary on the Book of Revelation*, ed. J. Otis Yoder [Scottdale, PA: Herald, 1961], p. 331).
25. Walter Bauer, William F. Arndt, and F. Wilbur Gingrich, *A Greek-English Lexicon of the New Testament and Other Early Christian Literature*, 2d ed., rev. F. Wilbur Gingrich and Frederick W. Danker (Chicago: University of Chicago Press, 1957), pp. 805–6.
26. Robertson, *A Grammar of the Greek New Testament*, p. 598.

27. Smith, *A Revelation of Jesus Christ*, p. 331.
28. Thomas Hewitt, *The Epistle to the Hebrews: An Introduction and Commentary*, Tyndale New Testament Commentaries (Grand Rapids: Eerdmans, 1960), pp. 99–100.
29. Both Bruce and Lenski are correct in answering the question of how the Lord's prayers were answered since He went to the cross in spite of His prayers. "While Gethsemane provides 'the most telling illustration' of our author's words, they have a more general reference to the whole course of our Lord's humiliation and passion" (F. F. Bruce, *The Epistle to the Hebrews: The English Text with Introduction, Exposition and Notes,* New International Commentary on the New Testament [Grand Rapids: Eerdmans, 1964], p. 100). "Jesus prayed for deliverance from death only with an 'if ': 'if it be possible' (Matt. 26:39); 'if this cup may not pass away from me, except I drink it' (v. 42). The real burden of his prayer was: 'Nevertheless, not what I will, but what thou wilt' (Mark 14:36). So also Matt. 26:39, 42, 'thy win be done,' and this prayer of Jesus was fully and truly granted" (R. C. H. Lenski, *The Interpretation of the Epistle to the Hebrews and the Epistle of James* [Minneapolis: Augsburg, 1943], p. 164).
30. Walter W. Wessel, "The Epistle of James," in *The Wycliffe Bible Commentary*, ed. Charles F. Pfeiffer and Everett F. Harrison (Chicago: Moody, 1962), p. 1439.
31. As Morris puts it: "'Keep thee from (ek) the hour of temptation' might mean 'keep thee from undergoing the trial' or 'keep thee right through the trial.' The Greek is capable of either meaning" (Leon Morris, *The Revelation of St. John: An Introduction and Commentary*, Tyndale New Testament Commentaries [Grand Rapids: Eerdmans, 1969], p. 80). Cf. Henry Alford, *The Greek Testament*, rev. Everett F. Harrison, 4 vols., (Chicago: Moody, 1958), 4:585; James Moffatt, "The Revelation of St. John the Divine," in *The Expositor's Greek Testament*, ed. W. Robertson Nicoll, 5 vols. (London: Hodder & Stoughton, 1900–10), 5 (1910): 368.
32. *Theological Dictionary of the New Testament*, s.v. "τηρέω," by Harald Riesenfeld, 8:142.
33. Though τοῦ πονηροῦ may be either masculine or neuter, it is most likely masculine and a reference to Satan, according to Johannine usage (cf. John 12:31; 14:30; 16:11; 1 John 2:13–14; 3:12; 5:18–19).
34. Gundry, *The Church and the Tribulation*, p. 59.
35. Evidently, combining τηρέω with ἐκ modifies the meaning of the preposition from the primary meaning of motion out from within to the secondary meaning of outside position (S. Lewis Johnson,

Vital Prophetic Issues

Jr., class notes in 228 The Revelation, Dallas Theological Seminary, fall 1976).
36. Gundry, *The Church and the Tribulation*, p. 59.
37. For evidence that πειρασμός was associated with θλῖψις in the New Testament, compare Luke 8:13 with Matthew 13:21 and Mark 4:17.
38. Mounce thinks that the hour is "three and a half years of rule by Antichrist in Revelation 13:5–10. In fact, all the judgments from 6:1 onward relate to this final hour of trial" (Robert H. Mounce, *The Book of Revelation*, New International Commentary on the New Testament [Grand Rapids: Eerdmans, 1977], p. 119). However, it seems better in the light of the 70th week concept of Daniel 9:27 to see the hour as a seven-year period of time. Cf. Henry C. Thiessen, "Will the Church Pass through the Tribulation?" *Bibliotheca Sacra* 92 (January–March 1935): 45–50.
39. Henry C. Thiessen, "Will the Church Pass through the Tribulation?" *Bibliotheca Sacra* 92 (April–June 1935): 202–3.
40. Charles C. Ryrie, *A Survey of Bible Doctrine* (Chicago: Moody, 1972), p. 170.
41. Gundry, *The Church and the Tribulation*, p. 60.
42. *Theological Dictionary of the New Testament*, s.v. "ὥρα," by Gerhard Delling, 9:677.
43. Gundry, *The Church and the Tribulation*, p. 60.
44. That it is possible for ἀπό to indicate prior existence in its object (as ἐκ normally does) is demonstrated by its use in Psalm 69:14 (Septuagint, 68:14) and Psalm 140:1, 4 (Septuagint, 139:1, 4). According to Turner, in both the Septuagint and the New Testament ἀπό encroaches on ἐκ (James Hope Moulton, *A Grammar of New Testament Greek*, 4 vols. [Edinburgh: Clark, 1906–76]; vol. 3 [1963]: *Syntax*, by Nigel Turner, pp. 250–51).
45. Some posttribulationists insist that οἰκουμένη limits the hour of testing to the Roman world of John's day. Bell writes, "The seemingly universal terms are used elsewhere in the New Testament to mean the civilized world of that day, i.e. the Roman Empire. . . . The several empire-wide persecutions of Christians could easily satisfy the universal terminology" (William Everett Bell, Jr., "A Critical Evaluation of the Pretribulation Rapture Doctrine in Christian Eschatology" [Ph.D. diss., New York University, 1967], p. 304). But as Johnston notes, "οἰκουμένη may have a very wide reference. . . . Sometimes it is synonymous with αἰών and κόσμος. . . . Hence, *oecumenē* may mean also mankind as a whole. . ." (George Johnston, "Οἰκουμένη and Κόσμο" in the New Testament," *New Testament Studies* 10 [April 1964]: 353). This is exemplified by the use of οἰκουμένη in Matthew 24:14 and Acts 17:31. Commenting on the

use of οἰκουμένη in the Matthew passage, Michel writes, "It is certainly not to be linked here with political imperial style. The reference is simply to the glad message which is for all nations and the whole earth" (*Theological Dictionary of the New Testament*, s.v. "ἡ οἰκουμέ νη," by Otto Michel, 5:158). In both Acts 17:31 and Revelation 3:10 οἰκουμένη is set in an eschatological context that also seems to demand the widest possible reference.

Furthermore the next phrase in Revelation 3:10 τοὺς κατοικοῦντας ἐπὶ τῆς γῆς ("those who dwell upon the earth"), is used only pejoratively in Revelation (cf. 6:10; 8:13; 11:10; 13:8, 14; 17:8), thus indicating that unbelievers are designated by the phrase. This is fatal to Bell's view because, as Brown points out, "If the enemies of the Christian religion are to be affected . . . by the 'hour of trial,' it is clear that the author cannot be thinking of a persecution directed against Christians" (Schuyler Brown, "'The Hour of Trial' (Rev. 3:10)," *Journal of Biblical Literature* 85 [summer 1966]: 310).

46. Cf. *Theological Dictionary of the New Testament*, s.v. "πεῖρα κτλ," by Heinrich Seesemann, 6:23; and Thayer, *A Greek-English Lexicon of the New Testament*, p. 646.

47. Richard Chenevix Trench, *Synonyms of the New Testament* (New York: Redfield, 1854), p. 281m. Cf. *Theological Dictionary of the New Testament*, s.v. "πεῖρα κτλ ," 6:23.

48. Johnson, class notes.

49. Alva J. McClain, *The Greatness of the Kingdom* (Grand Rapids: Zondervan, 1959), p. 465.